States and the
Reemergence of
Global Finance

States and the Reemergence of Global Finance

FROM BRETTON WOODS

TO THE 1990S

Eric Helleiner

Cornell University Press

ITHACA AND LONDON

First published 1994 by Cornell University Press
First printing, Cornell Paperbacks, 1996

Printed in the United States of America

Library of Congress Cataloging-in-Publication Data

Helleiner, Eric, 1963–.
    States and the reemergence of global finance : from Bretton Woods to the 1990s / Eric Helleiner.
        p. cm.
    Includes bibliographical references and index.
    ISBN 978-0-8014-8333-2 (pbk. : alk. paper)
    1. International finance.   2. Monetary policy.   3. State, The.
I. Title.
HG3881.H418   1994
332'.042—dc20   93-39542

Cornell University Press strives to use environmentally responsible suppliers and materials to the fullest extent possible in the publishing of its books. Such materials include vegetable-based, low-VOC inks and acid-free papers that are recycled, totally chlorine-free, or partly composed of nonwood fibers. For further information, visit our website at www.cornellpress.cornell.edu.

5   7   9   Paperback printing   10   8   6

Contents

Preface

J<small>ACOB</small> V<small>INER</small> <small>ONCE NOTED THAT PEOPLE</small> "<small>ARE NOT NARROW IN</small> their intellectual interests by nature; it takes special and rigorous training to accomplish that end." I am indebted to those who introduced me to one academic field, international political economy (IPE), where special and rigorous training is compatible with the pursuit of some of the broadest intellectual questions. This field is, in Susan Strange's words, one of the few remaining "open ranges" in the social sciences today, "still unfenced, still open to all comers." In this book, I have tried to make a small contribution to the reversal of the enclosure movement within the social sciences by detailing a political history of the globalization of financial markets in the postwar period. Seemingly obscure and technical, the study of international finance has long been the narrow preserve of specialists in international economics. Popular in these circles is the view that the globalization of financial markets has been primarily a product of technological and economic developments. This book challenges such a perspective with the argument that the contemporary open global financial order could never have emerged without the support and blessing of states as well.

There are a number of people I thank for their contributions to this work. My most profound gratitude is to Jennifer Clapp for supporting me throughout this project in many more ways than even she knows. I also give special thanks to Gautam Sen and Robert Cox, who helped me begin the project. I also thank Louis Pauly for

vii

his suggestions and support in the process of revising the manuscript, as well as Roger Haydon for guiding the manuscript through to publication so smoothly. In addition, I am very grateful for the support, comments, and criticisms I received from the following people: Jeremy Adelman, Mark Brawley, Phil Cerny, Benjamin Cohen, Nilesh Dattani, Jeffry Frieden, Stephen Gill, Michael Hodges, David Leyton-Brown, Michael Loriaux, James Mayall, Matthew Martin, Julia McNally, Kathleen Newland, Leo Panitch, Piers Revell, Susan Strange, Geoffrey Underhill, Michael Webb, numerous students in the "Money in the International System" course at the London School of Economics, and one anonymous reviewer. I thank the Social Sciences and Humanities Research Council of Canada and the British government for providing me with generous financial support to conduct the research for the book. Various librarians at the U.S. National Archives, the Library of Congress, the Ford Presidential Library, and the British Library of Political and Economic Science were also extremely helpful and generous with their time. Finally, I thank my parents, to whom this book is dedicated, for their enormous support and encouragement over the years.

ERIC HELLEINER

Peterborough, Ontario

Abbreviations

ABA	American Bankers Association
AEI	American Enterprise Institute
BIS	Bank for International Settlements
BP	Arthur Burns Papers, Ford Presidential Library
C-20	Committee of Twenty
CED	Committee for Economic Development
ECA	Economic Cooperation Administration
EMS	European Monetary System
EPU	European Payments Union
G-10	Group of Ten
GATT	General Agreement on Tariffs and Trade
IBF	International banking facility
IET	Interest equalization tax
IMF	International Monetary Fund
IOSCO	International Organization of Securities Commissions
IPE	International political economy
NA	U.S. National Archives, Washington, D.C.
NAC	National Advisory Council on International Monetary and Financial Problems, U.S. government
OECD	Organization for Economic Cooperation and Development
OEEC	Organization for European Economic Cooperation
OPEC	Organization of Petroleum Exporting Countries
RG	Record group, records of the Treasury Department in U.S. National Archives

States and the
Reemergence of
Global Finance

CHAPTER ONE

Introduction

THE GLOBALIZATION OF FINANCIAL MARKETS HAS BEEN ONE OF the most spectacular developments in the world economy in recent years. Although international financial markets flourished in the late nineteenth and early twentieth centuries, they were almost completely absent from the international economy during the three decades that followed the financial crisis of 1931. Beginning in the late 1950s, however, private international financial activity increased at a phenomenal rate. Global foreign exchange trading, for example, was negligible in the late 1950s but by the early 1990s had grown to a daily value of roughly $1 trillion, almost forty times the daily value of international trade. Similarly, gross international capital flows totaled $600 billion by the end of the 1980s, a figure almost twice the size of aggregate global current account imbalances.[1]

Most explanations of the globalization of financial markets discount the role played by states. According to this view, unstoppable technological and market forces, rather than state behavior and political choices, were the prime movers behind the phenomenon. As Walter Wriston recently argued:

Today we are witnessing a galloping new system of international finance. Our new international financial regime differs radically from its precursors in that it was not built by politicians, economists, central bankers or fi-

1. Statistics from Goldstein et al. 1993:24; Turner 1991:9–10. Unless otherwise indicated, all amounts are in U.S. dollars.

nance ministers, nor did high-level international conferences produce a master plan. It was built by technology . . . [by] men and women who interconnected the planet with telecommunications and computers.[2]

In recent years, a growing number of scholars in the field of international political economy have challenged this historical account. They have not ignored technological and market developments, but they emphasize the importance of states in the process of globalization. Louis Pauly, for example, has argued that "a global village does not just spring up: it must be created. Politics within distinct state structures remains the axis around which international finance revolves."[3] Similarly, Jeffry Frieden has stressed that "political consent made the global financial integration of the past thirty years possible."[4] Susan Strange, too, has emphasized that "it is very easily forgotten that [international financial] markets exist under the authority and by permission of the state, and are conducted on whatever terms the state may choose to dictate, or allow."[5]

Existing IPE studies of the globalization of financial markets, however, tend to concentrate on certain stages of the process or on the experience of individual countries. I attempt to provide here a more synthetic "political" history of the globalization process which focuses primarily on the crucial role played by advanced industrial states. In addition to assuming this historical task, I have sought to answer a key analytical question: Why has such an open international financial order emerged in an era when states have retained numerous restrictive trade practices? Indeed, the divergent experience in the areas of international trade and international finance in recent years has given considerable strength to the argument that the globalization trend in finance has somehow been beyond politics. If

2. Wriston 1988:71. See also McKenzie and Lee 1991, Bryant 1987, O'Brien 1992, and Al-Muhanna 1988.
3. Pauly 1988:2. See also Goodman and Pauly 1990.
4. Frieden 1987:166.
5. Strange 1986:29. Other IPE scholars who have begun to emphasize the key role of states in the globalization process include Cerny (1989), Cohen (1986), Hawley (1984, 1987), Kapstein (1989, 1992), Loriaux (1991), Maxfield (1990), Moran (1991), Rosenbluth (1989), Spero (1980), Underhill (1991), Banuri and Schor (1992), Dale (1984), Versluysen (1981), and Wachtel (1986). Many IPE scholars writing on international monetary issues, such as Aronson (1977), Gowa (1983), Kelly (1976), and Odell (1982), have also touched on the globalization of finance. The importance of states has also been discussed in several other works on the globalization of finance, such as Mendelsohn 1980 and Hamilton 1986.

this view is to be successfully challenged, it is necessary to explain why state behavior in matters of international finance has been different from that pertaining to international trade. This explanation might also have broader relevance for IPE debates concerning state behavior relating to open, liberal international economic orders, debates that have until now focused primarily on state behavior with regard to the trade sector.

The book is organized in three parts, the first of which is an analysis of the relationship between the globalization process and the early postwar international economic order. The second part is an explanation of how and why states have promoted the globalization of financial markets since the late 1950s. The concluding chapter addresses the question of why state behavior in finance has been so different from that in trade in recent years. The arguments of each part are briefly summarized in this introductory chapter.

The Restrictive Bretton Woods Financial Order

Among policymakers and scholars concerned with international economic issues, there is a widely held view—even "an article of faith," as Paul Volcker has described it—that the United States used its overwhelming power in the early postwar years to establish an open, liberal international economic order.[6] Since the early 1980s, however, this conventional wisdom has come under attack. John Ruggie, for example, argued persuasively in an article published in 1982 that the United States did not in fact promote a purely liberal international economic order at the 1944 Bretton Woods Conference. Rather, it built an "embedded liberal" order in which restrictive economic practices required to defend the policy autonomy of the new interventionist welfare state were strongly endorsed.[7] A second influential revisionist work was Alan Milward's 1984 study, which asserted that the importance of Marshall Plan aid in the reconstruction of Western Europe had been greatly exaggerated.[8] More recently, other scholars have also questioned the notion that the United States used its power in the early postwar years to build a liberal international economic order.[9]

6. Volcker and Gyohten 1992:288.
7. Ruggie 1982.
8. Milward 1984.
9. Loriaux 1991, Ikenberry 1989, Maxfield and Nolt 1990, and Burnham 1990.

The first part of this book provides strong support for the revisionist school by demonstrating that the globalization of financial markets should not be seen as a direct consequence of the international economic order established under U.S. leadership in the early postwar years. As explained in Chapter 2, the Bretton Woods negotiators, under American leadership, explicitly opposed a return to the open, liberal international financial order existing before 1931. Indeed, they constructed a decidedly *non*liberal financial order in which the use of capital controls was strongly endorsed. As U.S. Treasury Department Secretary Henry Morgenthau told the conference, the goal of the Bretton Woods Agreement was to "drive the usurious moneylenders from the temple of international finance."[10] Chapter 3 makes clear that advanced industrial states remained strongly committed to this restrictive international financial order in the early postwar years, employing extensive capital controls throughout the 1940s and 1950s. Even U.S. policymakers, who chose not to use capital controls in this period, were remarkably accepting, and indeed supportive, of the use of capital controls abroad. In the late 1950s and early 1960s, when Western Europe and Japan finally restored the convertibility of their currencies, the United States also fully supported their decision not to extend convertibility to the capital account.

Four explanations can be given for the widespread use of capital controls and the wariness of states throughout the advanced industrial world to accept a liberal international financial order in the early postwar period. First, following Ruggie's analysis, the use of capital controls was prompted in part by the prominence of an embedded liberal framework of thought in this period. Although they acknowledged the validity of the liberal case that some capital movements were beneficial, "embedded" liberals argued that capital controls were necessary to prevent the policy autonomy of the new interventionist welfare state from being undermined by speculative and disequilibrating international capital flows. The embedded liberal normative framework in finance was strongly backed by a new alliance of Keynesian-minded state officials, industrialists, and labor leaders who had increasingly replaced private and central bankers in positions of financial power in the advanced industrial world during the 1930s and World War II. Whereas the bankers continued to

10. Quoted in Gardner 1980:76.

support a liberal ideology in finance, members of this new alliance favored more interventionist policies that would make finance the "servant" rather than the "master" in economic and political matters.[11]

The second explanation of the support for the restrictive Bretton Woods financial order was the widespread belief in the early postwar period that a liberal international financial order would not be compatible, at least in the short run, with a stable system of exchange rates and a liberal international trading order. This belief stemmed from the experience of the interwar period, when speculative capital movements had severely disrupted exchange rates and trade relations. It also reflected early recognition of a point that has increasingly been emphasized in recent years by Robert Gilpin and others: that different elements of a liberal international economic order are not necessarily compatible.[12] Faced with a choice between creating a liberal order in finance and building a system of stable exchange rates and liberal trade, policymakers in the early postwar period generally agreed that free finance should be sacrificed. As Lawrence Krause notes, the financial sector was thus assigned a kind of "second-class status" in the postwar liberal international economic order.[13]

The third explanation concerns the sympathetic attitude adopted by the United States toward the use of capital controls in Western Europe and Japan. Although this stance in part reflected the first two factors, it also stemmed from American strategic goals in the cold war after 1947. On one hand, U.S. strategic thinkers were reluctant to alienate their West European and Japanese allies by pressing for unpopular liberalization moves. On the other, as Michael Loriaux has also recently pointed out, U.S. strategic thinkers actively supported financial interventionism abroad as part of a larger effort to promote economic growth in Western Europe and Japan.[14] Indeed, U.S. officials were often more enthusiastic advocates of embedded liberal financial policies abroad than were the policymakers in these countries for this reason. The cold war thus prompted the United States to assume an accommodating or "benevolent" form of hegemony over Western Europe and Japan after 1947; it both

11. Gardner 1980:76.
12. Gilpin 1987:367. See also the discussion in Chapter 9 of this volume.
13. Krause 1971:536.
14. Loriaux 1991:chap. 4, 300–303.

yielded to their preference for capital controls and actively supported measures that might foster their prosperity.

There was, however, one brief interval after the Bretton Woods
conference and before the onset of the cold war when U.S. foreign
financial policy took a different tack. Between 1945 and 1947, leading members of the New York financial community dominated U.S.
foreign economic policy and tried to create a more open international financial order by applying more aggressive pressure on Western European countries to liberalize their exchange controls and restore monetary stability. The 1947 economic crisis in Europe,
however, marked the failure of the initiative. Although the crisis has
usually been attributed to the severity of the economic dislocation in
Europe following the war, Chapter 3 suggests that a key cause was
the behavior of the New York bankers themselves. Their refusal to
cooperate with West European governments in curtailing enormous,
disruptive capital flight from Europe to the United States in this period contributed substantially to Europe's economic difficulties.
Their behavior stemmed primarily from their direct interest in receiving the capital as the leading international bankers after the war.
This shortsightedness constitutes the final explanation for why a
more open international financial order did not emerge in the early
postwar years.

Explaining the Globalization of Finance

If states were so wary of international movements of private capital in the early postwar years, what explains the reemergence of
global financial markets since the late 1950s? Most histories of the
globalization of finance stress the influence of technological changes
and market developments. The growth of global telecommunications
networks is shown to have dramatically reduced the costs and difficulties of transferring funds around the world. At least six market
developments are said to have been significant. The first was the
restoration of market confidence in the safety of international financial transactions in the late 1950s. This confidence had been shaken
by the 1931 crisis and the subsequent economic and political upheavals. The second was the rapid increase in the demand for international financial services that accompanied the growth of international trade and multinational corporate activity in the 1960s.

Third, private banks responded quickly to the global financial imbalances caused by the 1973 oil price rise, encouraging enormous deposits by oil-producing states and the borrowing of those funds by deficit countries. Fourth, the adoption of floating exchange rates in the early 1970s encouraged market operators to diversify their assets internationally in the new volatile currency markets. Fifth, the disintegration of domestically focused postwar financial cartels throughout the advanced industrial world in the 1970s and 1980s forced financial institutions to enter the international financial arena to supplement their declining domestic profits; such a move also enabled them to evade remaining domestic regulatory constraints. Finally, the market innovations that were created in this increasingly competitive atmosphere, such as currency and interest rate futures, options and swaps, also reduced the effective risks and costs of international financial operations.

According to this interpretation, states have played only a minor role in the globalization process. In particular, they are said to have been unable to stop the trend because of the impossibility of controlling international capital movements, which in turn is said to have stemmed from two characteristics of money: its mobility and its fungibility. As Lawrence Krause explains, "[Money] can be transmitted instantaneously and at low cost—indeed, with the mere stroke of a hypothetical pen. It can be inventoried without physical deterioration and without warehousing cost. It can change its identity easily and can be traced only with great effort, if at all."[15] Increasing international economic interdependence and technological change only multiplied the opportunities for market operators to evade controls, particularly those in the form of "leads and lags" in current account payments. It has thus become common to argue that the endorsement of capital controls at the Bretton Woods Conference was largely useless in that it exaggerated the capacity of states to control capital movements.[16]

As will be discussed in Part 2, this attempt to downplay the importance of states is not convincing. International financial markets were able to develop only within what Stephen Krasner and Janice Thomson refer to as "a broader institutional structure delineated by the power and policies of states."[17] Two questions arise: *How* were

15. Krause 1971:525.
16. For example, Gardner 1980:217.
17. Krasner and Thomson 1989:203.

the actions and decisions of states important to the globalization process? *Why* did states increasingly embrace an open liberal international financial order after having opposed its creation in the early postwar years?

What Role Did States Play in Globalization?

Advanced industrial states made three types of policy decisions after the late 1950s that were important to the globalization process: (1) to grant more freedom to market operators through liberalization initiatives, (2) to refrain from imposing more effective controls on capital movements, and (3) to prevent major international financial crises.

The policy decision to allow market operators a greater degree of freedom through liberalization moves has received the most attention in the growing body of IPE literature. It was first in evidence in the 1960s when Britain and the United States strongly supported growth of the Euromarket in London. This market served as an offshore regulation-free environment in which to trade financial assets denominated in foreign currencies, predominantly U.S. dollars. In a world of extensive capital controls, it was a kind of "adventure playground" for private international bankers, marking a significant break from the restrictive financial relations that had characterized the early postwar period.[18] Although the market has sometimes been described as "stateless,"[19] it could not have survived without the backing of Britain and the United States. Britain's support for the Eurodollar market was crucial because locating the market in London meant that it could operate free of regulation. The support of the United States was equally important because of the dominant presence of American banks and corporations in the market. Although it had the power to do so, the United States did not prevent these institutions from operating in the market.

States also granted market operators an extra degree of freedom after the mid-1970s when they began to abolish their postwar capital controls. Once again, the United States and Britain played a leading role. In 1974, the United States initiated this liberalization trend by removing the various capital controls it had introduced briefly in

18. Quote from Strange 1990:264.
19. Wriston 1986:133.

the mid-1960s. Britain followed in 1979, eliminating its forty-year-old capital controls. The American and British actions were copied by other advanced industrial nations in the 1980s. In 1984–85, Australia and New Zealand abolished capital controls that had been in place for almost a half-century. Many European countries initiated financial liberalization programs in the mid-1980s, and by 1988 all countries in the European Community had agreed to remove their controls completely in two to four years. The Scandinavian countries announced similar commitments in 1989–90, and Japan gradually dismantled its tight postwar capital controls throughout the 1980s. By the end of the decade, an almost fully liberal financial order had been created in the OECD region, giving market operators a degree of freedom they had not had since the 1920s.

The second type of policy decision of states—to refrain from imposing more effective capital controls—has not received extensive analysis in IPE literature. Although it is true that states find it difficult to control capital movements, the authors of conventional histories of the globalization process have generally overlooked the fact that the Bretton Woods architects discussed these difficulties and outlined two specific mechanisms for overcoming them. First, they argued that capital controls could be made to work through cooperative initiatives in which controls were enforced at both ends, that is, both in the country that sent the capital and in the country that received it. Second, they concluded that evasion of capital controls could be prevented through the use of comprehensive exchange controls in which all transactions—capital account *and* current account—were monitored for illegal capital flows. Because both mechanisms found their way into the final Bretton Woods Agreement, it is necessary to explain why states chose not to use them in an attempt to render their capital controls more effective.

In fact, there were a number of episodes in the 1970s and early 1980s when policymakers seriously considered, but ultimately rejected, the use of these mechanisms to reverse the globalization trend. Despite the lack of attention given to these decisions in histories of the globalization of finance, each represented a key turning point in the globalization process. The first such turning point was in the early 1970s, when the increase in speculative capital flows threatened the Bretton Woods stable exchange rate system. Because limited capital controls had failed to contain these speculative capital movements, governments in Japan and Western Europe pressed for the introduction of cooperative controls on capital movements as a way of preserving the stable exchange rate system. Controls were to be imposed both in countries receiving capital flows and in countries sending them, as well as in "throughflow" countries such as those housing Euromarket centers. This ambitious initiative would have dealt a strong blow to the embryonic globalization trend. Although the proposal had considerable support, the U.S. refused to endorse it. Indeed, the United States not only opposed cooperative controls in this period but also began, for the first time since 1945–47, to urge other countries to follow its lead in abolishing existing capital controls. Without U.S. support, other countries were forced to abandon the initiative. Given the importance of the United States in international finance, its cooperation was clearly necessary for such a regulatory effort to succeed.

The second turning point occurred in the late 1970s and early 1980s, in four instances when policymakers gave serious consideration to the implementation of more effective capital controls. Whereas the Japanese and West European initiative in the early 1970s had been driven by a desire to defend the Bretton Woods stable exchange rate system, these initiatives were intended to preserve the Bretton Woods commitment to policy autonomy in the increasingly open global financial environment. In the first two instances, the British government in 1976 and the French government in 1982–83 contemplated the introduction of comprehensive exchange controls in order to defend their expansionary macroeconomic programs from the disruptive effects of speculative capital flight. Only after extremely divisive internal debate was the option ultimately rejected by each government. These decisions were important in the history of the globalization process. As participants at the time recognized, the introduction of tight exchange controls by a major advanced industrial state in this period would have seriously challenged the underlying trend. The introduction of exchange controls in Britain, in particular, would have removed one of the key pillars of the emerging global financial order, the Euromarket centered in London.

The other two instances in this period involved the United States. During the 1978–79 dollar crisis, U.S. policymakers briefly considered the reintroduction of capital controls in order to preserve some degree of policy autonomy in the face of speculative market pressures. Despite the severity of the crisis, they rejected the idea. This decision marked an important turning point because it demonstrated the strength of the U.S. commitment to the emerging open international financial order, a commitment that had been increasing since the 1960s and that would become more overt in the 1980s. In 1979–80, the U.S. Federal Reserve made a brief attempt to persuade central bankers in other Western nations to cooperate in reregulating the Euromarket in order to prevent its operations from interfering with U.S. domestic monetary policy. Had this initiative succeeded, it would have significantly reduced the market's size and weakened some of the key forces contributing to the liberalization trend in the 1980s. It failed, however, because of strong domestic opposition and the opposition of Britain and Switzerland.

The importance of the third type of policy decision—to attempt to prevent major international financial crises—is rarely acknowledged by those who point to the inevitability of the globalization trend in the face of market and technological pressures. The danger posed by these crises is that, if uncontained, they would likely encourage market operators to retreat to their domestic markets and prompt states to introduce tight capital controls. Both developments, for example, followed the 1931 crisis, thus bringing down the liberal international financial order of the 1920s.

Three major crises struck the emerging open financial order in the postwar period: the international banking crisis of 1974, the international debt crisis of 1982, and the stock market crash of 1987. All three crises were prevented from spiraling out of control because states acted decisively to contain them through lender-of-last-resort action; that is, the extension of emergency assistance to institutions, countries, or markets that were experiencing a sudden withdrawal of funds. In 1974 and 1982, the United States played the key role. U.S. policymakers were also supported in each case by Britain as well as by the close cooperation of central banks from the G-10 countries.[20] In 1987, the G-10 central banks acted together in the lender-of-last-resort role. Their action was also bolstered by decisive steps that the Japanese government took in its own markets. In addition to these crisis-management activities, G-10 central banks—prompted by the United States and Britain—also made important moves to

20. The original G-10 countries were the United States, Canada, Japan, the Federal Republic of Germany, France, Italy, the United Kingdom, Sweden, the Netherlands, and Belgium. Switzerland also joined the G-10 after its formation, although the group's name remained unchanged.

prevent further crises from occurring in the 1970s and 1980s. In the mid-1970s, they bolstered the confidence of private international financial operators by reassuring them that lender-of-last-resort action would extend to new international financial markets such as the Euromarket. Throughout this period, they also expanded their supervision and regulation of international financial activities in an effort to curtail imprudent market behavior.

Why Did States Support Globalization?

Why did states increasingly embrace an open, liberal international financial order in these ways beginning in the late 1950s, after supporting the restrictive Bretton Woods order in the early postwar years? There are four explanations (discussed more fully in Part 2) for this change in attitude.

First, attempts to preserve the Bretton Woods order met with several inherent political difficulties. The creation of the Euromarket showed the ease with which individual states (the United States and Britain) could significantly undermine the order unilaterally by offering mobile financial traders a location in which to operate without regulation. Equally important, individual states—once again the United States and Britain—could unleash competitive pressures that indirectly encouraged liberalization and deregulation throughout the system. When these two states supported growth of the Euromarket in the 1960s and then liberalized and deregulated their financial markets in the 1970s and 1980s, foreign financial centers increasingly witnessed their business and capital migrating to these more attractive markets. To compete effectively for this mobile financial business and capital, they were forced to follow the lead of Britain and the United States by liberalizing and deregulating their own financial systems. This "competitive deregulation" in finance was a central reason for the flurry of liberalization activity throughout the advanced industrial world in the 1980s.[21]

Political difficulties also hindered implementation of the two mechanisms outlined at the Bretton Woods conference for more effectively controlling capital movements. The introduction of cooper-

21. Other scholars have also pointed to the competitive deregulation dynamic in finance, such as Goodman and Pauly (1990), Cerny (1989), Hawley (1987:142–43), Moran (1991), Plender (1986–87:41), Strange (1988:108), Walter (1991:207, 232), Hamilton (1986), Dale (1984:40), Kapstein (1989:324), and Bryant (1987:139).

ative controls could easily be vetoed by a major state or group of states, as shown by the United States in the early 1970s and Britain and Switzerland in 1979–80. The use of comprehensive exchange controls would impose large economic and political costs, especially in the increasingly interdependent world economy of the 1970s and 1980s, as policymakers in Britain and France in 1976 and 1982–83 were forced to recognize. Thus, although it may have been technically possible to control capital movements more effectively by means of the two mechanisms suggested at Bretton Woods, both were politically difficult to implement in practice. Indeed, these political difficulties had been encountered in the early postwar years as well and were then temporarily handled only by the creation of costly offsetting financing networks (as described in Chapters 3 and 4), a solution that proved difficult to sustain in the 1970s and 1980s.

The second explanation for the unraveling of the Bretton Woods financial order relates to the strong interest of the United States and Britain after the late 1950s in promoting a more open international financial order. The United States abandoned its early postwar support for the restrictive Bretton Woods order in large part because of its changing global position. In the early postwar years, the economic strength of the United States and its strategic interests in the cold war encouraged it to assume a "benevolent" hegemonic position in the Western alliance. Many analysts have suggested that beginning in the 1960s, the United States gradually adopted a more self-centered or "predatory" foreign economic policy because of growing current account and budget deficits. In particular, the United States began to seek foreign help in financing and adjusting to these deficits, in order to maintain its policy autonomy.[22] This more aggressive foreign policy strategy relied largely on what Susan Strange calls the unique "structural power" of the United States within the emerging open global financial order.[23] Its hegemonic position in trade may have been declining, but the United States retained a dominant position in this financial order well into the 1980s because of the relative attractiveness of U.S. financial markets, the preeminence of U.S. financial institutions and the dollar in global markets, and the relative size of the U.S. economy. This hege-

22. See, for example, Gilpin 1987; Calleo 1982, 1987; and Strange 1988. The distinction between predatory and benevolent hegemony is from Gilpin 1987:90, 345.

23. For a discussion of "structural power," see Strange 1988:24–31 and Moran 1991:131.

monic position in the emerging open global financial order provided
the United States with a fundamental reason for promoting the globalization process from the 1960s through the 1980s.[24]

Whereas U.S. support for globalization reflected its existing hegemonic position in world finance, British support was rooted in a
"lagging" hegemonic financial policy.[25] Long after Britain had lost
its nineteenth-century position as a financial hegemon, British financial authorities remained wedded to the notion that London should
be an international financial center. This commitment stemmed from
the strength of what Geoffrey Ingham has called the "Bank of En-
gland-Treasury-City nexus" in British politics.[26] From the 1931 sterling crisis to the 1950s, London's international financial position
was ensured because the city served as the financial center for the
closed sterling bloc. As the long-term viability of this bloc came increasingly into question in the late 1950s, however, British financial
authorities realized that London's international position might be
better preserved if it were to act as a financial center for offshore
dollar transactions. This realization led to their support for the Eurodollar market in the 1960s and more broadly for the globalization
process in the 1970s and 1980s.

It was not just the United States and Britain whose interests in
promoting globalization were related to their respective positions of
power (present and past) in world finance. Japan's leadership role in
stabilizing the 1987 stock market crash and its financial liberalization program in the 1980s were also associated with its growing
importance in the international financial order in this decade.
Whereas Britain's actions reflected the lagging behavior of a power
in decline, Japan's represented the "leading" behavior of a financial
power on the rise. Three considerations encouraged Japan to take a
keen interest in financial openness in the 1980s before it had
achieved a hegemonic financial position. First, and most important,
its rapid and enormous accumulation of external financial assets beginning in 1981 gave Japan an important stake in global financial
stability. Second, its strong political and economic dependence on
the United States encouraged Japanese policymakers to respond to
U.S. pressure for financial liberalization and to act promptly when

24. This argument concerning U.S. behavior is somewhat similar to that of Walter
(1991).
25. Krasner (1976:341–43) developed the notion of "lagging" hegemonic financial
policy.
26. Ingham 1984.

the 1987 crisis threatened U.S. financial stability. Third, Japan's financial liberalization was also accelerated by an upheaval in the domestic financial system beginning in the mid-1970s caused primarily by an increase in government deficits.

In addition to the inherent political difficulties associated with maintaining the Bretton Woods financial order and the unique "hegemonic" interests of these three powers, the third explanation for states' growing enthusiasm for the globalization process was the increasing rejection of the embedded liberal framework of thought (on which the Bretton Woods financial order was based) in favor of a neoliberal framework in the 1970s and 1980s.[27] Neoliberal advocates favored a liberal international financial order on the grounds that it would enhance personal freedom and promote a more efficient allocation of capital both internationally and domestically. Neoliberals also rejected the two reasons outlined at Bretton Woods for justifying capital controls. First, they disregarded the postwar concern that speculative capital flows would disrupt the Bretton Woods exchange rate system by arguing strongly in favor of floating exchange rates. Second, they did not seek to preserve the policy autonomy of the interventionist welfare state but rather supported freer domestic markets and more orthodox fiscal and monetary policies. Indeed, neoliberal advocates praised international financial markets for prompting states to adopt these policies.

Although the ideological shift to neoliberalism took place at varying rates of speed and degrees of intensity in different countries, several factors explain its prevalence throughout the advanced industrial world. Many policymakers began to embrace neoliberal ideas for the practical reason that they found it increasingly difficult to continue to support embedded liberal policies in the increasingly open financial environment of 1970s and 1980s. The shift was also encouraged by important thinkers such as Milton Friedman and Friedrich Hayek who developed neoliberal ideas and helped to build intellectual networks, often transnational in scope, in order to promote them, as had Keynes and his supporters in the 1930s and 1940s.[28] The neoliberal movement gained added strength from the economic slowdown in the 1970s and 1980s, which, like that in the

27. Other scholars, such as Pauly (1987a, 1988), Schor (1992:8), and Plender (1986–87:40), also emphasize the importance of changing normative frameworks in explaining the increasing support of states for financial openness in the 1970s and 1980s.

28. The transnational spread of the earlier Keynesian revolution is well analyzed by Hall 1989.

1930s, eroded support for existing economic paradigms and created an intellectual climate in which neoliberal ideas were more easily embraced. Finally, neoliberal ideas were also supported by a coalition of social groups throughout the advanced industrial world in the 1970s and 1980s that differed considerably from that which had supported embedded liberal ideas in the early postwar period. This coalition included representatives of multinational industrial firms, who increasingly favored a liberal international financial order as their operations became more internationalized, and officials of private financial institutions, who had, for the most part, supported financial liberalization throughout the postwar period but whose enthusiasm was strengthened by the competitive financial environment of the 1970s and 1980s.[29] The neoliberal financial message also found strong support among officials of central banks, finance ministries, and international financial organizations, who had often been wary of the interventionist financial practices of the early postwar years.[30]

The fourth explanation for state support for globalization is that the important cooperation of central bank officials from G-10 countries in preventing major international financial crises was aided enormously by the existence of an increasingly sophisticated "regime" based around the Bank for International Settlements (BIS) in Basel.[31] These central bankers were the most cautious of the neoliberal advocates in their endorsement of a fully liberal, deregulated global financial order. They not only worried that the operations of

29. The reasons given for the support of private financial firms and multinational industrial interests for neoliberal ideas in the 1970s and 1980s suggest that there is some validity to the argument that market pressures (such as increased financial competition and the growth of multinational corporations) can explain the globalization process. Whereas some see such pressures as promoting globalization *directly*, however, I am arguing that the influence was *indirect*; the support of neoliberal advocates by private financial firms and multinational corporations encouraged states to turn away from the restrictive Bretton Woods financial order.

30. My emphasis on this neoliberal coalition, as well as its earlier embedded liberal counterpart, is comparable to Maxfield's (1990) discussion of two competing "policy alliances or currents." Frieden (1991:442) also discusses the importance of distinguishing "two camps": "integrationist" forces, consisting of "the financial sector, owners of financial assets, and integrated multinational firms"; and "anti-integrationist" forces, consisting of "firms specific to a particular industry and location" (see also Frieden 1987:166–70). See also Goodman and Pauly 1990. Similarly, Moran (1991:12, 130–31) points to the importance of a common "bloc" of financial officials and private financial interests promoting globalization in each country. Pringle (1989) and Epstein and Schor (1992) also emphasize the centrality of financial interests.

31. For a discussion of the concept of a "regime," see Keohane 1984 and Krasner 1983.

such an order would conflict with domestic monetary policies but, more important, they feared instability and crises in the new global financial markets. To prevent such crises, they cooperated closely in a number of ways that have already been noted. This close pattern of cooperation was facilitated not only by U.S. and British leadership, but also by the BIS-centered regime. The BIS had been set up by private and central bankers in 1930 to help reduce the international financial instability and reparations problems of that era by providing a forum where the world's leading central bankers could be brought together for monthly meetings. Although it failed to prevent the 1931 crisis, the institution acted as a helpful meeting place for central bankers in the 1970s and 1980s to devise cooperative means of minimizing financial instability. Understandings built through the frequent BIS meetings proved crucial in fostering cooperative central bank responses to each of three major crises in this period. Moreover, in the wake of each crisis, central bankers met within the BIS to construct an increasingly sophisticated set of norms, rules, and decision-making procedures for handling and preventing future crises. These norms, rules, and procedures identified and allocated responsibilities for both international lender-of-last-resort action and the regulation and supervision of international financial markets. These provisions did much to diminish problems of collective action involved in maintaining global financial stability by changing expectations, providing information, and institutionalizing cooperation among central bankers.

The prominence of this BIS-centered regime dedicated to the principle of preserving stability in international financial markets reflected a further way in which the international financial order had changed from that outlined at Bretton Woods. The Bretton Woods authors, after all, outlined no specific mechanisms for preventing international financial crises, save that of imposing capital controls. Furthermore, the association that many Bretton Woods negotiators drew between the BIS and the pre-1931 liberal era of international finance had led them to pass a motion at the conference calling for the institution's abolition "at the earliest possible moment." This resolution, however, was never enforced. Saved from abolition, the institution reemerged to perform the function that the international bankers of the pre-1931 era had hoped it would. As Fred Hirsch said, it was "a link between the old financial world and the new."[32]

32. Hirsch 1967:239.

Why Have States Acted So Differently in Trade and Finance?

In the concluding chapter the discussion returns to the question of why states increasingly embraced an open, liberal international financial order at a time when they retained numerous restrictive trade practices. Five explanations are given for this difference in state behavior. First, the unique mobility and fungibility of money ensured that policymakers were not faced with the same collective action problems in creating and maintaining an open international financial order that existed in the area of trade. A more open financial order could be *created* by a state that unilaterally provided resourceful financial market operators an extra degree of freedom, as did Britain and the United States when they supported the Euromarket in the 1960s. The competitive deregulation dynamic also demonstrated that collective action problems were less relevant to the liberalization process because the key benefit of financial openness—attracting footloose global financial business and funds to a country's own market—was "consumed" through unilateral rather than collective action. The task of *maintaining* an open financial order also presented few collective action problems. For example, there was less need to create a collective regime to police against unilateral moves toward closure because such moves were unlikely, given the high cost of introducing comprehensive exchange controls in the 1970s and 1980s. The other mechanism for more effectively controlling capital movements—cooperative controls—was equally problematic because individual states could veto such an initiative. Indeed, in this sense, collective action problems were more relevant to creating a closed financial order than to maintaining an open one.

Although collective action problems were not present in these respects in finance, they did exist with respect to two activities necessary to prevent financial crises: international lender-of-last-resort action and international prudential supervision and regulation.[33] These problems were partly overcome with the consolidation of the central bankers' regime centered around the Bank for International Settlements. This regime could be strengthened at a time when the postwar trade regime was increasingly encountering difficulties in part because central bankers as a group had much in common with what

33. See, for example, Dale 1984, Guttentag and Herring 1983:11–16, Kapstein 1989, Bryant 1987:chap. 8, and Spero 1980:185.

Peter Haas has termed "transnational epistemic communities."[34] To a much greater degree than trade officials, they shared a similar knowledge base, common causal and principled beliefs, and the collective policy project of seeking to prevent international financial crises. This contrast in the nature of the interaction of central bankers and that of trade officials constitutes the second explanation for the differing pattern of state behavior in international finance and trade.

The successful handling of financial crises, as well as the consolidation of the BIS-centered regime, also related to the third explanation: the unique "hegemonic" interests of the United States, Britain, and, more recently, Japan in the financial sector. In assuming a leadership role in these areas, and in promoting financial openness in other important ways, these three states displayed a particular enthusiasm for the emerging open, liberal financial order, a sentiment that was stronger than their support for open, liberal trade in this period. A key reason for their different approach to the two sectors was that each had "hegemonic" interests in finance that they did not have with respect to trade. In contrast to its declining position in international trade, the United States retained its hegemonic position in the emerging open global financial order well into the 1980s, a position from which it derived important benefits. The hegemonic lag that explained British support for globalization was politically more sustainable in finance than in trade primarily because the Euromarket provided London bankers with a mechanism by which to regain their leading position in international finance. Japan's leadership was more evident in finance as the decade of the 1980s progressed than in trade, largely because of its rapid accumulation of external financial assets after 1981.

The fourth explanation is that the neoliberal advocates had more influence in the international financial sector than in the trade sector in the 1970s and 1980s, for the most part because of the relatively low domestic political visibility of the issue of financial liberalization among politicians and the general public.[35] Financial liberalization attracted relatively little attention partly because of the seemingly complex and highly technical nature of international financial issues.

34. Haas 1992. Like Kapstein (1992), I am wary of describing central bankers as constituting a full-fledged transnational epistemic community, for reasons given in Chapter 9.
35. Duvall and Wendt (1987:46) and Bertrand (1981:21) have also commented on the low political visibility of international financial issues.

Consequently, supporters of neoliberal ideas in academia, financial bureaucracies, and the private sector had considerable autonomy to determine policy outcomes in this area. Another reason for the issue's low political visibility is that the liberalization of financial movements, unlike trade liberalization, did not negatively affect any specific societal group in an easily recognizable way; rather, its impact was largely at the less visible and more dispersed macroeconomic level.

The fifth explanation for the difference in state behavior with regard to trade and finance is that there is a relationship between the two. As policymakers noted in the early postwar years, a liberal international financial order is not necessarily compatible with a liberal international trading order. The Bretton Woods negotiators worried that speculative and disequilibrating capital movements would disrupt trade patterns and encourage protectionist pressures. Recent experience has to some extent borne out these fears. Many observers have attributed the increase in restrictive trade practices in the 1970s and 1980s to the globalization of financial markets. Robert Gilpin has argued that "as international finance has more tightly integrated national markets, states have responded by increasing the level of trade protectionism."[36] Similarly, Rimmer De Vries concluded in 1990 that "there is a certain tension in maintaining both free capital and free trade. The difficulty of repressing capital flows makes for a tendency to compensate ill effects by giving ground on free trade."[37] In this sense, the difference in state behavior in trade and finance lends strength to the assertion that different parts of a liberal international economic order are not necessarily compatible.

Chapter 9 presents three broad theoretical issues that arise from these five explanations of the differences between state behavior in trade and finance. First, as suggested by three of the explanations, states may be more likely to embrace an open, liberal order in some sectors of the international economy than in others because of inherent sector-specific characteristics. Such an order was easier to create and maintain in finance than in trade because of the unique mobility and fungibility of money, the relatively cooperative attitude of central bankers, and the low domestic political visibility of the issue of financial liberalization. Second, the leadership of the United States, Britain, and, more recently, Japan in promoting globalization sug-

36. Gilpin 1987:367.
37. De Vries 1990:9.

gests that "hegemonic" states do play an important role in the creation of a liberal international financial order.[38] Three qualifications of the traditional hegemonic stability theory must be mentioned, however: (1) U.S. hegemonic behavior in finance was driven by less benevolent objectives than predicted by some versions of the theory; (2) the Japanese and British roles can be understood only by allowing for "leads" and "lags" in hegemonic behavior; (3) the concept of hegemony must be differentiated by sector, because each state's hegemonic interest in financial openness did not correspond with its interests in trade. Third, the apparent incompatibility of liberal orders in trade and in finance suggests that IPE scholars should be careful when using the term "liberal international economic order" to describe the structure of the international economy as a whole in any given period.

This book builds on recent work by IPE scholars to provide a more synthetic political history of the globalization of financial markets in the postwar period. It presents three broad arguments. First, globalization cannot be seen as a direct product of the early postwar international economic order. Rather, throughout the 1940s and 1950s, states were committed to a restrictive financial order outlined at Bretton Woods because of the strength of an embedded liberal framework of thought, U.S. strategic goals in the cold war, and the perceived need to sacrifice financial liberalism in order to promote free trade and exchange rate stability. The shortsightedness of the New York bankers in 1945–47 also helped undermine the one brief effort to construct a more open financial order in this period.

Second, advanced industrial states have played an important role in the globalization process since the late 1950s by (1) granting freedom to market operators, both through encouraging growth of the Euromarket in the 1960s and through liberalizing capital controls after the mid-1970s; (2) choosing not to implement more effective controls on capital movements in the early 1970s and in four instances in the late 1970s and early 1980s; and (3) preventing three major international financial crises, in 1974, 1982, and 1987. Their support can be explained by the political difficulties involved in implementing more effective controls and in preventing unilateral liberalization moves; the respective hegemonic interests of the United

38. Proponents of this view include Krasner (1976), Gilpin (1987), and Kindleberger (1973, 1986).

States, Britain, and Japan in creating and maintaining a stable, open international financial order; the growing influence of neoliberal advocates in international financial policymaking; and the existence of an increasingly sophisticated regime centered around the BIS and designed to prevent and contain international financial crises.

Third, states embraced a more open liberal international financial order at a time when they retained numerous restrictive trade practices for five reasons: (1) The mobility and fungibility of money ensured that the collective actions necessary to create and maintain an open trade order were less relevant in finance. (2) The BIS-centered regime drew strength from the fact that central bankers, unlike trade officials, exhibited many of the characteristics of transnational epistemic communities. (3) The United States, Britain, and Japan supported the globalization trend in finance particularly strongly because their power and interests in trade and in finance differed considerably. (4) Neoliberal advocates were able to exert strong influence in finance in part because of the low domestic political visibility of the issue of financial liberalization. (5) State behavior in trade and in finance may have been interrelated, thus reinforcing the early postwar view that free trade and free finance are not necessarily compatible.

PART I

THE RESTRICTIVE
BRETTON WOODS
FINANCIAL ORDER

CHAPTER TWO

Bretton Woods and the
Endorsement of Capital Controls

IT IS SOMETIMES ASSUMED THAT THE GLOBALIZATION OF FINANCIAL markets had its roots in the 1944 Bretton Woods Agreement. As the constitution of the postwar international economic order, the agreement is said to have promoted both a liberal order in international trade *and* finance.[1] In fact, the agreement set up a rather restrictive financial order in which capital controls were not only permitted but encouraged. Far from setting the stage for the globalization of financial markets in more recent years, the Bretton Woods Agreement was a dramatic rejection of the liberal financial policies that had been prominent before 1931. As the chief British negotiator, John Maynard Keynes, put it, "Not merely as a feature of the transition, but as a permanent arrangement, the plan accords to every member government the explicit right to control all capital movements. What used to be a heresy is now endorsed as orthodox."[2]

In addition to the need to clarify this misconception, it is also important to study the Bretton Woods negotiations concerning international financial movements because they clearly laid out many of the central issues that would confront policymakers in this field in the following decades.[3] Recent debates concerning the costs and ben-

1. See, for example, Ilgen 1985:10.
2. Keynes 1980b:17.
3. The authors of the classic texts on the Bretton Woods negotiations (e.g., Van Dormael 1978, Block 1977, Gardner 1980, and Eckes 1975) refer only briefly to the discussions concerning international private finance. Somewhat more detailed examinations can be found in De Cecco 1979, Gold 1977, Goodman and Pauly 1990, and Crotty 1983.

efits of a liberal international financial order were foreshadowed by
those at Bretton Woods, for example. The Bretton Woods negotiators also discussed in detail the issue of to what degree and by what
mechanisms capital movements could actually be controlled—discussions that would be repeated in the 1970s and 1980s. The political forces aligning for and against controls at Bretton Woods were
also similar to those that would emerge on either side of the issue in
subsequent decades.

The first section of this chapter situates the Bretton Woods discussions in the context of the financial history of the interwar period,
concentrating on the growing support for capital controls after the
international financial crisis of 1931. The second section presents
the Bretton Woods proposals as initially formulated in 1941–42 by
the chief negotiators of the two major allied powers, Keynes from
Britain and Harry Dexter White from the United States. Far from
disagreeing, the two negotiators agreed on the need for restrictions
on international capital movements in the postwar world. The third
and fourth sections focus on how these proposals were modified because of opposition from the New York financial community.

The Break with the Liberal Tradition in
International Finance after 1931

To understand the Bretton Woods discussions concerning capital
movements, we must return briefly to the history of international
finance in the interwar period, which can be conveniently divided in
two segments, with the 1931 international financial crisis marking
the divide. The decade of the 1920s was dominated by an initiative
by private and central bankers throughout the advanced industrial
world to restore the pre-1914 liberal international monetary and financial order in which they had been so prominent.[4] Beginning at
international monetary conferences such as those at Brussels in 1920
and at Genoa in 1922, these bankers called for a return to balanced
budgets, independent central banks, free capital movements, and
above all, the international gold standard. This political initiative
was led by the two most powerful groups of bankers of the postwar
world: those in London and in New York. Working closely together,

4. See, for example, Costigliola 1984, Hogan 1977, Leffler 1979, and McNeil 1986.

they offered large loans to governments willing to adopt these policy changes. Indeed, by the mid-1920s, they had largely succeeded in resurrecting the international gold standard and reviving an active circuit of international private lending.

The bankers' victory was short-lived, however. After 1929, the confidence of private international lenders rapidly deteriorated as a result of the U.S. stock market crash of that year, the subsequent worldwide depression, the continuing reparations and war debt muddles, and large underlying payments imbalances. Hoping to preserve what they had built, bankers in the advanced industrial nations tried desperately to prevent a crisis through initiatives such as the creation in 1930 of the Bank for International Settlements, a body that was supposed to facilitate central bank cooperation as well as to depoliticize the debt and reparations issue.[5] But they were unable to prevent the complete collapse of market confidence in 1931. In the middle of that year, enormous speculative capital flight and a total cessation of long-term lending from the United States forced Germany and Austria to introduce exchange controls. In September, speculative pressures forced Britain to abandon the gold standard. By the end of the year, the bankers' project of restoring the pre-1914 monetary and financial order lay in ruins.[6]

The 1931 international financial crisis was important not only because it brought about the collapse of international capital markets and abandonment of the international gold standard but also because it marked the beginning of an important break with liberal tradition in financial affairs. As one German financier noted at the height of the crisis: "What I have just experienced means the end of a way of life, certainly for Germany and perhaps other countries as well. . . . The common vision of the future has been destroyed."[7] Their views largely discredited by the crisis, the private and central bankers who had dominated financial politics in the 1920s were increasingly replaced at the levers of financial power in the industrial world by a new coalition of social groups that included industrialists, labor leaders, and Keynesian-minded state officials. Whereas the bankers had advocated a laissez-faire approach to domestic financial issues and the automatic following of "rules of the game" in the international financial sphere, these new groups favored a more in-

5. Costigliola 1972; Simmons 1992.
6. See Kindleberger 1973 and Clarke 1967 for accounts of the crisis.
7. Quoted in Kunz 1987:71.

terventionist approach that would make domestic and international finance serve broader political and economic goals. As Fred Hirsch and Peter Oppenheimer have put it, "monetary standards no longer imposed. Rather, overriding political and economic circumstances determined monetary standards."[8]

Although the break with liberal tradition in financial affairs was prompted by the 1931 crisis, it was part of a reaction against liberalism that had been growing throughout the industrial world since the late nineteenth century.[9] In the areas of labor policy and international trade, the liberal traditions of the mid-nineteenth century had come under challenge since the 1870s. In international finance, however, the abandonment of the liberal tradition came much later and more abruptly. The relative longevity of liberalism in this area was due in part to the complex and technical nature of the issues involved. The prominent British socialist Sidney Webb, for example, is said to have been so mystified by international financial affairs that on learning of Britain's decision to abandon the gold standard, he stated: "Nobody told us we could do that."[10] The complexity of international financial issues gave them low political visibility, allowing private and central bankers sympathetic to financial liberalism to dominate international finance well into the 1920s. Only with the financial crisis and the depression of the 1930s was the predominance of the bankers and of liberal thought in financial matters ended.

The increasing use of capital controls in the 1930s was an important part of the break with liberal tradition in finance. The period before 1931 had not been completely free of capital controls. France and Germany had frequently restrained capital exports before World War I by controlling flotations of foreign securities. Even the strong supporters of the liberal financial order in the 1920s, Britain and the United States, had subtly attempted to regulate the flow of international capital at various times.[11] What was new, however, was the comprehensiveness and permanence of the controls. Before 1931, states had generally used capital controls on a temporary basis to achieve certain foreign policy goals (for example, denying enemy

8. Hirsch and Oppenheimer 1976:643. See also Kunz 1987, Van Der Pijl 1984, Polanyi 1957, and Aronson 1977:41 on the structural break.

9. See, for example, Cox 1987:151–89 and Polanyi 1957.

10. Quoted in Eichengreen and Cairncross 1983:5.

11. Feis 1964 (1930); Viner 1951; Leffler 1979:122, 174–77; and Einzig 1970:286.

states access to capital markets); they were now introduced as a permanent aspect of new interventionist economic strategies.

Not surprisingly, the first states to use comprehensive capital controls were those that departed most quickly and dramatically from liberal practices in other areas: Japan and Germany.[12] Although such controls were initially designed for the practical purpose of maintaining the balance of payments during and after the 1931 crisis, in these two countries they soon came to be seen as a permanent component of economic policy. Facing severe domestic economic crises, both Japan and Germany began to experiment with unorthodox domestic financial policies such as deficit financing and active monetary policy. Moreover, as the pressures of militarization increased during the 1930s, both states began extensive direct intervention in their domestic financial systems to ensure that scarce capital resources were allocated according to national objectives. Both macroeconomic management and state-directed financial planning forced a change in attitudes with regard to international capital movements. Macroeconomic management could easily be disrupted by speculative capital movements or by the flight of capital from artificially low interest rates. Similarly, government attempts to ration and allocate capital would be undermined if borrowers and investors had access to foreign capital markets. Capital controls thus became an integral part of the new domestic economic interventionism.

At the other extreme from Japan and Germany were the gold bloc countries—Switzerland, France, Belgium, and the Netherlands. The absence of severe balance-of-payments constraints and the stronger influence of orthodox ideas in these countries caused the change in their economic policies to be more gradual and less radical.[13] In the early 1930s, their exchange markets continued to be relatively free and they imposed few controls on capital movements. Only after the exchange crises in the second half of the decade did economic policy in these countries begin to change course. After its election in 1936, Léon Blum's Socialist government in France brought the Bank of France under increased public control and created a government financial institution to finance public works projects. By 1938, the French government was seriously considering the introduction of a system of exchange controls similar to that in Germany in order to more actively pursue an expansionary domestic policy. Not until

12. See Child 1954 and Dowd 1953.
13. Bloomfield 1950:9–10.

France and the other gold bloc countries were faced with the financial exigencies of World War II, however, did they fully institute domestic financial planning and capital controls.[14]

The shift away from liberal policies with respect to international capital movements in the United States and Britain can be said to have fallen between these two extremes. In the United States, the economic and financial crises of the early 1930s were a catalyst for a significant realignment of political coalitions that culminated in the election of Franklin D. Roosevelt as president in 1932. Supported by an alliance of farmers, labor groups, and sympathetic business leaders, the Roosevelt administration held the New York financial community, and especially the Morgan financial empire, responsible for much of the economic chaos of this period. Several important initiatives were launched in an effort to bring financial and monetary policy under stricter governmental control. Domestically, financial regulations were introduced to moderate competition, increase investor protection, and reduce Morgan's power. Reforms were also instituted to make the Federal Reserve System more politically accountable, and Marriner Eccles, a non–New York banker with decidedly nonorthodox views, was appointed to head it. Internationally, Roosevelt took the United States off the gold standard in April 1933, describing it as one of the "old fetishes of so-called international bankers."[15] Moreover, in a move that is particularly important for an understanding of the Bretton Woods discussions, control over international monetary policy was shifted from the Federal Reserve Bank of New York to the Treasury Department, which, under the leadership of Henry Morgenthau, had become a center of New Deal radicalism.

Initially, little effort was made to interfere with international movements of capital. Although Congress broadened the president's power to control foreign exchange transactions and prohibited loans to foreign governments that were in default to the United States, these initiatives were of minor practical consequence.[16] By 1936, however, the inflationary effect of increasingly large inflows of flight capital from Europe led many government officials, in the Treasury

14. Bloomfield 1950:187–88. Hall (1989:387) also stresses the importance of the war in spreading Keynesianism. On the Blum government's initiatives, see Brown 1987:89–90, Rosanvallon 1989:182–83, and Kuisel 1981:124–25.

15. Quoted in Hathaway 1984:284. See Hyman 1976 on Eccles's pre-Keynes Keynesian views.

16. Williams 1939:18–20.

Department in particular, to favor the introduction of exchange controls.[17] Their proposals were strongly opposed (as they would be during the Bretton Woods discussions) by more liberal thinkers in the federal government as well as by members of the financial community, who worried that New York's position as an international financial center would be weakened.[18] In place of exchange controls, the Treasury Department initiated a program intended to sterilize the monetary effect of the inflows after December 1936. At the same time, the department initiated discussions with Britain concerning possible cooperative efforts to control this "hot money" that might not require the use of exchange controls (again foreshadowing the Bretton Woods proposals).[19]

Both the coming of war and the initiation of planning for the postwar international economic order had the effect of encouraging a decisive shift away from liberal financial tradition in the federal government. The war demonstrated the potential effectiveness of exchange controls, and indeed of many kinds of domestic financial intervention which had become an integral part of the war effort.[20] The initiation of postwar planning encouraged creative and ambitious thinking within the Treasury Department. In particular, Morgenthau made it clear that he would use the postwar planning effort to build "a New Deal in international economics" designed to curtail the power of the bankers at home and abroad that had dominated international finance in the 1920s.[21] As he put it, the objective would be "to move the financial center of the world from London and Wall Street to the United States Treasury, and to create a new concept between nations in international finance."[22] Morgenthau chose Harry Dexter White to oversee the planning largely because of White's willingness to question orthodox financial thinking. On the question of capital movements, for example, White had shown an early skepticism (in his 1933 Ph.D. thesis) regarding classical argu-

17. The volume of these inflows was enormous; the Treasury Department estimated that between 1935 and 1937, as much as $100 million was entering New York per month (Warren 1937:339). See also Bloomfield 1950 on European capital flight to the United States in the 1930s.

18. Bloomfield 1950:182, 186–88, 195; Williams 1939:20–21; and League of Nations 1944:165n1. Kindleberger 1987a:24 also mentions discussions of this issue within the Federal Reserve Bank of New York in 1938.

19. Williams 1939:20–21.

20. Kindleberger 1943:348; Bloomfield 1950:187–88.

21. Quote from Van Dormael 1978:52.

22. Quoted in Gardner 1980:76.

ments that favored a liberal international financial order.[23] By 1937, White had become a convert to Keynesian economics as well as to the idea that "centralized control over foreign exchange and trade" might be necessary to protect national planning strategies.[24]

Important domestic political changes also took place in Britain after the September 1931 exchange crisis forced it to abandon the gold standard. As in the United States, the Treasury assumed more influence over monetary affairs, and the Bank of England and private financiers in the City of London lost much of the power they had held in the 1920s.[25] Important changes in policy soon followed. The Treasury insisted on a more accommodative monetary policy, oriented toward domestic goals instead of the external balance of payments. Internationally, an Exchange Equalization Account was set up under the Treasury's jurisdiction to facilitate intervention in exchange markets that could offset the effects of short-term gold movements on the domestic monetary situation. Moreover, in June 1932, public loans to overseas borrowers were prohibited in order to protect the pound sterling. Although this prohibition was relaxed later that year for Commonwealth and Empire borrowers, strict surveillance of the foreign lending of private London financial firms continued, and "foreign issues were permitted only if there was a compelling case that they would benefit British industry."[26]

These changes seemed dramatic, but the Treasury in fact remained largely wedded to orthodox principles in the 1930s.[27] The goal of its low-interest-rate policy, for example, was not macroeconomic management but rather reduction of its own debt service costs. Similarly, in the fiscal realm, the Treasury remained largely committed to balanced budgets. As in the United States, not until the war did attitudes change considerably. The war not only made it necessary to introduce exchange controls but, more important, brought an influx of academic economists to the Treasury who were committed to more activist and interventionist economic policies. The most important of these economists was Keynes. Having rapidly become a dominant figure in the British Treasury during the war, Keynes took on the task of devising the plans for the postwar international economy

23. White 1933:301.
24. White quoted in Kees 1973:79. On his conversion, see Kees 1973:64–65.
25. See, for example, Kunz 1987:6, 189.
26. Eichengreen and Cairncross 1983:22.
27. Ham 1981:chaps. 4–5.

that would be discussed with the Americans. Like Morgenthau and White, Keynes hoped to establish an order that would consolidate the financial and economic experiments of the 1930s. He felt particularly strongly about the need for capital controls. As early as 1933, he had advised governments to "let finance be primarily national" on the grounds that their policy autonomy had to be protected from the disruption of international capital flows.[28] In 1941–42, Keynes also strongly endorsed the Germans' interventionist proposals for the international economy of the postwar world and made clear that, like the Germans, he believed that "control of capital movements, both inward and outward, should be a permanent feature of the post-war system."[29]

The Early Proposals of Keynes and White

The Bretton Woods negotiations are often portrayed as a battle of wills between Keynes and White, who are said to have held different views on how the postwar international economy should be organized. Although this was the case with respect to many issues discussed in the negotiations, on the question of international movements of private capital, both strongly supported the use of capital controls. In their respective early drafts written in 1941–42, Keynes and White gave two basic explanations for their endorsement of such controls.

First, they each argued that international movements of capital could not be allowed to disrupt the policy autonomy of the new interventionist welfare state. Their key concern was to protect the new national macroeconomic planning measures that had been developed in the 1930s. White noted that capital controls "would give each government much greater measure of control in carrying out its monetary and tax policies" by preventing "flights of capital, motivated either by prospect of speculative exchange gain, or desire to avoid inflation, or evade taxes."[30] Keynes also feared such "short-term speculative movements or flights of currency." In particular, he

28. Keynes 1933:758. See also his recommendations to the 1931 Macmillan Committee (Moggridge 1986:58).

29. Quote from Horsefield 1969c:13. See also Van Dormael 1978:6–7, 33; Pressnell 1986:18.

30. Horsefield 1969c:67, 66.

worried that "movements of funds out of debtor countries which lack the means to finance them" would impose an undue balance-of-payments constraint on domestic macroeconomic objectives.[31] More broadly, Keynes pointed out that it was not just "abnormal" capital flows—that is, those motivated purely by speculation—that disrupted national macroeconomic planning, but also "normal" flows responding to interest rate differentials between countries.[32] He worried that a country with a current account deficit that attempted to maintain interest rates lower than the existing international norm would be subject to substantial disequilibrating capital outflows. If interest rates were to be determined by domestic macroeconomic priorities and not by considerations of external balance, he argued that such capital movements would have to be controlled in order to avoid external constraints on policy:

> Freedom of capital movements is an essential part of the old *laissez-faire* system and assumes that it is right and desirable to have an equalisation of interest rates in all parts of the world. . . . In my view the whole management of the domestic economy depends upon being free to have the appropriate rate of interest without reference to the rates prevailing elsewhere in the world. Capital control is a corollary to this.[33]

Keynes also pointed out that, as Japan and Germany had discovered, domestic financial regulatory measures designed to facilitate industrial and macroeconomic planning would be undermined if savers and borrowers had access to external financial markets. He explained to the British House of Lords that the endorsement of capital controls in the Bretton Woods Agreement would ensure that "our right to control the domestic capital market is secured on firmer foundations than ever before."[34] Moreover, both Keynes and White argued that the new welfare state had to be protected from capital flight initiated for "political reasons" or induced by a desire to evade the "burdens of social legislation."[35] As Keynes put it,

---

31. Quotes from Horsefield 1969c:32 and Van Dormael 1978:8. In earlier drafts, White had also been concerned with the "reserve position of the capital losing country" (Horsefield 1969c:49). See also Keynes 1980b:16–17; Van Dormael 1978:8.

32. The distinction between "abnormal" and "normal" movements was frequently made at the time (e.g., Fanno 1939, Bloomfield 1950:33–35), although Keynes did not use these terms.

33. Keynes 1980a:149. See also Keynes 1980a:212, 275–76.

34. Keynes 1980b:17.

35. Horsefield 1969c:31, 67.

"Surely in the post-war years there is hardly a country in which we ought not to expect keen political discussions affecting the position of the wealthier classes and the treatment of private property. If so, there will be a number of people constantly taking fright because they think that the degree of leftism in one country looks for the time being likely to be greater than somewhere else."[36] Similarly, White argued that capital flows should not be permitted to "operate against what the government deemed to be the interests of any country," even if this involved restricting "the property rights of the 5 or 10 percent of persons in foreign countries who have enough wealth or income to keep or invest some of it abroad."[37]

The second reason that Keynes and White advocated capital controls was their belief that a liberal international financial order was not compatible with a stable exchange rate system and a more liberal international trading system, both of which they hoped to establish. With respect to stable exchange rates, White noted that speculative capital movements were "one of the chief causes of foreign exchange disturbances," and would have to be controlled if a stable exchange rate system were to be maintained.[38] With respect to a liberal trading system, Keynes argued that large and volatile movements of capital could force "painful and perhaps violent" offsetting adjustments in the less flexible trade account that would likely increase political pressure for protectionist measures.[39] Capital controls would thus be needed to prevent capital flows from "strangling" international trade instead of playing "their proper auxiliary role of facilitating trade."[40]

The worries of Keynes and White in this regard were widely shared by their contemporaries, largely because of the experience of the interwar years. The difficulty of maintaining stable exchange rates in an open financial order had been demonstrated during the 1931 crisis, when enormous speculative capital movements had forced many states to abandon the gold standard. This experience led even members of the orthodox Gold Delegation of the League of Nations Financial Committee to recommend in their 1932 report

36. Keynes 1980a:149. See also Keynes 1980a:31.
37. Horsefield 1969c:67.
38. Horsefield 1969c:67.
39. Keynes 1930:335.
40. Quotes from Van Dormael 1978:33, 10. White was also concerned about "the rapidity with which the mechanism of adjustment in the balance of payments is operating" (Horsefield 1969c:49). See also Keynes 1980a:16–17.

that short-term capital flows be controlled and that only equilibrating capital flows that were used for "productive purposes" be permitted.[41] By World War II, there was widespread consensus—well publicized in Ragnar Nurkse's 1944 League of Nations report—that capital controls were needed to defend a stable exchange rate system.[42] When Germany and Japan resorted to systems of exchange control because of enormous capital flight in 1931, it seemed to point to the incompatibility of a liberal international financial order and a liberal trading system. Many also saw speculative capital flows in the 1930s as having severely disrupted traditional trading patterns. The U.S. Department of Commerce, for example, concluded in 1943 that "unless brought under control in the future, capital movements of this [speculative] nature might readily nullify other efforts to attain greater stability in international transactions and would decrease the amount of dollars available to foreigners for purchases of American goods and services."[43]

Although Keynes and White advocated capital controls, it is important to note that they did not oppose all types of international capital movements. Whereas "disequilibrating" movements of capital were to be controlled, both Keynes and White argued that "equilibrating" capital flows from countries with a surplus on their current account to those with a deficit were to be favored because they would "help to maintain equilibrium" in the international monetary system.[44] Furthermore, although speculative flows were to be controlled, White agreed with the League of Nations Gold Delegation that international flows of "productive" capital should be encouraged.[45] Keynes, too, favored "legitimate" capital movements that would "satisfy practical needs" in international commerce and provide "genuine new investment for developing the world's resources," as international investment had done before 1914.[46] Both Keynes

41. Flanders 1989:230–31.
42. League of Nations 1944. See also Ohlin 1936:82, Henderson 1936:168, and Robinson 1944:436. In 1936, the Treasury Department had also encouraged the new Blum government in France to introduce capital controls to prevent capital flight from forcing a devaluation of the franc (Brown 1987:74).
43. Quoted in Robinson 1944:434–45. See also Bloomfield 1946:687, 1950:182.
44. Keynes quoted in Horsefield 1969c:13, 32. For White's views, see Horsefield 1969c:176, 49–50.
45. White asserted that "the desirability of encouraging the flow of productive capital to areas where it can be most profitably employed needs no emphasis" (Horsefield 1969c: 46).
46. Horsefield 1969c:32, 11, 13.

and White made clear in their drafts that they hoped the various activities of the Bretton Woods institutions would promote equilibrating and productive capital flows by reducing exchange rate instability and by restoring confidence in international economic conditions.[47]

Although these two types of capital movement were to be encouraged, both Keynes and White made clear that the overriding principle in their drafts was to give states the right to control capital movements. The priority given to capital controls partly reflected the importance they attached to the goal of defending the policy autonomy of the new interventionist welfare state. The particularly disruptive nature of speculative and disequilibrating capital movements made a liberal financial order less easy to reconcile with the policy autonomy of the new interventionist welfare state than a liberal trading order. For this reason, their "embedded liberal" ideology was pushed in the "embedded" direction in the financial sector.

The priority given to capital controls also reflected the secondary status of liberal finance in their vision of a liberal international economic order. Faced with the prospect of a liberal financial order that would disrupt stable exchange rates and an open trading system, they agreed that the former should be sacrificed to preserve the latter. Their skepticism concerning the benefits of a liberal international financial order had partly been prompted by the interwar experience, when the international lending of the 1920s had culminated in the financial disaster of the early 1930s.[48] It also reflected a widespread feeling among economists of their generation that the classical case in favor of free trade was less relevant to finance. White, for example, argued: "The assumption that capital serves a country best by flowing to countries which offer the most attractive terms is valid only under circumstances that are not always present."[49] Bertil Ohlin summarized the views of many international economists in 1936: "There is a decisive difference between the role of such transfers [capital movements] and the functions of an exchange of commodities. The latter is a prerequisite of prosperity and economic growth, the former is not."[50]

47. Horsefield 1969c:32, 46, 139, 176.
48. According to Harrod (1969:566; 1972:8), Keynes's lack of enthusiasm for encouraging flows of productive capital can be explained in part by the interwar experience.
49. Horsefield 1969c:67.
50. Ohlin 1936:90. Even Aldrich (1943:16), one of the key New York bankers who supported a liberal financial order, argued that international investment was not vital to

Keynes and White recognized that states had had difficulty controlling financial transactions in the 1930s. Their early proposals were important not only because they stated clearly the theoretical case for capital controls but because they also included two provisions designed to make such controls more effective. First, to prevent capital movements that were disguised as current account payments, all states were given the right to institute exchange controls to screen current account transactions for illegal capital movements. Keynes explained: "If control is to be effective, it probably involves the *machinery* of exchange control for *all* transactions, even though a general open licence is given to all remittances in respect of current trade."[51] Second, as discussed in meetings held between the United States and Britain in the late 1930s, Keynes and White recommended that countries be able to increase the effectiveness of their capital controls by cooperating in the enforcement of each other's regulations. As White put it, "Almost every country, at one time or another, exercises control over the inflow and outflow of investments, but without the cooperation of other countries such control is difficult, expensive and subject to considerable evasion."[52] Keynes, too, observed that control of capital movements "will be more difficult to [make] work, especially in the absence of postal censorship, by unilateral action than if movements of capital can be controlled *at both ends*."[53] Keynes strongly recommended cooperation in his drafts, but White went even further and made such cooperation *mandatory*. In his 1942 draft, governments were required "a) not to accept or permit deposits or investments from any member country except with the permission of the government of that country, and b) to make available to the government of any member country at its request all property in form of deposits, investments, securities of the nationals of that member country."[54]

---

global economic prosperity because "capital accumulation . . . is largely a product of domestic policy."

51. Quoted in Horsefield 1969c:13 [emphasis in the original]. White also endorsed the use of exchange controls as a means for controlling financial movements (Horsefield 1969c:63).

52. Quoted in Horsefield 1969c:66.

53. Quoted in Horsefield 1969c:13 [emphasis in the original]. See also Nurkse's influential views at the time 1944:188–89.

54. Quoted in Horsefield 1969c:44. For Keynes's recommendation, see Horsefield 1969c:13, 29, 31–32.

Opposition from the New York Bankers

The early proposals of Keynes and White concerning capital controls were not without controversy. They met with strong opposition from members of the New York financial community, who worried that countries not only would be *permitted* to use capital controls but might be *required* to do so under White's cooperative enforcement provisions. Any U.S. obligation to control speculative flows would remove what had been a lucrative business for New York banks in the 1930s—receiving flight capital from Europe. More broadly, a system that permitted other countries to control capital movements might prevent the rebuilding of an open, liberal international financial system from which they, as world's leading bankers after the war, would derive considerable benefit. In particular, they feared that Britain would use capital controls to prevent them from challenging London's dominant position within the sterling area.[55]

The bankers' objections were not motivated only by considerations of self-interest, however. Equally important was the desire to voice opposition to the embedded liberal ideology underlying the plans. They did not share the concern of Keynes and White with the adverse impact of disequilibrating speculative capital flows on the policy autonomy of the new interventionist welfare state. Whereas Keynes worried that disequilibrating flows responding to international interest rate differentials might disrupt domestic macroeconomic planning, the bankers saw such flows as merely a reflection of an inappropriate interest rate policy. Opposed to the idea of national fiscal and monetary planning, they argued that if rates were adjusted "appropriately"—that is, in accordance with the objective of maintaining *external balance* instead of achieving domestic macroeconomic goals—equilibrating flows of short-term capital would be attracted to cover the external imbalance. Indeed, such interest rate adjustments had been the basis of the functioning of the pre-1931 gold standard, which they hoped to restore.

The bankers also differed with Keynes and White on the question of speculative or "abnormal" flows. They were not blind to the damage that such flows had caused to stable exchange rates and

55. De Cecco 1976:382–83; 1979:52. See also Enkyo 1989:49.

liberal trading relations in the interwar period. For the most part, they agreed with Keynes and White that it would be necessary for many countries to control such flows to prevent this damage from recurring.[56] Where they differed was in their belief that such controls should be only *temporary*, restricted to a transition period until the root cause of the speculative flows could be eliminated. In addition to political instability and floating exchange rates, one of the principal root causes was, in their view, the unorthodox domestic economic policies introduced in the 1930s. Robert Warren, of the financial house of Case Pomeroy and Company, for example, noted that speculative capital movements resulted from the distrust of certain currencies. "These currencies are distrusted," he explained, "by reason of government deficits either financed by present inflation or threatened with the imminence of inflation."[57] Whereas Keynes and White sought to preserve and extend the ability of governments to pursue national planning at the macroeconomic level by controlling speculative flows, the bankers hoped to eliminate the flows by ending those very policies.

Some of the bankers also applauded speculative flows for the healthy discipline they exerted on governments attempting to pursue such "unsound" policies. Winthrop Aldrich of the Chase National Bank, for example, argued that a dollar free of all capital controls was needed to "check domestic inflationary pressures" that might result from government management of the national economy.[58] That the bankers viewed international financial markets as a positive influence in disciplining governments that pursued improper policies was reflected in their opposition to the creation of *public* international financial institutions such as the International Monetary Fund (IMF). They were highly doubtful that an institution run by governments could match the efficiency and rationality of a market-oriented system. The only international financial institution in which they had faith was the Bank for International Settlements because it was run not by Keynesian-minded government bureaucrats but by pragmatic central bankers.[59]

56. See, for example, Brown 1944:205, Riddle 1943:32, Bloomfield 1946, and Williams 1949:96–97; 1943:6.
57. Warren 1937:339–40. See also Warren 1937:342–43, Lutz 1943:19, Riddle 1943: 30–31 (who was an adviser to the Bankers Trust Company of New York), and Conolly 1936:367–68 (of the BIS).
58. Johnson 1968:282. See also Block 1977:53.
59. The American Bankers Association (1943:13), Fraser (1943), and Riddle (1943) all

The bankers were also concerned about the compatibility of capital controls with a liberal democratic form of government. Whereas Keynes and White had viewed controls on the investment behavior of a wealthy minority as essential for a government's political autonomy, their critics viewed such controls as overly "coercive" and reminiscent of the "Hitlerian monetary system."[60] As Jacob Viner explained, because of the difficulty of distinguishing between capital account and current account transactions, capital controls could be made effective only "by censorship of communications and by crushing penalties for violations," an idea that, he noted, "quite frankly, rather frightens me."[61] Another critic, Imre De Vegh, who was quoted approvingly by J. H. Riddle of the Bankers Trust Company of New York, noted: "A perpetuation and legalization of control over capital movements is not compatible with any notion of a world that supposedly combats violence and dictatorial forms of government."[62] Although Keynes attempted to rebut these statements, arguing that capital controls could be made effective without measures such as postal censorship (which he agreed would be a "gross . . . infringement on personal rights"), the bankers responded by emphasizing that Keynes and White were underestimating the difficulties of differentiating capital movements from other international transactions.[63]

What practical alternatives to Keynes's and White's proposals did the members of the New York financial community propose? As a final goal, they favored a system in which there was complete freedom for capital movements.[64] They conceded that in a transition period before internal and external stability was achieved, however, capital controls would be helpful in preventing speculative capital flows from disrupting trade and exchange rate stability. To minimize this transition period, they favored the "key currency" plan advo-

---

recommended centering international monetary cooperation in the BIS instead of the IMF. Chicago banker Edward Brown also strongly opposed the resolution to abolish the BIS at Bretton Woods (Van Dormael 1978:204).

60. Anderson 1943:13.
61. Viner 1943:103.
62. De Vegh 1943:539, quoted by Riddle 1943:14.
63. Keynes 1980a:276. For skeptical views of the possibility of distinguishing between current account and capital account transactions, see Aldrich 1944:11, Penrose 1953:54, and U.S. Department of State 1948:314.
64. See, for example, the *Wall Street Journal* editorial of July 1, 1944 (Eckes 1975: 166); also Riddle 1943 and Brown 1944:205.

cated by John Williams of the Federal Reserve Bank of New York. Williams argued that the quickest way to create a stable world economy would be to restore convertibility to the world's two most important currencies, the U.S. dollar and the British pound.[65] He urged the United States to remove all controls on the international use of the dollar and to extend a large loan to Britain in order to encourage it to do the same for the pound. The plan provided the New York bankers with an additional reason for opposing White's proposals concerning obligatory cooperative enforcement of capital controls. If the United States were forced to adopt capital controls, it would be prevented from assuming this "key currency" leadership role. As Winthrop Aldrich made clear, if the dollar were to provide "a sure anchorage for the currencies of other nations," it would have to be freed of all controls "including [those on] short- or long-term capital movements."[66]

Although White had not consulted the New York financial community in drafting his initial proposals in 1941 and 1942, three developments forced him to take their views more seriously.[67] The first was the success of the Republican party in the fall 1942 congressional elections. Because many Republicans were more supportive of the bankers' opinions than were their Democratic colleagues, White knew he would have to take the bankers' demands more seriously if a final deal were to stand a chance of getting through Congress.[68] The second was the outspoken opposition of Winthrop Aldrich. In contrast to other bankers who opposed the proposals, such as W. Randolph Burgess, Leon Fraser, and Thomas Lamont, Aldrich had

65. Williams (1936, 1943). Interestingly, Williams himself did not share the bankers' opposition to the capital controls provisions of Keynes and White. He not only favored the use of tight controls during the transition period, but supported the proposal of Keynes and White that *permanent* capital controls would be needed in the postwar world. In his opinion, this "modification" of the gold standard was necessary to prevent speculative flows from disrupting stable exchange rates; like Keynes and White, he believed it was also necessary to preserve states' policy autonomy. Unlike the other bankers, he had become an advocate of active fiscal and monetary policy, and he worried that "national business cycles" could be disturbed by panic flights of capital, as well as by capital movements that caused a "spreading of booms and depressions, or of a boom in one country feeding upon deflation elsewhere" (Williams 1944:45).

66. Aldrich 1943:11. See also Aldrich 1944:25–26 and American Bankers Association 1943:16.

67. By 1943, he was making a point of meeting periodically with the bankers (Eckes 1975:298n29). See also Pressnell 1986:121, Robbins 1971:199, Howson and Moggridge 1990:84, and Dam 1982:99.

68. Eckes 1975:74, De Cecco 1979:51, and Robbins 1971:199.

been an active supporter of the New Deal in its early years, and his statements carried considerable weight not only within the administration but also with the public at large.[69] Finally, after his initial drafts, White was forced to begin to discuss his plans with government officials outside of the U.S. Treasury, including those from the Federal Reserve System and the State Department, among whose personnel were prominent supporters of financial liberalism from the academic world such as Viner and Herbert Feis, as well as many Wall Street figures such as James Forrestal and Dean Acheson.[70]

The strong opposition to White's proposals from bankers within the administration, as well as from those (such as Aldrich) who had at first been active supporters of Roosevelt, reflected the still unresolved direction of New Deal financial politics. As Thomas Ferguson points out, these bankers had supported the early New Deal largely because of their desire to remove the House of Morgan from its prominent position in the New York financial community.[71] Once Roosevelt's financial reforms of 1933–35 had achieved this, the bankers' support for other radical initiatives in the financial area was limited. Although some bankers, such as Forrestal and Acheson, remained affiliated with the administration, others such as Aldrich increasingly distanced themselves from it, denouncing its excessive public spending, inflationary policies, and penchant for financial regulation.[72] As one Bretton Woods delegate noted, Aldrich and the other American bankers at the conference "regarded Mr. Morgenthau and Mr. White as representatives of a 'different world' since they were in favor of the active intervention of the state in financial policy."[73]

Interestingly, those industrialists who had provided Roosevelt with crucial business support in the 1930s—largely from capital-intensive, high-technology sectors—proved much more sympathetic

69. Johnson 1968:194–96, 212.

70. Acheson chaired the State Department's subcommittee on postwar monetary planning (Oliver 1971:15). On Herbert Feis's annoyance with the Treasury Department's international monetary proposals, see Howson and Moggridge 1990:63. For Viner's views, see Viner 1926 and 1943:103; and Oliver 1971:18. Representatives of the State Department and the Federal Reserve System would later be included in the U.S. delegation to the Bretton Woods Conference.

71. Ferguson 1984.

72. Aldrich resigned from the government-sponsored Business Advisory Council in 1935 (McQuaid 1976:179). See the Aldrich speeches in Johnson 1968:190–91, 210–11, 222.

73. I. Zlobin quoted in Johnson 1968:292.

than the bankers to the need for capital controls and Keynesian planning. Subscribing to an embedded liberal framework of thought, they felt that the orthodoxy of balanced budgets and adherence to a gold standard had been discredited by the upheavals of the 1930s.[74] The Department of Commerce, a stronghold of these "New Deal industrialists," showed an interest in the idea of joint capital controls in its postwar blueprint published in 1943.[75] Similarly, the Committee for Economic Development, created by several of them in 1942, was supportive of Keynesian strategies and saw a need for capital controls to preserve policy autonomy.[76] This division between industrialists and bankers regarding the desirability of governmental intervention and capital controls was paralleled in other industrial countries.

Some Modifications of the Early Proposals

The opposition of the New York bankers had an important impact on the evolution of the Bretton Woods proposals concerning capital movements. The bankers had pressed for a statement in the agreement making clear that one of its objectives would be to promote international movements of "productive" capital.[77] Reflecting this pressure, White's 1943 revised draft stated that one of the fund's purposes would be "to reduce the use of such foreign exchange restrictions, bilateral clearing arrangements, multiple currency devices, and discriminatory foreign exchange practices as hamper world trade and *the international flow of productive capital.*"[78] To the British, however, this new clause was very threatening. Because it included an explicit *obligation* to reduce barriers to the flow of productive capital, this clause might be used to limit their *right* to

74. For a general discussion of emergence of this group of industrialists, see Collins 1978, Ferguson 1984, and Hogan 1987:chap. 1.

75. Robinson 1944:434.

76. For its support for Keynesian ideas, see McQuaid 1982:117 and Salant 1989:46. See also the CED-sponsored research project by Duke University economist Calvin Hoover (1945:26–28, 32, 42, 56–57n1) and the official CED report (CED 1945:7, 20) for its sympathetic approach to capital controls.

77. Both Secretary of State Cordell Hull and the ABA had strongly pressed White (as had Jacob Viner for the Council on Foreign Relations) for measures to promote flows of productive capital. See, for example, Hull's memo (NA, RG 56, Records of the Assistant Secretary: Chronological Files of H. D. White, June 29, 1943).

78. Horsefield 1969c:86 [emphasis added].

control capital movements, particularly by the use of exchange controls.[79] Indeed, it was not just Keynes who strongly opposed this new clause. The Bank of England also made clear in early 1944 that the clause was unacceptable and insisted that an explicit guarantee of the right to use exchange controls to restrict capital movements be included in the final agreement.[80]

The Bank of England's position must have been particularly discouraging to the New York bankers, who were hoping to revive their pre-1931 political alliance with that institution to facilitate a return to a more liberal and orthodox world. But Bank of England officials, along with many London financiers, supported the restrictive proposals of Keynes and White. One reason for the Bank of England's stance was that, as chief administrator of Britain's exchange controls, the bank was aware of the extreme vulnerability of Britain's payments position. Equally important, however, was that in the wake of the 1931 crisis, the bank had increasingly become an advocate of a protectionist sterling area.[81] This shift, which began immediately after the crisis, rapidly accelerated during the war when the bank transformed the loose arrangements of the sterling area, into the more formal sterling bloc. By 1944–45, the bank was proposing that the consolidation and extension of this sterling bloc would be a more effective way than any proposal submitted at Bretton Woods to preserve London's international position and that of the pound sterling.[82]

Although the experience of the 1930s seemed to have shattered the pre-1931 alliance between the bankers of New York and London by pushing the latter into a restrictive sterling bloc, the Bank of England was in fact an ally of sorts of the New York financiers.[83] Like the New York bankers, the Bank of England opposed the creation of international public financial institutions such as the IMF on the grounds that the world of international finance should be governed by private and central bankers.[84] Moreover, as one contemporary observer noted, the bank had "an almost passionate in-

79. Kahn 1976:18; Gold 1977:13.

80. Pressnell 1986:140, 148–49; Fforde 1992:40–43; and Van Dormael 1978:114. Important Labour party figures such as Aneurin Bevan announced their refusal to consider any dilution of the right to control capital movements (Pressnell 1986:130).

81. Pressnell 1986:69, 72, 74, 142, 148; Fforde 1992:39–40; and Strange 1971.

82. Pressnell 1986:72, 96–97, 141, 148; Van Dormael 1978:131–32.

83. See, for example, Robbins 1971:197 and Fforde 1992:33, 39.

84. Harrod 1969:530, Pressnell 1986:141, and Fforde 1992:39.

terest in maintaining and restoring the position of London as a monetary center," an interest that proved important in the 1960s and after in encouraging a world in which private international financial activity could flourish.[85] The bank also remained a staunch defender of the need for austerity in domestic financial and monetary policy and for interest rates to be consistent with the maintenance of external balance.

Despite holding these views, Bank of England officials sided with Keynes on the issue of capital controls during the Bretton Woods negotiations and together they successfully resisted any dilution of the right to control capital movements with exchange controls. The objectionable phrase referring to the need to promote "productive" capital flows was eliminated from the Joint Statement issued by the British and U.S. delegations in April 1944. Moreover, in the final Bretton Woods Agreement arrived at two months later, Article 6-3 explicitly granted countries the right to use exchange controls to curtail capital movements: "Members may exercise such controls as are necessary to regulate international capital movements."[86] There was a qualification, however: "But no member may exercise these controls in a manner which will restrict payments for current transactions or which will unduly delay transfers of funds in settlement of commitments." After the Bretton Woods Conference, some officials (notably those of the Federal Reserve System and the State Department) argued that the wording of this article—in addition to that of Article 8-2a, which prohibited the imposition of "restrictions on the making of payments and transfers for current international transactions"—removed the right to institute a system of exchange controls as a way of controlling such financial transactions.[87] Those involved in drafting the sections, however, explicitly stated that this was not the case.[88] Indeed, archival documents make it clear that the U.S. bankers failed to convince the U.S. delegation to the Atlantic City conference that preceded Bretton Woods of the need to curtail the

85. Quoted in Van Dormael 1978:131.
86. Horsefield 1969c:194. This right had been introduced at the Atlantic City conference (NA, RG 56, Bretton Woods, Atlantic City Conference, document f-1, no. 172).
87. Horsefield 1969c:195; Van Dormael 1978:228–39.
88. U.S. Department of State 1948:314, 598. This meaning was also clarified at the Atlantic City conference; see NA, RG 56, Bretton Woods, Atlantic City Conference: Meeting of Subcommittee Two of the Preliminary Agreement Committee, June 23, 1944. See also Gold 1977:5, 14; Rasminsky 1972.

right to use exchange controls to make capital controls effective.[89] Still, it was not clear how exchange controls used to control capital movements could be prevented from restricting trade payments, especially in light of the difficulty of distinguishing between current account and capital account transactions.

The bankers had more success in toning down the proposal for obligatory cooperative controls. The first indication of this success was White's 1943 draft, which required cooperation in enforcing foreign capital controls *only* if the IMF had recommended it. Moreover, governments were no longer required to hand over "all property in form of deposits, investments, [or] securities" of the nationals of a requesting country but only "information" concerning this property.[90] By the time the April 1944 Joint Statement was issued, almost all mention of the obligation to cooperate in controlling undesirable flows had been removed.

At the Atlantic City and Bretton Woods conferences, there was considerable pressure from both the British and the Polish delegations to reinstate a provision concerning obligatory joint controls. The members of the U.S. delegation (especially the bankers, such as Edward Brown) strongly opposed these initiatives, however.[91] They wanted "to avoid having to bring before Congress a special law such as would be required to make black markets illegal."[92] In the end, a compromise was reached. The final agreement stated clearly that governments were *permitted* to cooperate in controlling capital movements (Article 8-2b). They were, however, *required* only to provide the IMF on request with information on capital movements and holdings, except to the extent that such information would disclose the affairs of individuals or companies (Article 8-5a).[93] In addi-

---

89. See the debate on this question within the U.S. delegation at the Atlantic City conference in NA, RG 56, Bretton Woods, Atlantic City Conference: Meeting of the American Technical Group, June 17, 1944—Attachment D.

90. Horsefield 1969c:96.

91. For the Polish and British proposals, see U.S. Department of State 1948:230, 334, 437; NA, RG 56, Bretton Woods, Atlantic City Conference: Minutes of Meetings, June 28, 1944. Inexplicably, at one point in the negotiations, the United States did propose a draft with a clause requiring cooperation (U.S. Department of State 1948:502, 542, 576), but the clause did not reappear.

92. Quote from Keynes 1980b:138. For Brown's opposition, see Brown 1944:205; and NA, RG 56, Bretton Woods, Atlantic City Conference: Minutes of Meetings, June 28, 1944; Meeting of the Financial Agenda Committee, June 29, 1944.

93. Horsefield 1969c:196–97; Bloomfield 1946:706n33.

tion, IMF members had to ensure that all exchange contracts that contravened other members' exchange control regulations were made "unenforceable" in their territory (Article 8-2b). The latter provision, although seemingly impressive, implied only a weak definition of cooperation, as the notes of a lawyer advising a leading delegation at Bretton Woods made clear: "This does not mean that one country owes any duty to police or enforce the exchange control regulations of another country. . . . [It means only that] if a suit is brought within the courts of one country involving a contract which violated the exchange control regulations of another country, the courts of the former will not enforce the contract."[94] Joseph Gold, the IMF's longtime legal counsel, said "the United States had seen the provision as one that . . . would protect it from any proposal that it should introduce capital controls in the interests of other members."[95]

Although the notion of cooperative capital controls was thus preserved in the final agreement, the United States bankers had in effect extracted the U.S. government from an explicit obligation to introduce them. At the Atlantic City conference, the U.S. delegation also succeeded in changing a clause that had allowed the IMF, as late as the 1944 Joint Statement, to "require" the imposition of capital controls if its resources were being drained by a member for the purpose of financing a deficit stemming from speculative capital movements. Keynes and White had granted the IMF this power to ensure that its resources would be used only for the purpose of financing deficits on the current account or those stemming from movements of productive capital.[96] Under U.S. pressure, the IMF's power was reduced so that it could only "request" controls to prevent such use, and a member refusing to cooperate would be declared ineligible to use the fund's resources (Article 6-1a). According to the U.S. technical group at the conference, this change was made because "the United States does not want to be forced to control an export of capital."[97] Indeed, the success the U.S. bankers had had in opposing White's

94. Quoted in Gold 1986:792n2.

95. Gold 1977:15–16. For a good summary of the history of the drafting of Article 8-2b, see Gold 1982:429–38.

96. See Horsefield 1969c:23, 49–50, 89–90, 133–34.

97. NA, RG 56, Bretton Woods, Atlantic City Conference: Meeting of the American Technical Group, June 17, 1944, Attachment D. Keynes had tried to convince U.S. officials that the United States could be subject to considerable capital flight immediately after the war if the economy fell into a depression (Bernstein 1984:15).

cooperative control proposals was brought home at a press conference held at Bretton Woods, when White himself explained that, although other countries were free to use capital controls, "the United States does not wish to have them."[98]

The globalization of financial markets that has occurred in more recent years was not a direct product of the international economic order outlined in the Bretton Woods agreement. Despite the various alterations made in response to opposition from the New York bankers, the final Bretton Woods agreement retained the restrictive approach to international capital movements taken by Keynes and White in their early drafts. To be sure, productive and equilibrating flows of capital were to be promoted by the activities of the World Bank and by the fact that IMF resources could be used to finance deficits arising from "capital transactions of reasonable amount required for the expansion of exports or in the ordinary course of trade, banking or other business" (Article 6-1b(i)). The overriding principle, however, was restriction: states were given the explicit right to control *all* capital movements. Capital controls were also encouraged because IMF funds could not be used to finance a "large or sustained outflow of capital" and because the IMF was empowered to request (but not require) a member to implement controls to prevent such use of its funds (Article 6-1a). Equally significant, the two mechanisms outlined by Keynes and White as necessary to make capital controls more effective were included in the final agreement. The agreement both endorsed the use of cooperative controls (albeit in a weak fashion) and permitted states to use exchange controls to search for and prevent illicit capital movements.

The restrictive financial provisions in the Bretton Woods Agreement partly reflected the prominence of an embedded liberal framework of thought, which gave priority to the defense of the policy autonomy of the new interventionist welfare state from international financial pressures. As John Ruggie has argued, many authors of conventional analyses of this period ignore the importance of this normative framework in guiding state behavior. Embedded liberal ideas in finance were not universally accepted in this period, however. Although they found strong support among industrialists, la-

98. Quoted in Van Dormael 1978:185.

bor groups, and Keynesian-minded state officials, they were often opposed by the private and central bankers who dominated financial politics before 1931. This division between embedded liberals and bankers existed throughout the advanced industrial world, and it ensured that the debate at Bretton Woods would be carried out partially on a transnational basis, with Keynes and White allied against the opposition of the New York bankers.[99] The strong endorsement of capital controls in the final agreement resulted from the fact that the upheavals of the 1930s and the wartime experience had given political prominence to the embedded liberal forces represented by Keynes and White, while weakening and fracturing the pre-1931 alliance between the bankers of New York and London.

The restrictive Bretton Woods financial provisions also reflected the shared belief among bankers and embedded liberals alike that a liberal financial order would not be compatible, at least in the short term, with a stable system of exchange rates and a more liberal trading order. This belief had grown out of the interwar experience. Perceiving liberal finance as a less important component of a liberal international economic order, they chose to sacrifice it in favor of preserving stable exchange rates and liberal trade. The New York bankers argued that these incompatibilities between the constituent parts of the liberal international economic order would be resolved with restoration of economic and political stability, but this proved more difficult than they had anticipated.

99. On the Keynes-White alliance, see Pressnell 1986:121, Robbins 1971:199, and Howson and Moggridge 1990:84. For a similar argument concerning the transnational nature of alliances during the Bretton Woods negotiations, see Ikenberry 1992.

CHAPTER THREE

Continuing Caution: The Slow and Limited Move to Convertibility

THE EARLY POSTWAR YEARS ARE COMMONLY PORTRAYED AS A PE-
riod in which the United States used its overwhelming power to
build an open, liberal international economic order. The argument
advanced in this chapter is that, except for a brief interval between
1945 and 1947, the United States in fact did little to promote the
construction of a liberal order in finance in the decade and a half
following World War II. Although American policymakers chose not
to employ capital controls in this period, after 1947 they supported
the use of such controls abroad, in keeping with the restrictive financial order they had helped construct at Bretton Woods.[1] In the absence of U.S. pressure, West European and Japanese governments
chose to retain the capital controls they had introduced in the 1930s
and during the war. Indeed, the control of capital movements remained such a central part of the foreign economic policy of these
countries in the early postwar years that when their currencies were
finally made convertible with dollars in the late 1950s and early
1960s, they chose to restrict convertibility to the current account.
This decision, too, was fully supported by the United States.

The chapter begins by investigating the failure of an effort by
the New York banking community between 1945 and 1947 to en-

1. The argument differs from that of Strange (1990), who suggests that the United
States pressured governments in West Europe and Japan to liberalize their capital controls
in the early postwar years, although she admits that her analysis is "deducible more by
inference than by reference to any specific act or document" (p. 264).

courage a rapid move toward convertibility throughout Western Europe. A hitherto neglected explanation is proposed for this failure that centers on the bankers' refusal to help European governments control disruptive capital flight in this period. The second and third sections of the chapter detail the change in U.S. foreign economic policy that took place with the introduction of the Marshall Plan in 1948. It is argued that U.S. policy with respect to finance in this period returned to the normative framework outlined at Bretton Woods. The fourth section demonstrates the cautious manner in which U.S. and European policymakers encouraged the restoration of dollar convertibility for European currencies in the 1950s. The final section briefly analyzes the even slower and more limited move to convertibility in Japan in this period.

Capital Flight and the Failure of the Key Currency Plan

Although the Bretton Woods Agreement was signed in July 1944, Congress did not consider it for approval until early 1945. Ironically, just as ratification was being granted, American foreign economic policy began to shift away from the Bretton Woods framework. The catalyst for this change was Franklin Roosevelt's death in April 1945. The architects of the Bretton Woods Agreement, Henry Morgenthau and Harry Dexter White, suddenly found themselves without influence in the new Truman administration, whereas the bankers who had opposed the agreement soon emerged in prominent positions and guided the making of foreign economic policy. Under the influence of figures such as Winthrop Aldrich, U.S. policymakers looked with favor on the key currency plan that the bankers had proposed when making known their opposition to the Bretton Woods proposals.[2]

The most important objective of this strategy was to pressure Britain to restore convertibility between the pound and the dollar. It was hoped that stability in the relationship between these two key currencies would revive international trade and reestablish traditional patterns of private international financing in London and New York. In July 1945, after cutting off aid under the Lend-Lease Act, the United States offered Britain a sizable loan if it would restore

2. For Aldrich's role, see Johnson 1968:317.

current account convertibility within eighteen months. The new British Labour government, faced with a serious financial crisis, listened to John Maynard Keynes's strong recommendations that the loan be accepted. Keynes then played a crucial role in persuading a skeptical House of Lords to accept the loan, which was approved by Parliament in tandem with the Bretton Woods Agreement in December 1945.

At the same time as they attempted to restore pound-dollar convertibility, the New York bankers sought to encourage restoration of more orthodox internal economic policies elsewhere in Western Europe that might speed the return to convertibility of other currencies. As part of this effort, they attempted to transform the Bretton Woods institutions, the IMF and the World Bank, into more conservative bodies by appointing orthodox American and West European bankers to important positions in them.[3] Moreover, they made a crucial decision not to enforce a resolution passed at Bretton Woods calling for the liquidation of the Bank for International Settlements "at the earliest possible moment."[4] The resolution had been proposed by the Norwegian government, which had argued that the Basel-based central bankers' institution was guilty of collaborating with Germany in the late 1930s and during the war. It had been strongly supported by Morgenthau and White, who were "bitterly opposed" to the bank and saw its abolition as a "matter of international propaganda" in their war against the international bankers who had dominated the pre-1931 financial order.[5] The New York bankers had strongly opposed the resolution, wanting to preserve the body that had been such a bastion of orthodox monetary thinking in Europe during the 1930s and that would facilitate a revival of central bank cooperation.[6] The Treasury Department initially had

3. Gardner 1980:298–99.

4. The phrase "at the earliest possible moment" apparently reflected the fact that the BIS was still within German-controlled territory at the time of the Bretton Woods Conference (Schloss 1958:119).

5. Schloss 1958:120; Eckes 1975:152–53. See also Schloss 1958:102–12, 118–21; 1970:22 and Beyen 1951:121–24, 156–57. Some have argued that the BIS could not have been abolished by the resolution at Bretton Woods because the body was chartered in Switzerland. Although this statement is strictly true, abolition could have been accomplished through indirect pressure. For example, proposals were made at Bretton Woods to prohibit governments from becoming members of the IMF unless their central banks worked to abolish the BIS (Keynes 1980b:96; Beyen 1951:156–57).

6. American banking figures in the administration, such as Dean Acheson, had strongly opposed the Bretton Woods resolution (Howson and Moggridge 1990:63).

tried to convince reluctant European central banks to enforce the Bretton Woods resolution but abandoned this effort in November 1946, thus opening the way for a resumption the next month of the monthly meetings of European central bankers that had been suspended in 1939.[7] The survival of the BIS was then assured when it was made the fiscal agent for the intra-European payments mechanisms being established under the Marshall Plan in 1947–48 and for the European Payments Union (EPU) after 1950.[8]

Although the bankers were able to save the BIS, their broader strategy of encouraging pound-dollar convertibility and the restoration of orthodox economic policy elsewhere had failed completely by mid-1947. Within six weeks of moving to convertibility, Britain was forced to resort to a system of tight exchange controls because of massive speculation against the pound. Elsewhere in Western Europe, efforts to implement orthodox economic policies and achieve liberalization were defeated as inflation accelerated rapidly and exchange controls were tightened to cope with large external deficits. Some governments, notably in Italy and France, even considered resorting to a floating exchange rate to cope with their external payments problems. These developments, moreover, prevented the restoration of confidence among private American investors who might have extended loans to European countries to help them overcome their external payments imbalances.

The cause of the 1947 crisis has been the subject of considerable debate. The conventional view is that the crisis was caused by a collapse of industrial production throughout Western Europe, brought about by the general economic dislocation following the war and the harsh winter of 1946–47. Alan Milward has challenged this explanation, however, effectively demonstrating that the crisis was merely one in the balance of payments generated not by the failure of European economic recovery but by its very success, which increased im-

7. Jacobsson 1979:188–90, Eckes 1975:152–53, and Schloss 1970:32. Jacobsson claims that the Treasury Department's assistant for international finance, Andrew Overby (who had come from the Federal Reserve Bank of New York), convinced Treasury Secretary John Snyder to stop attempting to enforce the Bretton Woods resolution. The NAC did not formally agree to stop trying to enforce the resolution until April 1948, however. Indeed, according to the NAC minutes, as late as October 1947, Treasury Secretary Snyder was still uncertain as to the institution's worth (NA, RG 56, Records of the NAC, NAC document no. 661; NAC Minutes, October 13, 1947, pp. 2–3, and April 21, 1948, p. 7).
8. West European central banks ensured that the BIS was given this role (Fforde 1992:177–78, 205–6).

ports of goods. Although the West Europeans might have solved their balance-of-payments troubles by instituting an orthodox deflationary program, all countries (except Belgium and to some extent Italy) were unwilling to sacrifice expansionary national economic programs to maintain external balance. The financial orthodoxy of the pre-1931 period was replaced by a new embedded liberal commitment to macroeconomic policy autonomy. As Milward puts it, "full employment, industrialization and modernization had become in different countries, as a result of the experiences of the 1930s and the war, inescapable policy choices."[9] The consequence, according to Milward, was that West European countries were forced to resort to increasingly rigorous external controls to protect their external payments position.

Although Milward's analysis serves as an important corrective of the conventional wisdom, his emphasis on imports as the source of Western Europe's balance-of-payments crisis in 1947 explains only part of the story. Another principal source of European balance-of-payments difficulties was the capital that fled European economic and political instability and ended up in the U.S. banking system. Because of the illicit nature of this capital flight, there are few reliable statistics on its exact volume. Many economic historians have commented on its central importance in this period, however.[10] The U.S. government was also actively researching the problem at the time. According to its internal study, on June 30, 1947, private assets in the United States held by citizens of West European countries totaled $4.3 billion (not including an additional $800 million of "blocked" assets from the war). The authors of the study acknowledged that these statistics were far from comprehensive. Although they noted that they had little knowledge of what percentage of this total had arrived since 1945, the National Advisory Council on International Monetary and Financial Problems (NAC) stated categorically that there had been a large increase in the private assets of foreigners in the United States since September 1946.[11]

9. Milward 1984:466.

10. For example, Bloomfield 1954 and De Cecco 1972:163, 170–71, 173; 1979:56, 58–59. Even Milward (1984:4, 44) briefly admits its importance. In addition to causing European capital flight, instability in Western Europe ensured that U.S. exporters and banks would be unwilling to accept European currencies, which further aggravated Western Europe's balance-of-payments problems.

11. NA, RG 56, Records of the NAC, staff document no. 189, October 10, 1947; NAC document no. 547, November 12, 1947; NAC document no. 580, January 14, 1948. For a more detailed discussion, see Helleiner 1992a.

Why was this capital flight not controlled? West European governments did in fact make extensive efforts to control it with exchange controls. As the U.S. bankers had predicted at Bretton Woods, however, the difficulties of distinguishing between capital account and current account transactions rendered these controls quite ineffective. Only by employing increasingly tighter exchange controls could they hope to prevent evasion through "leads and lags" in current account payments and by other illicit means.[12] It was precisely this move toward comprehensive exchange controls that conflicted with the American objective of creating a more open trading order. In the important case of Britain, the difficulties of controlling illegal capital flows had been compounded by the existence of large sterling balances accumulated by foreigners within the sterling bloc during the war. The loose individual arrangements made with the major holders of sterling balances proved difficult to enforce with convertibility.

Cooperative enforcement of controls on capital flight would have been more effective and more compatible with an open trading order, as Keynes and White had argued at Bretton Woods. In 1945–47, West European governments had displayed a keen awareness of the need for cooperative controls. The bilateral economic agreements reached between Britain and many continental European countries in 1945–46 had included provisions for the cooperative control of speculative capital movements.[13] More important in terms of the 1947 crisis, most West European governments repeatedly requested U.S. assistance to prevent the assets of their citizens from illegally entering the country and being held in U.S. banks.[14] As White had correctly predicted in 1942, U.S. help was central to resolving the 1947 crisis:

12. See, for example, Bloomfield 1954:23–28, 68–69. In addition to imposing controls, the Italians and the French attempted to repatriate capital unilaterally through schemes whereby capital held illicitly abroad could be used to finance imports with no questions asked. These schemes "yielded only modest results" (Bloomfield 1954:64, 54, 63; Ellis 1950:253–54, 292, 329). The French also hoped to repatriate capital by establishing a free gold market and a floating exchange rate for the capital account. The IMF, however, concluded that such measures would be much less effective than U.S. help (NA, RG 56, Records of the NAC, NAC document no. 602, January 19, 1948, p. 11).

13. Bloomfield 1946:705n32; 1954:64, 69–70.

14. Treasury Secretary Snyder acknowledged this request in his testimony to Congress in February 1948 (U.S. Congress 1948b:805). The French were pressing for such assistance as early as 1946 (U.S. Congress 1947:141).

It would seem to be an important step in the direction of world stability if a member government could obtain the full cooperation of other member governments in the control of capital flows. For example, after the war a number of countries could request the United States not to permit increases in the deposits or holdings of their nationals, or to do so only with a license granted by the government making the request. Or, some countries greatly in need of capital might request the United States to supplement their efforts to attract capital back to the native country by providing information, or imposing special regulations or even special taxes, on certain types of holdings of the nationals of the foreign countries.[15]

The bankers who dominated U.S. foreign economic policy in this period refused to consider controls on inflows of West European capital, just as they had during the Bretton Woods discussions. They argued that European governments were fully capable of preventing capital flight on their own by restoring deflationary internal policies to attract the capital back.[16] With European governments unwilling to sacrifice their expansionary economic programs, however, this was an unrealistic suggestion. It reflected a failure to acknowledge the new political commitment to embedded liberalism throughout Western Europe. Moreover, the bankers' prescription ignored the fact that European capital flight was a response not just to domestic inflationary conditions and the possibility of devaluation but also to Europe's *political* uncertainty.

In opposing cooperative controls the bankers were likely guided by their short-term self-interests, as they had been at Bretton Woods. The imposition of U.S. capital controls would interfere with their goal of making New York the key international financial center after the war; more important, such controls would hurt the banks' lucrative business of handling European capital flight. In pursuing these short-term interests, however, the bankers undermined their long-term goal of restoring the confidence in the international monetary system that was needed to build a more open financial order. Indeed, there was a basic contradiction in the key currency plan. The bankers had made clear during the Bretton Woods discussions that

15. Horsefield 1969c:66.
16. See, for example, U.S. Congress 1948a:1431. See also the 1946 monetary report of the International Chamber of Commerce prepared in part by important U.S. bankers (Jacobsson 1979:214). The IMF also argued in 1950: "To a large extent, of course, it is within the power of the their responsible authorities to limit capital flight through appropriate budget and internal credit policies" (Bloomfield 1954:72).

they were acutely aware of the problems that postwar capital flight might pose for international monetary stability. They had insisted that capital controls would be needed in a transition period until stable monetary conditions had been established. Yet the key currency plan required that the United States itself remove all such controls and restore a "free" dollar, thus rendering it unable to cooperate with West European governments in making their capital controls more effective.[17] This contradiction was a further cause of the 1947 crisis.

Marshall Plan Aid as Offsetting Financing

Only with the extension of Marshall Plan aid beginning in 1948 was the contradiction between these short-term and long-term goals overcome. The Marshall Plan has traditionally been viewed as having promoted Western Europe's economic recovery. Milward has effectively demonstrated that the principal economic significance of the aid was not that it promoted economic recovery—for recovery was already under way—but that it provided offsetting financing to resolve the European balance-of-payments crisis. Milward has in mind the offsetting of deficits caused by European imports; however, Marshall Plan aid was also crucial in offsetting capital flight from Europe to the United States. Indeed, according to the "able and authoritative" *New York Times* correspondent Michael Hoffman, the total volume of U.S. aid to Western Europe in the early postwar years was *exceeded* by the total volume of European capital moving in the other direction.[18] If this assessment is accurate, Marshall Plan aid was not only serving simply to offset such disequilibrating capital movements but was not even adequate to that task. According to this interpretation, the economic significance of Marshall Plan aid

17. There was at least one figure associated with the New York banking community, however: Arthur Bloomfield (who was with the Federal Reserve Bank of New York at that time), who pointed to the need for the countries receiving capital flight to aid the countries sending it, either by imposing exchange controls or, at the least, by sharing information (Bloomfield 1946:705).

18. Michael Hoffman, "Europe Feels Drop in Capital Flight," *New York Times*, July 25, 1953, p. 5. The description of him as "able and authoritative" is from Bloomfield 1954:59n87, who concludes, "It is evident . . . that a significant part of the foreign aid of the U.S. government has in effect gone to finance hot money movements from the recipient countries to the United States and elsewhere." See also De Cecco 1979:59.

was, in effect, simply to compensate for the U.S. failure to institute controls on inflows of hot money from Western Europe.[19]

American policymakers were in fact keenly aware of the link between Marshall Plan aid and European capital flight. In late 1947, particularly vocal demands from the French government for help in locating the concealed assets of its citizens in the United States increased the visibility of this issue in Congress. Many members wondered if the cost of the Marshall Plan to the American taxpayer could be reduced by forcing wealthy Europeans to keep their money at home. They deplored the "small, bloated, selfish class of people [in Europe] whose assets have been spread all over the place" and questioned "whether or not [the United States] should become a sanctuary for refugee money."[20] The view of the American Veterans Committee, for example, was that "the American taxpayer should not be obliged to provide the necessary funds for the program while well-to-do Europeans continue to hold on to their private hidden investments in the United States."[21] Administration officials favoring the more interventionist policies of the New Deal also sympathized with this point of view. Officials of the Commerce Department and the newly created Economic Cooperation Administration (ECA), for example, were supportive of the idea in January 1948.[22] Marriner Eccles, President Roosevelt's appointment as chairman of the Federal Reserve Board, also appeared to be sympathetic, as when he stated: "The question was whether this Government was going to protect the private rights of foreign citizens as against the effort of their governments to survive."[23]

The American banking community, however, continued successfully to oppose moves to forcibly repatriate existing concealed as-

19. In a broader sense, however, Marshall Plan aid *was* undoubtedly important in reducing capital flight because it restored private-sector confidence in Western Europe's economic and political future.

20. Quotations from U.S. Congress 1948a:399; 1947:141. See especially the statements of Senator Henry Cabot Lodge, U.S. Congress 1948a:223, 393–99. See also congressional bills H.R. 4576 and H. J. Res. 268, introduced in the House on November 25, 1947, and December 2, 1947, respectively, to support the French request. On French pressure, see NA, RG 56, Records of the NAC, NAC Minutes, November 8, 1947, p. 12; November 24, 1947, pp. 7–8; January 6, 1948, pp. 2–3. For more detail on congressional discussions, see Helleiner 1992a.

21. U.S. Congress 1948b:936.

22. See especially the discussion in the NAC in January 1948: NA, RG 56, Records of the NAC, NAC Minutes, January 6, 1948, pp. 2–4.

23. NA, RG 56, Records of the NAC, NAC Minutes, January 22, 1948, p. 3.

sets, arguing that such moves would infringe on the property rights of foreigners and violate the traditional secrecy of the American banking community.[24] The bankers were supported within the administration by the Treasury Department, which after Morgenthau's departure had become a center of more orthodox thinking, first under the cautious Fred Vinson and then under the St. Louis investment banker John Snyder. In his testimony to Congress, Snyder made explicit his worries that efforts to control capital inflows would require exchange controls, which "would do maximum violence to our position as a world financial center and to our policy of keeping the dollar substantially free of restrictions."[25] In the end, the bankers accepted a deal whereby the United States would offer to help West European governments locate funds that had been blocked during wartime. There would, however, be no controls on the much larger flows that had "freely" entered the United States since December 1945 or on those which would enter in the future.[26] Although Congress also insisted on including a clause requiring recipients of aid under the Marshall Plan to attempt to "locate and identify and put into appropriate use" the foreign assets of their citizens, the clause appeared to impose no obligation on the U.S. government to assist such efforts.[27]

Although the failure to force the bankers to agree to joint enforcement of capital controls reflected the pattern of U.S. policymaking since the Bretton Woods discussions, the extension of financing in the form of Marshall Plan aid to offset capital flight represented an important departure from past American policy. In 1946, the United States had insisted that the IMF not be allowed to provide any financing for deficits stemming from capital movements on the grounds, as Joseph Gold explains, that "the resources of the Fund . . . might be squandered in financing capital flight from mem-

24. See, for example, U.S. Congress 1948a:1040–42, 1431. Strong bank opposition can also be noted in U.S. Congress 1948b:805; NA, RG 56, Records of the NAC, NAC Minutes, November 24, 1947, and March 18, 1948, p. 5; and Records of the NAC, document no. 580.

25. U.S. Congress 1948b:806. See also Snyder's testimony on p. 804 and in U.S. Congress 1948a:394.

26. Announced by Snyder on February 2, 1948 (U.S. Congress 1948b:804–6).

27. Quote from Bloomfield 1954:65n98. Although the ECA argued that the wording implied such an obligation, the Treasury and State departments insisted that it did not (NA, RG 56, Records of the NAC, NAC Minutes, May 5, 1948, p. 5). See the more extended discussion in Helleiner 1992a.

bers that maintained overvalued currencies."[28] Because of the seriousness of the 1947 crisis, however, the United States decided to assume this burden itself through the extension of Marshall Plan aid. Marshall Plan aid was important more broadly in that it established a new mechanism for handling speculative capital flows that was politically more acceptable to the makers of U.S. foreign economic policy than the two mechanisms proposed by Keynes and White at Bretton Woods. Cooperative capital controls had proven unacceptable to the American banking community. Efforts throughout Western Europe to tighten exchange controls as a way to control capital flight had worried U.S. policymakers, who favored a more open trading order. A third option for coping with disruptive capital flows—floating exchange rates—was also unacceptable, given the U.S. goal of constructing a stable exchange rate system. The provision of offsetting financing, however, prevented the disruptive impact of capital flight in a way that was compatible with an open trading order, stable exchange rates, and the liberal inclinations of the American financial community. This new mechanism was to prove important as a supplement to efforts to control the speculative flows that continued to disrupt payments within the EPU in the 1950s.[29] It also would become central to efforts to handle increasing speculative capital movements in the 1960s, as discussed in the next chapter.

The use of financing to offset disruptive capital flows had in fact been discussed during the Bretton Woods negotiations. Most observers, however, had considered it less practical than exchange controls or cooperative controls, given the large sums of money that would be required. As Nurkse put it in discussing the role of the IMF in his 1944 report for the League of Nations: "If, in addition to trade and other normal transactions, such a fund had to cover all kinds of capital flight, it might have to be endowed with enormous resources. In fact, no fund of any practicable size might be sufficient

28. Gold 1977:23. The date of this "unduly restrictive" interpretation (Gold's words) is September 26, 1946.

29. The EPU's funds were made available explicitly for the purpose of offsetting speculative capital flows. (Kaplan and Schleiminger 1989:130; Zacchia 1976:584). See Bloomfield (1954:14–21, 58–59, 68–69) and Mikesell (1954:191–205) for the continuing difficulties caused by disequilibrating flows in the late 1940s and the 1950s.

to offset mass movements of nervous flight capital."[30] Ironically, Nurkse also questioned whether the United States would be willing to provide financing to a fund simply to offset capital flight: "While the United States, for instance, may be quite prepared to hold temporarily at any rate, foreign balances resulting from an increase in exports, it may be questioned whether the United States Treasury would be willing to hold, directly or indirectly, large amounts of, say, Austrian shillings merely to enable Austrian citizens to hold United States dollars."[31] Having rejected Nurkse's alternative solution of cooperative controls, the United States did take on this enormous financial burden of covering such speculative flows, however. The enormity of Marshall Plan aid thus did not so much reflect the resources required to rebuild Europe, as is assumed in conventional histories of the period, but rather the volume of funds that were needed to offset the "mass movements of nervous flight capital" that Nurkse accurately predicted would materialize.

Foreign Aid as Leverage?
The Stabilization Programs of the Late 1940s

The Marshall Plan, or European Recovery Program, was important not only because it established a new mechanism for handling speculative capital movements but also because its introduction marked a second important shift in U.S. foreign economic policy. It might be presumed that the United States would have used Marshall Plan aid as leverage enabling it to continue to push for policy changes in Western Europe similar to those the bankers had sought in 1945–47. On the surface, this presumption would seem accurate. The institution of the European Recovery Program coincided with several key changes in West European economic policy that are frequently seen as having paved the way for the move to multilateral convertibility with the dollar in 1958. A closer look at the historical record, however, reveals that American foreign economic policy shifted after 1947 to reflect more closely the embedded liberal ideas propounded by Keynes and White at Bretton Woods.

One important change in West European economic policy in this

30. League of Nations 1944:188. Henderson (1936:168) also discussed the use of financing to offset disruptive capital flows.
31. League of Nations 1944:188.

period was the introduction of orthodox stabilization programs throughout continental Europe between 1947 and 1949. By reversing the rapid expansionary policies that had generated the payments crisis of 1947, these programs corrected external imbalances and laid the groundwork for an early move to multilateral convertibility with the dollar. Although the United States might be presumed to have encouraged this significant change in European economic policy, recent scholarship has made it clear that the United States played a rather ambiguous role. The ambiguity stemmed from a deep split within U.S. foreign economic policymaking circles after 1947 concerning how Marshall Plan aid should be used. Bankers in the Treasury Department and the IMF wanted to use the aid to force recipient countries to undertake orthodox stabilization programs and to move quickly toward convertibility. The bankers met considerable and usually overwhelming opposition from officials within the State Department and the ECA (the administrative arm of the Marshall Plan), however. These officials felt that Marshall Plan aid should be used first to encourage economic growth and that only after substantial gains in production had been achieved should any stabilization programs or liberalization be encouraged.[32]

The latter, more accommodative approach to European expansionary policies reflected in part the greater influence on foreign economic policy of the "New Deal industrialists" who, as we saw in Chapter 2, were more sympathetic than the New York bankers to the need for Keynesian planning and external capital controls. Although these business figures had become increasingly influential in government in the 1930s and during the war, their influence on foreign economic policy reached a peak with the introduction of the Marshall Plan. One of their most prominent members, Paul Hoffman of the Studebaker Corporation, was selected to head the ECA, and he brought many of his colleagues from the Committee for Economic Development to serve in important positions in that governmental body.[33] The cold war also ensured that economic growth, not deflation, was a prime objective for U.S. strategists in the State Department as a means of fostering political stability in Western Europe and offsetting the strength of the Communist party in countries such as Italy and France. The cold war also ensured that Euro-

32. On these disagreements, see especially Hogan 1987:chap. 2, 249, 253, 420, 437 and Maier 1987a:136; 1987b:175.
33. Schriftgeisser 1960:128–33.

pean economic and political integration was given priority over the goal of restoring complete multilateral convertibility with the dollar. Overly strong arm-twisting, of the sort used in the British loan discussions, was also ruled out because it risked alienating key allies.[34]

This division in U.S. foreign economic policymaking circles between the bankers in the Treasury Department and the IMF, on the one hand, and New Deal industrialists and strategic thinkers in the ECA and the State Department on the other meant that "American hegemony" under the Marshall Plan was often a rather puzzling matter for Europeans.[35] The British Labour government, for example, could often count on the support of the State Department and the ECA in opposing the demands of the U.S. Treasury Department and the IMF (as well as European conservatives) for deflationary policies and early moves to convertibility.[36] Similarly, when the Italians, West Germans, and Belgians devised orthodox plans, much to the liking of the U.S. Treasury Department, they faced opposition from the ECA, which tried to convince them to accept the new Keynesian thinking.[37] For this reason, it is difficult to describe the United States as actively using Marshall Plan aid as leverage to promote the sudden policy changes in 1947–49 throughout continental Europe. Whereas one branch of the U.S. government advocated a return to orthodoxy, the other pressed for expansionary policies. Indeed, if anything, it was the goal of increased industrial production that won the day in U.S. policymaking circles; the bankers' objective of internal financial and monetary stability ran only "a close second."[38]

More important than U.S. pressure in encouraging the policy shift

34. Hogan 1987:23, 27, 228; Dobson 1988:117, 119.

35. Although the division between the ECA and State Department versus the IMF and Treasury Department did, to a large extent, reflect a split between industrialists and bankers (Maier 1987a:138–39), bankers such as William Averell Harriman (in the ECA), Robert A. Lovett, and Dean Acheson (both in the State Department) found themselves in the first camp, opposing the harsh proposals of their banking colleagues in the Treasury Department (Wexler 1983:100; Kaplan and Schleiminger 1989:80–82, 151–53; Hogan 1987:71–74, 262). In each case, however, their commitment to accommodating policies can be traced to strategic cold war considerations. As we saw in Chapter 2, the "New Deal" bankers' commitment to the Democratic party rarely extended to an acceptance of unorthodox financial policies.

36. Hogan 1987:67–68, 294, 420.

37. See, for example, Hogan 1987:153–54, 197, 356, 436; De Cecco 1972:178–79; Milward 1984:18; Harper 1986:162–63; Kaplan and Schleiminger 1989:54.

38. Quotation from Wexler 1983:97. This is also the theme of Hogan 1987.

in continental Europe were domestic political developments in many of those countries. In particular, the seriousness of the 1947–48 economic crisis on the continent led many prominent politicians, intellectuals, and bankers in Western Europe to demand a return to more orthodox economic policies. Faced with the stark alternatives presented by the crisis, Europe's middle classes gave their support to these figures. Elections in 1947–48 throughout continental Europe marked this shift; the shaky middle-left coalitions of 1945–47 gave way to strong center-right governments. By 1948, of the sixteen countries involved in the European Recovery Program, only three (Britain, Norway, and Sweden) were headed by socialist governments.[39]

It was perhaps understandable that this resurgence of orthodox thinking was particularly strong in the former gold bloc consisting of the Benelux countries, Switzerland, and France.[40] After all, proponents of orthodoxy had retained considerable authority in these countries in the 1930s. The resurgence of orthodox thinking in Italy and West Germany had slightly different roots, however. Many politicians and intellectuals, reacting to the fascist experience, were unwilling to accept the compromise between left and right represented by the embedded liberal ideas being promoted by ECA officials. Instead, they sought to move toward more free market policies. These "neoliberals," inspired by thinkers of the Freiburg and Austrian schools such as Wilhelm Ropke and Friedrich Hayek, assumed prominent positions in their respective countries and stressed that more strict monetary discipline and a move toward free market convertibility were necessary if a return to totalitarianism was to be avoided.[41] In Italy, the central bank governor, Luigi Einaudi, sup-

39. For a similar view on the importance of changes in domestic politics throughout continental Europe in promoting the return to orthodox policies, see, for example, Milward 1984:chap. 3, Maier 1987b:173–74, Heilperin 1968:232, and Hogan 1987:444. On the importance of European bankers in promoting orthodox views, see, for example, Jacobsson 1979:208 and Block 1977:90, 240n48.

40. On the orthodoxy of these countries, especially Belgium, in the Marshall Plan years (1948–52), see Hogan 1987:64, 226, 294; Milward 1984:262; Maier 1987a:138; and Diebold 1952:22, 39, 141. Proponents of orthodoxy in France, however, frequently found themselves fighting the bureaucratic-political alliance of "modernizers" that emerged after the war and was committed to economic planning and a strategy of rapid economic growth.

41. On the rise of the neoliberal school, see Johnson 1989, Lenel 1989, Zweig 1980, and Friedrich 1955. The two most important works were Wilhelm Ropke's *The Social Crisis of Our Time*, first published in 1942, and Friedrich Hayek's *The Road to Serfdom* (1944).

ported by a collection of liberal economists who had been prominent in the 1920s, played a vital political role in pushing for the deflation of 1947–48 and implementation of the liberalization policies of the Marshall Plan years.[42] Ludwig Erhard (economics minister, 1949–63), a central figure in the secret neoliberal revival in Germany during the war, achieved a similar goal with regard to the 1948 currency reform (which he had introduced), as well as the liberalization program that followed.[43]

Two other Europeans, Hayek and Per Jacobsson, were also prominent in encouraging the return to orthodox economic thinking in this period. In April 1947, at the height of the uncertainties in Western Europe, Hayek organized the first meeting of what came to be called the Mont Pelerin Society. It brought together neoliberal thinkers and political figures from the countries of Western Europe (as well as many Americans such as Milton Friedman) in a kind of transnational private forum that, as Friedman later put it, served as a "rallying point" for the neoliberal cause.[44] After its initial success, it continued to promote neoliberal ideas and met almost every year in different countries under Hayek's leadership; important individuals such as Einaudi and Erhard were members.[45] Jacobsson was chief economic adviser to the BIS from 1931 to 1956 and had been a tireless European defender of orthodoxy in the 1930s. In the late 1940s and early 1950s, he used his position at the BIS to try to ensure that Marshall Plan aid was used not to perpetuate inflationary conditions but to facilitate a return to more orthodox policies. To this end he lobbied U.S. officials and pressured European central bank governors, who are said to have been "heavily influenced" by

42. See De Cecco 1972, 1989.

43. See, for example, Allen 1989. The United States clearly exerted strong influence in advocating the 1948 currency reform (Klopstock 1949:281n10) and in sponsoring Erhard's rise—he referred to himself as an "American discovery" (Hardach 1976:143n5). The support of domestic neoliberals was crucial to Erhard's success, however, and in the 1948 liberalization program, he went even farther than the Americans wanted (Bark and Cress 1989:206–7).

44. Quoted in Nash 1976:26. See also Stigler 1988:116–17, 142 and Hayek 1967: 148–57. The founding members of the society (which Hayek had thought of calling the "Acton-Tocqueville Society") included Einaudi, Howard Ellis, Walter Eucken, Friedman, Frank Graham, Eli Heckscher, Frank Knight, Frederick Lutz, Ludwig von Mises, Fritz Machlup, Karl Popper, Lionel Robbins, Ropke, Jacques Rueff, Walter Rustow, and George Stigler.

45. Machlup 1976:xi–xiii; Nash 1976:25–27. Hayek relinquished the presidency in 1960 and was succeeded by Wilhelm Ropke in the early 1960s, Frederick Lutz (1964–67), and Milton Friedman (1970–72).

his constant insistence on the need to enforce discipline in monetary policy and move toward early free market convertibility.[46] West European governments, such as Italy, even employed him on occasion to serve as their advocate in debates with the Keynesian ECA concerning appropriate domestic policy.[47]

The Cautious Move to European Dollar Convertibility in the 1950s

It is often said that after the stabilization programs of the late 1940s, the United States laid the foundation for the move to European dollar convertibility by encouraging various developments, including the European devaluations of 1949, the establishment of the EPU in 1950, and liberalization during the 1950s. This interpretation is not fully convincing, however. A development endogenous to Europe—the turn to multilateralism by British financial figures—was more important in encouraging the move to convertibility in the 1950s. It is convenient first to look more closely at the role of the United States.

The 1949 devaluations throughout Western Europe, led by that of the British pound in September, were important because they helped to correct Europe's external payments imbalances, thus permitting liberalization to occur in the 1950s. It is frequently argued that the United States (along with the IMF) forced the crucial devaluation of the pound by deliberately "talking down" that currency in public pronouncements. Because of the "leaky" nature of Britain's exchange controls, these public statements unleashed capital flight that proved difficult to control.[48] This argument is not entirely persuasive, however. Although the U.S. Treasury Department and the IMF favored the devaluation, U.S. policy was once again split; the State Department urged caution out of fear of alienating the strategically important Britain.[49] More important, the case that U.S. officials were actively encouraging capital flight is weakened by fact that the Fed-

---

46. Kaplan and Schleiminger 1989:64. See also Kaplan and Schleiminger 1989:103; Jacobsson 1979:98–99, 198, 209–10, 246–58; Ridgeway 1959:179–82, 281; Schloss 1958:98, 141; and Wexler 1983:28–29, 261–62n16.
47. De Cecco 1989:221; Jacobsson 1979:228.
48. See, for example, De Cecco 1979:59–60 and Hogan 1987:228, 253.
49. Dobson 1988:119–21.

eral Reserve and the Treasury Department agreed in 1949 to help the Bank of England defend the pound by cracking down on "cheap sterling" transactions in New York foreign exchange markets. Such transactions, which were illegal under the regulations governing British exchange controls, were increasing rapidly in New York and elsewhere, and the Bank of England could do little to prevent them without foreign help. The assistance given by U.S. authorities in 1949 included exactly the sort of cooperative action that the New York banking community had strongly opposed at Bretton Woods and in 1947–48, and it was a dramatic gesture of support for British efforts to control speculative capital flows.[50] Moreover, in August 1949, the IMF released a statement repeating the obligations of member countries under Article 8-2b to make "unenforceable" those foreign exchange dealings in their territories that contravened other members' exchange controls. This statement suggested that IMF officials were also seeking ways to combat speculation against the pound.[51]

The establishment of the EPU in 1950 restored a somewhat limited regional convertibility between central banks and is said to have been decisive in helping Western Europe achieve a more open system of trade and exchange payments. Recent historical scholarship, however, makes it clear that this was not the view of either European neoliberals or American bankers in the Treasury Department and the IMF, who considered the EPU an unnecessary barrier to the early restoration of full multilateral, market-based convertibility. In their view, the EPU would be a "soft" currency bloc that encouraged unsound policies; it would also prevent individual countries from moving on their own to full convertibility if they so desired. Their proposals for a rapid move to convertibility, or at least a "harder" currency union, met stiff opposition in the ECA and the State Department. Seeking to foster European cooperation for strategic reasons, and concerned more with expanding industrial production than with achieving immediate multilateral convertibility, the ECA and the State Department insisted on the establishment of the EPU and sided with the socialist governments of Britain and Scandinavia in the view that it should be a relatively "soft" currency bloc.[52]

50. Fforde 1992:227, 229–30, 235; *Business Week*, September 3, 1949, p. 94.
51. Horsefield 1969a:210 and Gold 1950:329–30. See Chapter 2 for the origins of Article 8-2b. The statement specified that the obligation applied even if the currencies involved had not yet been made convertible under Article 8.
52. Kaplan and Schleiminger 1989:38–43, 49–53, 58, 64–65, 151–53, 340; Hogan 1987:253, 261–62; Diebold 1952:409–10; Milward 1990.

The ambivalent position of the United States during the EPU negotiations was made even more evident by its reaction to a request
from British financial authorities in late 1949 for a loan in order to
make the pound rapidly convertible. The plan was proposed by officials in the Bank of England and British Treasury who were deeply
worried about London's future as an international financial center
for the sterling bloc. The increase in illegal "cheap sterling" transactions abroad was depriving London of international financial business. Furthermore, the EPU would not only threaten the continued
existence of the closed sterling area but also place international
monetary and financial affairs under the control of European governments instead of London market operators. Faced with these
challenges, British financial authorities saw a "dash" to sterling convertibility, supported by a U.S. loan, as the best way to preserve
London's international financial position. This plan represented a
significant reversal of the post-1931 support in British financial circles for a protectionist sterling area. Recognizing the possibility of
finally restoring the financial alliance with Britain that had existed in
the 1920s, American bankers in the Treasury Department strongly
supported the proposal; indeed, it seemed remarkably similar to
their own key currency plan of 1945–47. The ECA vetoed it, however, arguing that the initiative undermined efforts to foster European cooperation within the new EPU.[53]

Recent scholarship also makes clear that the United States made
no special effort to promote convertibility after the EPU's creation.
It opposed a second, higher-profile scheme—"Operation Robot"—
proposed by the Bank of England and top British Treasury officials
in 1952–53 for a rapid restoration of the pound's convertibility.
Once again, the British scheme was supported by the U.S. Treasury
Department but was vetoed by the head of the Mutual Security Administration (which succeeded the ECA in 1951), who argued that it
would disrupt European unity.[54] The United States also gave little
support to countries such as West Germany, Belgium, and the Netherlands that held substantial surplus positions in the EPU in the early
1950s and that began to call for a move to dollar convertibility as
early as 1953. Indeed, in their recent study of the EPU, Jacob Kaplan
and Gunther Schleiminger demonstrate that the United States did

53. Kaplan and Schleiminger 1989:68–71, 74, 78 and Diebold 1952:100. For the
Bank of England's changed views, see Fforde 1992:221, 228–29, 242, 247–48.
54. Kaplan and Schleiminger 1989:164–65, 174, 181, 195–96 and Dobson 1988:
147–49.

not attempt, at this time or at any other time in the 1950s, to encourage EPU countries to restore dollar convertibility.[55]

This hands-off approach was confirmed by the 1954 Randall Commission, which conducted a full review of U.S. foreign economic policy. Having rejected Jacobsson's testimony, in which he called for a rapid move to full convertibility, the commission concluded that any such move should be gradual and that the timing should be left entirely to the West European governments.[56] It also strongly opposed any unilateral attempt to achieve convertibility outside the EPU structure, such as the effort proposed by Britain. A quick move to convertibility might, as Randall put it, cause a "sharp and sudden reduction of the standard of living" throughout Europe that "could create perils for the United States in the matter of security that we could not wisely risk."[57]

After the early 1950s, the decisive leadership in encouraging Western Europe to move to dollar convertibility came from Britain rather than the United States. With the rejection of Operation Robot, the Bank of England and the British Treasury became resigned to Britain's membership in the EPU and began to work "from within" to restore a world of market-based full convertibility in which London could flourish.[58] The first step in this direction, the reopening of London's foreign exchange markets, was taken in 1951. The next significant move came in 1953 when the Bank of England convinced other EPU members to let authorized private banks of each country deal in other countries' currencies. One year later, Britain reopened the London commodity markets in standardized products such as grain and gold, a move that had the effect of reestablishing a limited dollar convertibility throughout Europe because currencies could be exchanged by means of commodity shunting. Moreover, having extensively liberalized sterling area transactions in 1954, the Bank of England began in early 1955 to intervene in foreign exchange markets in New York and Zurich to support the pound's value abroad within one percent of the official rate, thereby making pounds effectively convertible into dollars and other currencies.[59]

55. Kaplan and Schleiminger 1989:162, 183, 195–96, 204–5, 210.
56. U.S. Government 1954a:72. See also Randall 1954:10–11, 17. Jacobsson's testimony was cited in the minority report (U.S. Government 1954b:13).
57. Randall 1954:16; Kaplan and Schleiminger 1989:43–44.
58. Hinshaw 1958:18–20; Kaplan and Schleiminger 1989:207.
59. Rees 1963:153, 156–59, 182, 188–89, 191–93; Strange 1971:64–65; Hinshaw 1958:22–24; Kaplan and Schleiminger 1989:194.

Although these moves had brought Western Europe close to market-based dollar convertibility by 1955, another three years would be required before it was actually achieved. This delay reflected the persistent worries of European governments that convertibility would externally constrain their policy autonomy. They preferred to wait until their monetary reserves were large enough to buffer the market forces—particularly speculative capital movements—that would be released by convertibility with the dollar. The economic boom that began in Europe in 1954–55 only worsened its external balance with the United States, thus reinforcing these worries and demonstrating the vulnerability of many countries' external payments position. Britain's announcement in 1955 that it would delay its move to dollar convertibility effectively ended discussions in Europe concerning an immediate move to convertibility. As in the past, the British decision was strongly supported by the United States (although it was actively opposed by the Bank of England).[60]

When Western Europe's balance-of-payments position strengthened in 1958, European governments finally agreed to restore the convertibility of their currencies with dollars.[61] Although this move revived confidence among private international market operators and led them to reenter the international financial arena, it is often forgotten that in all countries but West Germany, convertibility was restored only with regard to current account transactions. This decision angered West European neoliberals, who had demanded throughout the 1950s that convertibility be restored for both the current account *and* the capital account. Like the U.S. bankers at Bretton Woods, they emphasized that capital controls, like any type of foreign exchange control, represented, as Hayek had said in 1944, "the decisive advance on the path to totalitarianism and the suppression of individual liberty." Such controls, he continued, represented "the complete delivery of the individual to the tyranny of the state, the final suppression of all means of escape—not merely for the rich, but for everybody."[62] European neoliberals also pointed to the importance of capital movements in encouraging sound economic policy. As Ropke observed, "the more quickly and thoroughly an en-

60. Kaplan and Schleiminger 1989:210; De Vries in Horsefield 1969b:274.
61. Katz 1961 and Hinshaw 1958.
62. Hayek 1944:92n2. See also Ropke 1959:240–41, 248–49; Heilperin 1968:236; Hayek 1937:71–72; Robbins 1937:68–71; Kaplan and Schleiminger 1989:186–87; and Flanders 1989:134–36.

tirely new situation is created through the abolition of exchange control, the less will be the danger that through change of Government the course of economic policy might once more become uncertain. . . . It would be exceedingly difficult for any subsequent Government to destroy what has already been achieved, by a return to a 'leftist' course of economic policy."[63]

Although most West European governments welcomed productive and equilibrating flows of capital, they continued to fear the power of speculative and disequilibrating capital movements to curb their policy autonomy and disrupt the Bretton Woods stable exchange rate system. Moreover, their decision to maintain capital controls was supported by a 1956 IMF decision that reaffirmed countries' right to control capital movements "for any reason."[64] The American Randall Commission had also specifically discouraged the restoration of convertibility for the capital account on the grounds that "the risks of massive capital flight are still quite great."[65] Thus, although the restoration of dollar convertibility was an important moment in the building of the postwar international liberal economic order, both the American government and West European governments remained committed to the restrictive Bretton Woods financial order.

The Slow and Limited Move to Japanese Convertibility

This commitment to the Bretton Woods financial order was even more evident in U.S. policy toward Japan after the war. Planning concerning Japan's role in the postwar world began soon after Pearl Harbor and was dominated initially by New Dealers who sought to bring the principles of the New Deal to Japan.[66] To implement this goal domestically, between 1945 and 1947, they initiated a series of broad political, economic, and social reforms. At the international level, rather than pressing for a rapid move to convertibility, as the United States was doing in Western Europe in this period, the American Occupation authorities constructed a system of exchange controls "more exhaustive than any that had been maintained by the Japanese government itself prior to the surrender." Not only were

63. Ropke 1959:245.
64. For the IMF decision, see Horsefield 1969c:246.
65. U.S. Government 1954a:467. See also U.S. Government 1954a:73–74, 77.
66. Cohen 1987:32–48 and Welfield 1988:26.

all Japanese banks and offices overseas closed but the Occupation authorities went so far as to initially suspend all contact "between Japanese and foreigners at either the government or private level."[67]

In 1947–48, the cold war—in combination with the resurgence in Washington of the "old Japan lobby," consisting of representatives of U.S. businesses with prewar economic links to Japan—brought about a "reverse course" in U.S. policy toward Japan. The United States halted its program aimed at radically reforming Japanese society and began to cultivate the allegiance of Japan's business leaders. With respect to Japan's international economic policy, U.S. policymakers at this point were divided in two groups, as they were with regard to U.S. policy toward Western Europe. Dominant initially were figures, often with a banking background, in the Treasury Department, the Federal Reserve, some parts of the State Department, and the IMF who favored limited economic aid and a rapid move to convertibility by deflationary means.[68] In 1948, they backed a plan devised by William Draper, who had been vice-president of the Wall Street investment house Dillon, Read. His plan consisted of a strict internal domestic stabilization program and a substantial liberalization of external economic relations. Detroit banker Joseph Dodge, president of the American Bankers Association, was asked to implement the plan, a task that he achieved with notable effectiveness. Although Dodge's plan met with considerable domestic opposition, he had the support of, and cultivated links with, Japanese bankers who had been prominent before the war such as Viscount Hisaakira Kano, who had been vice-chairman of the BIS.[69]

These bankers were actively opposed on strategic grounds by some members of the State Department and especially by the Occupation authorities led by General Douglas MacArthur. MacArthur argued that the "weakness of the Japanese governmental structure" meant that deflationary and liberalizing policies could easily bring domestic political instability, which would hurt U.S. security interests.[70] These officials sought instead to encourage expansionary poli-

67. Hollerman 1979:710, 708.
68. Borden 1984:80–81, 88–89, 138; Cohen 1987:166, 406, 415; Schonberger 1977, 1989:chaps. 6–7; Iriye 1977.
69. Schonberger 1989:200 and Cohen 1987:180, 441–42. Sebald (1965:91), however, notes some opposition in the Japanese banking community.
70. NA, RG 56, Records of the NAC, NAC document no. 714, June 25, 1948, p. 4. See also Borden 1984:14; but note the more orthodox views of the finance section of the Occupation in Mitsuru 1977:419.

cies in much the same way that the ECA had in Western Europe. In late 1949 and early 1950, they began to gain influence as the Japanese economy showed signs of collapse and the risks of the bankers' strategy became more apparent. Growing recognition of the vulnerability of Japan's foreign exchange position led to the introduction of two important laws—the 1949 Foreign Exchange and Trade Control Act and the 1950 Law Concerning Foreign Capital—that recentralized government control over international payments.[71] Although these laws were intended as temporary measures to encourage more efficient allocation of scarce foreign exchange resources as well as to control capital flight, their practical effect was to establish the legal basis for Japan's restrictive foreign exchange regime, which lasted until 1980.

The coming of the Korean War caused a policy shift further away from the position of the bankers because it reinforced the strategic importance of Japan and thus softened U.S. pressure for tough economic programs. It also resulted in a large inflow of U.S. economic aid; Chalmers Johnson described the war as "the equivalent for Japan of the Marshall Plan."[72] At the end of the war, a more accommodating U.S. policy was firmly in place. Based primarily on security considerations, it stressed continued economic aid without pressure to liberalize. The domestic political instability that accompanied the deflation and the currency crisis of 1954 only confirmed to U.S. policymakers the importance of this new strategy.[73]

In the absence of strong U.S. pressure, the timing of Japan's move to currency convertibility was left to Japanese policymakers. They chose to retain a high degree of control over external transactions, limiting foreign exchange holdings to the government and a small number of specially designated foreign exchange banks. This restrictive approach was necessary in part because the variability of their foreign exchange earnings made the Japanese extremely vulnerable to, and thus wary of, speculative capital flows.[74] Rigid exchange controls were also needed to prevent capital flight from undermining artificially low interest rates, which were used to promote growth in

71. Borden 1984:96, Hollerman 1967:225–26, Ozaki 1972:78–81, Adams and Hoshii 1972:492–93.

72. Johnson quoted in Borden 1984:146. On Japan's new strategic importance, see Welfield 1988:49–50, 88–89.

73. Borden 1984:176–80.

74. Hollerman 1967:110–11; Adams and Hoshii 1972:511.

the industrial sector. Moreover, Japanese companies and individuals had to be prevented from evading the government's credit restraints by borrowing abroad.

It was not until the early 1960s that Japan began to liberalize its external financial relations. In 1964, the Japanese government announced the restoration of convertibility of its current account. In the same year, it joined the Organization for Economic Cooperation and Development (OECD) and thus accepted its various Codes on Liberalization, including the Code of Liberalization of Capital Movements (to be discussed in the next chapter). These moves were in part a result of pressure by the United States and the IMF, which had begun in the early 1960s when Japan's external payments position finally showed signs of strong improvement; in part they reflected Japan's desire to enter the ranks of the developed nations.[75] These were only limited moves, however. Japan restored convertibility on a much more restrictive, government-to-government basis than the "market" convertibility West European governments had chosen in 1958. Private citizens still were not permitted to hold foreign exchange, and all current account and capital account transactions continued to be handled by the government or by the specially authorized foreign exchange banks. Moreover, the restrictive 1949–50 foreign exchange laws remained in place, thus giving the government considerable discretionary power over market operators.[76] The Japanese also diluted the effects of the Code of the Liberalization of Capital Movements by taking many more exemptions—eighteen in all—than the West European governments had on joining. Although this move caused much "irritation and discontent" abroad, it was accepted by the United States.[77] In sum, as Leon Hollerman remarked, "the structure of the control system itself remained latent and intact."[78]

Although the early postwar years are commonly depicted as a period in which the United States used its overwhelming power to build a liberal international economic order, it did not construct a liberal pattern of economic relations in the financial sector in this era. This chapter has presented four explanations for this develop-

75. Fujioka 1979:23–36; Hollerman 1967:155, 204, 223, 228; Ozaki 1972:77.
76. Adams and Hoshii 1972:492–93; Hollerman 1967:155–56, 230.
77. Ozaki 1972:78; Adams and Hoshii 1972:463.
78. Hollerman 1967:230.

ment. First, although the New York bankers who dominated U.S. foreign economic policy between 1945 and 1947 sought to promote a more open, liberal international financial order, they sabotaged their efforts by refusing to support attempts to curtail European capital flight. As the bankers themselves acknowledged at Bretton Woods, this capital flight had to be curtailed in the short term to reduce West European payments imbalances and restore international monetary stability, both of which were necessary for the establishment of a more open, liberal financial order in the long term. Their refusal to support such efforts stemmed from their desire to continue to receive European funds and to maintain New York's openness as a financial center.

Second, as at Bretton Woods, policymakers in the United States considered it necessary to sacrifice financial liberalism to prevent disequilibrating speculative capital movements from threatening the construction of an open trading order and maintenance of stable exchange rates. The 1947 crisis confirmed that states would be forced to consider the introduction of trade-inhibiting exchange controls as well as floating exchange rates unless the disruptive impact of such flows could be minimized. Although the extension of offsetting financing in the Marshall Plan and in the E.P.U. helped minimize such disruption, capital controls were viewed as an essential tool for this task.

Third, policymakers throughout the advanced industrial world continued to be influenced by an embedded liberal framework of thought. American support for the use of capital controls abroad after 1947 partly reflected the political strength of New Deal industrialists who supported embedded liberal ideas. Although these industrialists were opposed by bankers and orthodox intellectuals, they had important allies abroad—a replication of the transnational politics that characterized the Bretton Woods negotiations.[79] New Dealers also were important in constructing Japan's tight exchange controls between 1945 and 1947.

Fourth, the New Dealers found strong support for their approach to foreign economic policy among those concerned with U.S. strategic goals in the cold war. These strategic thinkers were sympathetic to embedded liberal ideas because of their goal of promoting economic growth and political stability in Western Europe and Japan.

---

79. The transnational nature of politics in this period is noted by Hall 1989:388n64.

They also worried that aggressive efforts to encourage Europe and Japan to liberalize might alienate these key U.S. allies. The foreign economic policy of the United States with regard to its allies thus should be viewed not in isolation but rather in the broader context of its conflict with the Soviet Union after 1947.[80]

In general, the developments described in this chapter confirmed the strength of the restrictive Bretton Woods financial order in the early postwar years. There were, however, several developments in this period which also foreshadowed its unraveling. The first was the rise of the neoliberal intellectual movement in central Europe in the late 1940s. This movement would gain momentum and by the 1970s and 1980s would present an important challenge to supporters of the embedded liberal normative framework outlined by Keynes and White at Bretton Woods. The second was the decision to preserve the BIS, an institution that would, as the U.S. bankers had hoped, play an important role in maintaining stability in the international financial markets that emerged after the late 1950s. Third, the 1947 economic crisis revealed the fundamental political difficulties of using either of the Bretton Woods mechanisms to control disequilibrating speculative capital movements. Cooperative controls were easily vetoed by a major power, whereas comprehensive exchange controls were not compatible with an open world economy. These difficulties would reappear in the 1970s and 1980s. Moreover, the solution reached after 1947 for handling disruptive capital movements—the extension of offsetting financing—would prove to be of only temporary utility. The fourth development was the reorientation of British financial authorities in favor of multilateralism as an alternative to the protected sterling bloc in the late 1940s. As the New York bankers anticipated at Bretton Woods, the commitment of British financial authorities to the preservation of London's position as an international financial center would prove crucial in facilitating the emergence of a more open international financial order in the 1960s. That is the subject of the following chapter.

80. See also Haggard and Simmons 1987:503–4.

PART II

THE REEMERGENCE
OF GLOBAL FINANCE

CHAPTER FOUR

Support for the Euromarket in the 1960s

Most explanations of the globalization of financial markets after the late 1950s emphasize the importance of technological and market pressures, which states are said to have been forced to accept because of the impossibility of controlling international capital movements. But states have played a much more central role in the reemergence of global finance. By easing controls, states have given market operators more freedom than they otherwise would have had. At critical junctures, states have also chosen not to use comprehensive exchange controls and cooperative controls, the two mechanisms proposed by Keynes and White in their early Bretton Woods drafts for overcoming the difficulties of controlling capital movements. In addition, states have prevented international financial crises by taking lender-of-last-resort action and by cooperating in international regulatory and supervisory activities. The subject of this chapter is the support provided by Britain and the United States for the Euromarket in the 1960s, the first episode in which states provided market operators with an extra degree of freedom.

Although the restoration of current account convertibility encouraged a resumption of private international financial activity, the widespread use of capital controls created enormous obstacles for international market operators. Fred Hirsch and Peter Oppenheimer noted that the international financial system in the 1960s "was rather like a mini-golf course, with some hole or other always accessible, but others shut off and a variety of shifting obstacles to be negotiated."[1] In the midst of these obstacles, the Euromarket, created in the late 1950s and based primarily in London in the 1960s, allowed international financial operations to be conducted relatively freely; transactions could be made in nonlocal currencies, especially dollars, completely free of state regulations. Although this "offshore" market remained strictly separate from national financial systems, it still represented the most liberal international financial environment that private market operators had encountered in several decades. Its rapid growth in the 1960s indicated the extent to which bankers took advantage of this new freedom.

The Euromarket has often been described as a "stateless" financial market created by market operators outside the control of any national government.[2] Although market operators were instrumental in its creation and growth, the Euromarket was heavily dependent on state support from the outset.[3] Two states, in particular, Britain and the United States, strongly supported the market in its early years. Britain provided a physical location for the market, permitting it to operate in London free of regulation. U.S. support was equally important because American banks and corporations were a dominant presence in the market in the 1960s. Although it had the power, the United States chose not to prevent them from participating in the market. In fact, by the mid-1960s, U.S. officials were actively encouraging American banks and corporations to move their operations to the offshore London market.

Although the creation of the Euromarket marked an important shift away from the restrictive Bretton Woods financial order, this order retained considerable strength throughout the 1960s. Most advanced industrial states continued to employ capital controls, for example. Indeed, even the United States and Britain used such controls at the same time that they were supporting the offshore Eurodollar market. The decade was thus one of transition. The political reasons for British and American support for the Euromarket in the 1960s are discussed in the first two sections of this chapter. The third section describes the continuing reluctance of states to depart more fully from the restrictive practices of the early postwar years.

1. Hirsch and Oppenheimer 1976:661.
2. See for example, Wriston 1986:133.
3. See, for example, Frieden 1987:116, Kelly 1976:41, and Strange 1971:209.

British Support for the Euromarket

In the 1950s, the British government, more than other West European governments, hoped that the move to convertibility would bring freedom for capital movements, in order that London's international activities could be bolstered. British financial authorities were thus understandably frustrated when, convertibility having finally been achieved, a series of balance-of-payments crises forced them to impose increasingly tighter restrictions on the international use of sterling in capital transactions. The exchange crisis of 1957 had signaled the beginning of these difficulties even before full convertibility had been restored. The crisis was triggered almost entirely by capital flight in response to rumors of a German revaluation and to a loss of confidence in British economic policy.[4] The Conservative government responded to the crisis initially in an orthodox manner by increasing interest rates and cutting government spending. Strong domestic opposition to further austerity measures, however, forced the government to combine these policies with controls on outflows of capital from the sterling area. It restricted the use of trade credits in sterling to finance trade outside the sterling area and imposed controls on the purchase of foreign-currency securities from sterling area residents.

These restrictions suggested to bankers in London that the British government's commitment to the Keynesian welfare state in the face of substantial balance-of-payments difficulties would mean that they would not be able to operate freely at the international level after restoration of convertibility. This prediction was confirmed twice: in 1961, when the Conservative government, faced with a more severe exchange crisis, again increased restrictions on capital movements in and out of the sterling area; and in 1964–67, when exchange crises caused the government to impose increasingly tighter controls on capital outflows from the sterling area. The introduction of voluntary controls on capital outflows *within* the sterling area in 1966 indicated to London bankers that London's international business could no longer be based on even a protected sterling area.

The failure of the strategy initiated by British financial authorities in the early 1950s—trying to regain London's international position

4. Katz 1961:20.

on the basis of a multilaterally convertible sterling—did not result in a total defeat for London's international bankers, however. During the 1957 sterling crisis, they stumbled upon the Eurodollar market as a solution to their problems. The catalyst for the market's development were the restrictions on British banks' use of sterling to finance trade between countries outside the sterling area.[5] Customers whose trade had been financed by sterling acceptance credits continued to demand from London financiers a new mechanism for financing such trade. The London bankers found they could satisfy this demand by offering dollar loans against their dollar deposits of overseas residents. This business proved so attractive that when the restrictions were removed in early 1959, the bankers continued their new Eurodollar activity. By shifting their business to a dollar basis, the London operators had found a way to preserve their international business without being encumbered by British capital controls.

The Eurodollar market created by the private operators was actively encouraged by British financial authorities. To them, it represented a solution to the problem of how to reconcile the goal of restoring London's international position with the Keynesian welfare state and Britain's deteriorating economic position. The Bank of England was the most active proponent of the Eurodollar market.[6] It not only refrained from imposing regulations on market activity, but took several important measures, such as its 1962 decision to allow the issue of foreign securities denominated in foreign currencies in London, thereby permitting the growth of a Eurobond market. The move was particularly well timed to enable London to replace New York as the leading international capital market after the United States instituted a capital controls program in 1963.

Two Bases of American Support for the Euromarket

The early success of Britain's strategy to establish London as a Eurodollar center was largely due to the plan's coincidence with the U.S. capital controls program, which was intended to be a solution to the country's growing balance-of-payments problems in the 1960s. Because West European governments had chosen to postpone con-

5. Strange 1976:180.
6. Kelly 1976:42–45, 57–82.

vertibility until such time as the foreign liabilities of the United States began to exceed its gold reserves, Europe's move was followed by growing speculative attacks against the dollar. Market operators no longer had full confidence in the dollar's convertibility into gold. The difficulties these attacks posed for U.S. policy first surfaced in October 1960, when there was a run on the dollar. The orthodox response would have been to raise interest rates to attract funds back to the United States and to institute adjustment measures such as cutting back on domestic spending. Washington policymakers were not willing to change domestic policy in response to what was perceived as a temporary external payments problem, however. Instead, they chose a limited initiative to attract short-term funds back to the United States—"Operation Twist"—which involved the raising of short-term interest rates without affecting long-term rates.

Because the external deficit showed no sign of diminishing and market confidence continued to erode, the Kennedy administration was forced to consider more serious measures. Some within the administration advocated the introduction of exchange controls to restrict short-term capital flight,[7] but attention focused instead on curtailing long-term foreign lending from New York capital markets. After convertibility, there had been a large increase in long-term foreign lending by New York bankers, who had finally achieved the position of lender to the world that they had sought since 1945. But in light of the weakening U.S. external position, Washington policymakers considered these loans undesirable disequilibrating capital flows that were exacerbating the country's external payments problems.

The first initiative taken to curtail such flows was the imposition, in July 1963, of the interest equalization tax (IET) on all new issues of foreign securities and equities sold in the United States. The tax had been designed by two bankers in the administration, Douglas Dillon and Robert Roosa, who hoped that it would serve as a market-oriented alternative to the direct controls that others were urging President John F. Kennedy to consider.[8] Dillon and Roosa combined their advocacy of the IET with an active campaign to encourage West European governments to liberalize and deregulate their own capital markets, arguing that the imperfections of those markets had encouraged many European companies to borrow unnecessarily from

7. Odell 1982:107; Conybeare 1988:157.

8. Conybeare 1988:82–85, 101, 107; Hawley 1987:23, 48, 53. There were others who also supported the IET on this basis. See U.S. Congress 1963c:362, 376–77.

the New York markets. Liberalization and deregulation abroad, they claimed, would lead to an international capital market that functioned more properly—one in which international interest rate differentials would more accurately reflect national differences in the productivity of capital. This, in turn, would reduce disequilibrating flows of capital from the United States to Europe and reduce the need for U.S. controls.[9]

Although Dillon and Roosa attempted to steer U.S. policy in a more liberal direction, two measures were soon introduced to tighten capital restrictions: in 1964, the IET was extended to cover bank loans with a duration of one year or more as well as nonbank credits of one to three years; and, in 1965, a voluntary controls program was established to discourage the export of capital by American banks and corporations. These two measures were introduced in part because of the worsening of the U.S. balance-of-payments situation that resulted from the escalation of the Vietnam War and the initiation of President Lyndon Johnson's Great Society program. They were also intended to close some of the alternative paths that financial institutions had found for continuing to export capital. In particular, the IET had been circumvented by the shifting of foreign lending to bank loans that initially had not been covered by the tax. Indeed, in opposing direct controls, Dillon and Roosa had warned— as had their banking counterparts at Bretton Woods—that capital restrictions would easily be evaded and would be made effective only by introducing increasingly tighter restrictions that eventually would, in Roosa's opinion, "literally congeal the bloodstream of American capitalism."[10]

Although these initiatives imposed the first U.S. barriers to capital movements of the postwar period, they did reflect a similar skepticism among U.S. policymakers concerning the benefits of a liberal financial order as had been demonstrated in the 1940s and 1950s. The 1967 *Economic Report of the President*, for example, justified capital controls on the grounds that financial flows were not producing an optimum distribution of the world's scarce capital but

9. Hawley 1987:48–49. A 1964 presidential task force took up this argument and recommended in its report that the State and Treasury departments encourage the IMF and the OECD to promote the elimination of controls abroad (ABA 1968:246). See also OECD 1966:16–17; ABA 1968:203; Volcker and Gyohten 1992:33.

10. Quoted in Conybeare 1988:157. See also remarks by Dillon in U.S. Congress 1963a:28.

rather were responses to differences in national monetary policies, taxation, financial structures, and cyclical economic trends. Even the American Bankers Association was forced to admit in 1968 that the case for free capital movements was weak, given that many such movements were speculative, unproductive, and tax-avoiding.[11]

The capital controls program also demonstrated a continuity in U.S. foreign economic policy in that the interests of U.S. bankers continued to be subordinated, as they had been since 1947, to the priorities of New Deal economics and global strategic objectives. As an alternative to the capital controls program, representatives of the American banking community advocated a combination of orthodox deflationary measures and cutbacks in foreign military and aid commitments throughout the 1960s.[12] Neither, however, was seriously considered in Washington political circles. The Kennedy and Johnson administrations were not prepared to limit or decrease America's global role by cutting foreign aid and military spending. Moreover, having converted publicly to Keynesianism in the early 1960s, these Democrat administrations were not prepared to sacrifice interventionist domestic policy in order to correct an imbalance in the external accounts. Indeed, like Keynes and White, many of Kennedy's advisers saw the whole issue in a highly political light, "as a struggle over general financial policy between the national government on the one hand and on the other European bankers supported by domestic conservatives who had always opposed Democratic administrations."[13] The priority given to strategic considerations and domestic monetary and fiscal autonomy by these administrations was also strongly supported by Congress as well as by supporters of New Deal policies such as the AFL-CIO and, at least initially, industrial leaders in the Committee for Economic Development (CED).[14] Further evidence of the bankers' relative political

11. ABA 1968:203–6, 225, 229, 246, 252. Tax evasion was a particularly important part of Eurobond activity in the 1960s (Cooper 1971:204; Genillard 1970:326).

12. U.S. Congress 1963b:309; Conybeare 1988: chap. 5, 190–208, 226–27; Hawley 1987:53–56, 75–76.

13. Odell 1982:106. Indeed, President Kennedy is supposed to have remarked that it was "absurd" to reduce government programs for the sake of maintaining the freedom of private capital flows (Conybeare 1988:154). See also Conybeare 1988:69–70, 79, 101 and Hawley 1987:21, 64–65. Even bankers such as David Rockefeller accepted the view that capital controls were preferable to cutting back expenditures for national security (Hawley 1987:36).

14. For AFL-CIO and congressional views, see Conybeare 1988:132–36, 181–86. The CED was willing to accept capital controls but only on a temporary basis (CED 1961:65;

weakness was that their international activities were controlled more strictly than those of the industrialists. Although the Kennedy administration had initially favored controls on the foreign direct investment of U.S. industrial corporations, it had been forced to back down in 1962 because of strong political pressure from Commerce Secretary Luther H. Hodges and powerful industrial interests.[15] The New York banking community had proved to be an easier target with regard to the IET. The controls on banks after 1965 were also implemented more stringently than those on multinational industrial corporations. John Conybeare notes that the banks were very conscious of their "political vulnerability" and "historical weakness" in this period.[16]

Although they had little success in preventing the capital controls program, the U.S. bankers—like their London banking colleagues after 1957—found temporary relief from their problems by participating in the emerging Eurodollar market. By moving their international dollar business to London, they were able to avoid the restrictions placed on their international activities by the capital controls program and to retain their dominant place in international finance. Indeed, once the bankers had recognized the availability of this option, their opposition to the program diminished considerably.[17] They soon discovered that the Euromarket also enabled them to evade *domestic* New Deal financial regulations such as reserve requirements and interest rate ceilings. During the domestic credit squeezes of 1966 and 1969–70, for example, domestic financial business was "roundtripped" through the Euromarket to avoid interest rate ceilings.

The bankers had considerable domestic political support for their move offshore. Foreign currency loans of foreign branches of U.S. banks were explicitly exempted from the IET from the start and in 1967, following considerable bank pressure, offshore *dollar* loans were spared as well. The bankers also succeeded in ensuring that the

---

Hawley 1987:39, 74–75). Ferguson and Rogers (1986:51–57, 237n21) point to strong New Deal industrialist support for the emphasis Kennedy and Johnson placed on domestic growth and security issues.

15. Hawley 1987:chap. 2.
16. Conybeare 1988:110, 114, 117; De Cecco 1976:394.
17. Hawley 1987:60–61; Conybeare 1988:109–13, 118. The ABA in 1968 noted that the Euromarket had allowed U.S. institutions to take steps to offset the capital controls program, but it argued that such measures had not "fully offset the harm done by controls" (ABA 1968:243).

voluntary lending restraints did not apply to offshore bank activity. Moreover, divisions of the federal government traditionally sympathetic to the bankers' interests, such as the Federal Reserve and the Treasury Department, actively encouraged the banks' offshore activity and imposed few regulations on the establishment of new bank branches abroad. A legacy of the pre-1931 era—the 1919 Edge Act, which had been passed specifically to encourage U.S. foreign lending after World War I—also helped American banks expand their operations abroad.[18] After 1965, the bankers benefited from the relatively greater political strength of U.S. multinational industrial corporations. When it imposed the voluntary capital controls program on these corporations, the Johnson administration overtly encouraged them to use the Euromarket to finance their overseas operations, in order to discourage their opposition to the program.[19]

The influx of U.S. banks and multinational industrial corporations transformed the Eurodollar market from a short-term money market into a full-fledged international capital market serving needs that had previously been met by the New York market. For the U.S. financial community, the London Euromarket provided a setting where they could conduct their international activities unencumbered by an increasingly unfriendly federal government. In a way that the American bankers could not have predicted when they sought an alliance with London bankers in the early postwar years, the traditional openness of the City contributed to the creation of a more liberal international financial order. Indeed, with the creation of the Euromarket, bankers in both countries stumbled on a solution to the problem of how to reconstruct the London–New York financial axis that had been prominent in the 1920s, in the face of domestic political constraints. Treasury Secretary Henry Fowler accurately described the accidental nature of this discovery when he noted that "the Free World has backed inadvertently into a developing international capital market rather than effected a rational and conscious entry."[20]

18. On this regulatory support, see Conybeare 1988:116, 120, Odell 1982:127, Aronson 1977:62, Hawley 1987:52, ABA 1968:245, Spero 1980:47–48, Robinson 1972:182–84, and Kelly 1976:87.

19. Indeed, Versluysen (1981:31) argues that were it not for the Euromarket, the Johnson administration would never have imposed the 1968 mandatory controls on the multinational industrial corporations (to be discussed in Chapter 5).

20. Fowler in Roll 1971:61.

The American government's support for the emerging Eurodollar market did not derive simply from a concern for the interests of the country's banks and corporations. Also significant was its realization that the market provided a way of increasing the attractiveness of dollar holdings to foreigners. Ever since the first dollar crisis in late 1960, the government had attempted to postpone adjustment measures by persuading foreign central banks to finance its external deficit through dollar holdings. As the deficit grew, these requests to refrain from converting dollars into gold became more complex and increasingly related to such issues as U.S. military expenditures abroad.[21] There were, however, two important limitations to this strategy. First, many governments objected that the United States was, in effect, asking them to accept a paper dollar standard. Foreign governments—especially the French—increasingly perceived the U.S. government to be abusing its seigniorage privileges as issuer of the key currency in the system. They also worried about the inflationary effect of the dollar holdings on their domestic money supplies. Second, U.S. pressure on foreign governments did little to influence the increasingly important private international financial operators. As U.S. deficits grew, their confidence in the dollar's convertibility into gold was undermined. Moreover, with no interest paid on sight deposits in the United States at that time, and with the Federal Reserve's Regulation Q limiting interest payments on all other short-term deposits, dollars were a relatively unattractive asset for them to hold.

The United States attempted to enhance the dollar's appeal to foreigners with initiatives such as exempting foreign central banks' dollar holdings from the restrictive Regulation Q, but the emergence of the Eurodollar market proved more helpful in this regard. The absence of interest rate regulation in that market meant that dollar holdings, both official and private, could receive market rates of interest that were higher than those in the United States or in continental Europe. In addition, both the liquidity and the absence of regulation in the Eurodollar market made it an attractive place to hold investments. That the market encouraged dollar holdings was widely understood by American policymakers. Marcello De Cecco notes that as early as 1960, Dillon told Congress that the market provided "quite a good way of convincing foreigners to keep their

21. Coombs 1976:8; Strange 1976:chap. 9.

deposits in dollars, thus stopping the US gold drain."[22] The American Bankers Association also attempted to persuade U.S. officials not to regulate the Eurodollar market by stressing this benefit.[23]

United States' support for the Eurodollar market was thus related not only to the response of American banks and corporations to the capital controls program but also to the country's changing position in the world economy. Faced with growing external deficits, the government sought to avoid undertaking adjustment measures by encouraging foreign governments and private investors to finance these deficits. Central to this strategy was the attractiveness of the Eurodollar market to foreigners. Taking an approach that would prevail through the 1970s and 1980s, Washington policymakers fostered a more liberal international financial system as a way of preserving their policy autonomy in the face of growing external constraints.

Coping with Increasing Openness

The emergence of the Euromarket, combined with the revival of market operators' confidence in international financial transactions after the move to convertibility, brought a degree of financial openness in the 1960s not witnessed in several decades. Except for the support of Britain and the United States for the Euromarket, however, advanced industrial states remained wary of international capital movements for the reason discussed at Bretton Woods: disequilibrating speculative capital movements could restrict their policy autonomy and disrupt both the Bretton Woods system of stable exchange rates and liberal trading relations. To minimize this potential disruption, states utilized the two mechanisms that had proved effective in the late 1940s and 1950s: unilateral capital controls and offsetting financing.

Unilateral Capital Controls

The use of unilateral capital controls by both Britain and the United States as a means to preserve their policy autonomy and exchange rate parity has already been noted. Most continental Euro-

22. De Cecco 1987b:187. See also Strange 1971:209 regarding U.S. support on this basis.
23. ABA 1968:5, 240, 252–53.

pean governments (as well as Japan, as discussed in Chapter 3) also imposed restrictions on both long-term and short-term capital movements throughout the 1960s for the same reasons. In general, these governments employed direct controls, but some (such as West Germany, Austria, and Switzerland) preferred more indirect measures such as special reserve requirements for the foreign accounts of domestic banks and regulations concerning the payment of interest to nonresident deposit accounts.[24]

The specific concerns of these European governments were not always identical to those of Britain and the United States, however. Whereas the latter countries used capital controls to prevent capital *outflows* from exacerbating their balance-of-payments deficits and disrupting *expansionary* monetary and fiscal programs, many continental European governments in the 1960s sought to prevent capital *inflows* from upsetting domestic *anti-inflationary* policies. For these countries, the move to convertibility had coincided with a period of both domestic inflation and large external payments surpluses. In the financially open environment of the 1960s, this combination presented their central banks with a conflict between internal and external goals. A tightening of monetary policy to reduce domestic inflation would have the effect of attracting short-term capital, thus increasing their external payments surplus. But a drop in interest rates, aimed at balancing external accounts, would only encourage domestic inflation.[25]

Faced with this dilemma, European central bankers chose—in accordance with the Bretton Woods framework—to give priority throughout the 1960s to domestic macroeconomic objectives and to balance the external accounts by restricting the disequilibrating inflows of capital that their tight money policies attracted.[26] The commitment of European central bankers to policy autonomy demonstrated that, although the move to convertibility had been preceded

24. For a general survey of West European capital restrictions in the 1960s, see especially Katz 1969 and Mills 1976. Strong normative commitments to financial freedom among central bankers in Austria, West Germany, and Switzerland prevented these countries from employing direct controls. See, for example, the views of Austrian National Bank President Reinhard Kamitz (Thurn 1972:163–64).

25. Gilbert 1963 and Katz 1969. Before restoration of convertibility, conflicts between external and internal goals had been minimized because of limited capital movements and the unique circumstances of inflation-deficit and deflation-surplus combinations. See Bloomfield 1968:31 and Gilbert 1963.

26. Katz 1969:4, 32, 42, 44.

by a struggle between embedded liberals and more orthodox private and central bankers throughout Western Europe, the latter group had in fact come a long way from the orthodoxy of the period before 1931, when the goal of monetary policy had been, at least in theory, the preservation of the external balance of payments. The upheavals of the 1930s had had the effect of prompting central bankers to begin to pursue the goal of preserving domestic macroeconomic stability through monetary planning.[27] This emphasis on monetary planning was supported by many prominent neoliberal thinkers. Having experienced the inflation of the 1920s and the depression of the 1930s, they argued that one of the central conditions for the continued existence of a market economy was the maintenance of monetary stability by independent central banks following strict monetary rules.[28]

Central bankers remained committed to the principle of financial liberalism, however, and emphasized that the use of capital controls would be only temporary. Controls had been made necessary, they argued, by the "imperfect" nature of the international monetary system; the United States was, in effect, exporting inflation to them because of a lack of discipline on its own policies. West European monetary authorities argued that capital restrictions were justified as a second-best solution to preserve policy autonomy until a more appropriate international monetary system could be established that placed more constraints on U.S. behavior.[29]

Financial openness threatened European policy autonomy in other ways that also provided a motivation for the use of capital controls in the 1960s. In some countries, such as France, Italy, and the Scandinavian countries, the revival of international financial markets threatened to undermine the artificially low interest rates and credit-rationing arrangements that had become key tools in their overall economic planning and industrial strategies in the postwar period.[30] External controls were needed to prevent domestic market operators from evading such domestic financial regulatory mechanisms by borrowing and investing abroad. Similarly, the effectiveness of a domestic monetary policy that relied on discount rate changes could be

27. See Katz 1969:45, Bloomfield 1959:24, and Goodhart 1985.
28. Bernholtz 1989, Barry 1989:109, and Hardach 1976:143. This was part of a broader modification by neoliberals of the pure laissez-faire approach of the Manchester liberals of the nineteenth century.
29. See, for example, Kloss 1972:105–6.
30. See, for example, Zysman 1983.

undermined by the growing volume of internationally mobile speculative funds. A tight money policy, for instance, could be completely disrupted by the way in which higher interest rates would attract internationally mobile capital and thus drive down domestic rates. This was, for example, the experience of West Germany between mid-1959 and mid-1960, an experience that led the monetary authorities in Frankfurt seriously to consider reintroducing exchange controls.[31]

With governments in Western Europe, the United States, and Japan all placing restrictions on the free movement of capital, it is somewhat surprising that a Code of Liberalization of Capital Movements was created within the OECD when that organization was established in 1961.[32] In fact, the limited nature of the code only confirmed the general wariness of states with regard to international capital movements in this period and their continuing commitment to the Bretton Woods framework. Article 1 of the code made clear that the obligation to liberalize capital flows must be fulfilled only "to the extent necessary for effective economic cooperation." The effect of this qualifying clause was that, as pointed out by Raymond Bertrand, the former director of financial affairs at the OECD, "the basic commitment of the Code is in effect voluntary."[33] Therefore, it did not conflict with the right to control capital movements included in the IMF Articles of Agreement. In addition, any country, upon signing the code, could register reservations concerning any of its items until a future date.[34] The code also included an escape clause (Article 7) allowing the code's provisions to be temporarily suspended in the case of a "serious economic and financial disturbance" or "[i]f the overall balance of payments of a Member develops adversely at a rate or in circumstances . . . which it considers serious." As Raymond Bertrand notes, "These two causes of derogation together are broad enough to encompass any specific justification."[35] The liberalization campaign was also aimed at direct in-

31. Katz 1969:12.
32. See OECD 1971:41–43 for the code. A precursor of the code was created in 1959 within the Organization for European Economic Cooperation.
33. Bertrand 1981:6.
34. To encourage liberalization, the code was modified in 1964 to include a list of specific types of flows concerning which reservations could be added and dropped whenever a country so wished.
35. Bertrand 1981:8. Derogations are to last no more than eighteen months, but this provision has often been ignored (Bertrand 1981:8–9).

vestment, not financial flows. Whenever financial flows were addressed, the distinction introduced by Keynes and White between desirable flows of productive capital and undesirable flows of disequilibrating speculative capital was maintained and only the former were targeted for liberalization. Short-term capital flows (except commercial credits), for example, were excluded from the code because, as one OECD report noted, "they are the vehicle for hot money and because control of such flows is often considered necessary to buttress domestic monetary policy."[36] Liberalization with respect to medium and long-term capital flows was encouraged only if such flows related directly to trade, regular banking affairs, and personal issues.[37] Although the code also targeted the liberalization of securities transactions across borders, there was no obligation to permit such flows if they were disequilibrating. Even with this qualification, more than half the reservations registered by countries on agreeing to the code concerned the liberalization of securities transactions.[38]

In short, as Hans Lundstrom notes, the code did not represent a new consensus concerning the desirability of a liberal international financial system.[39] Rather, it largely reflected the continuing efforts of financial officials in the OECD to promote financial liberalization in some tangible way. During the 1950s, financial officials in the Organization for European Economic Cooperation (OEEC), the OECD's predecessor, had also called for member governments to liberalize financial transactions, despite the absence of a requirement that they do so.[40] Similarly, throughout the 1950s, financial officials on the EPU's Managing Board had strongly encouraged governments to remove capital controls, even though the right to control capital movements was included in the EPU's constitution.[41] The OECD code thus primarily reflected the neoliberal orientation of many financial officials in international organizations rather than the departure by any government from the Bretton Woods financial framework.

36. OECD 1971:38.
37. OEEC 1961:34–36.
38. Lundstrom 1961:136; OEEC 1961:33.
39. Lundstrom 1961:134, 136. See also Goodman and Pauly 1990:10.
40. See, for example, the recommendations of the OEEC's Committee for Invisible Transactions in 1955 (Rees 1963:216), as well as those of the OEEC Managing Board (OEEC 1954:79; 1957:38).
41. Kaplan and Schleiminger 1989:34, 235; Diebold 1952:106n31.

Offsetting Financing

Another indication of the continuing wariness of most states with regard to international capital movements in the 1960s was their establishment of extensive networks of offsetting financing. Their principal motivation was the same as it had been during the years of the Marshall Plan and the EPU: to preserve the policy autonomy of states experiencing disequilibrating speculative capital outflows and to prevent them from having to resort to trade-inhibiting exchange controls as a means of making their capital controls more effective.[42] Two developments in this period helped to make funds available for offsetting financing.

The first was the provision of IMF funds to offset capital movements. This had required a reversal of the excessively strict 1946 interpretation of Article 6-1 of the IMF Articles of Agreement, which stipulated that IMF resources could not be used to finance deficits caused by capital flows (see Chapter 3). The key figure in obtaining this reversal in 1961 was Per Jacobsson, the IMF managing director since 1956. He favored such financing not only because it would prevent the use of trade restrictions but because it would reduce the need for capital controls and facilitate the creation of a more liberal international financial system.[43] Jacobsson also pushed for an increase in IMF funds to offset capital movements. His success was reflected in the creation of the General Arrangements to Borrow (GAB) facility within the IMF in 1962, as well as in the increase of IMF quotas in 1964–65, both of which were expressly intended to make funds available to offset capital movements.[44]

The IMF's cumbersome decision-making structure made the quick provision of large sums somewhat difficult, however. To meet the need for a front line of defense against speculative capital flows, a more flexible institution was necessary: the Bank for International

42. Horsefield 1969a:505, Jacobsson 1979:363, and Schweitzer 1966:53–54.
43. Gold 1977:25. In fact, the IMF had been financing deficits arising from capital movements as early as 1954 (Horsefield 1969b: 412–14).
44. Chalmers 1972:19, De Vries 1985a:513, Horsefield 1969c:245, and Strange 1976: 97, 107. Strictly speaking, Article 6-1 of the Bretton Woods Agreement had intended IMF financing to be used only to offset productive capital movements, not those of a speculative nature. Jacobsson, however, interpreted the IMF's Articles of Agreement liberally in making IMF funds available during the 1960s. Moreover, when the Articles of Agreement were amended for the first time in 1969, Article 6-1 was rewritten to allow IMF financing of *all* capital movements (Gold 1971:22; 1977:27).

Settlements. After being rescued by the American banking community from abolition in the late 1940s, the institution had played only a minor regional role in Europe in the 1950s as the agent for the EPU. This strictly regional function was made clear when Japan was "prevailed upon" at the signing of the 1952 San Francisco Peace Treaty to renounce its membership in the institution.[45] Moreover, no official U.S. representatives attended the BIS monthly meetings in the late 1940s and the 1950s. Following the 1960 dollar crisis, however, the Europeans invited a representative of the Federal Reserve Board to attend the BIS meetings, reviving the pre-1931 tradition of transatlantic central bank cooperation that had, as Charles Coombs said, "withered away" after the early 1930s.[46] The Bank of Canada and Bank of Japan were also welcomed into the institution as observers in the early 1960s and as full members in 1970.[47] In the informal, clublike atmosphere of the BIS, the representative of the Federal Reserve Board led the effort to organize a series of short-term credits and swaps between the leading central banks of the advanced industrial states to offset speculative movements of capital. By 1965, agreements had been arranged between eleven central banks; their cooperation proved to be important in efforts such as the defense of sterling between 1964 and 1966.[48]

The emergence of offsetting financing networks in the IMF and the BIS in the 1960s was not entirely without controversy. The Canadian Louis Rasminsky was wary of the 1961 reinterpretation of Article 6-1 and correctly predicted that offsetting financing would permit increased freedom for speculative capital movements, which would ultimately threaten the stability of the exchange rate system.[49] The French government, supported by the Dutch and the Belgians, had also unsuccessfully opposed the article's reinterpretation, as well as the creation of the GAB, on the grounds that the financing was a substitute for necessary adjustment. With most financing being used

45. Schloss 1970:34. West Germany was readmitted as a member in April 1950. East European governments remained members of the BIS after the war.

46. Coombs 1976:22. The United States attended BIS meetings as an observer after 1960, having never picked up the stock allocated to it when the institution was created. The U.S. representatives to the BIS in the 1930s had been private bankers.

47. Adams and Hoshii 1972; Plumptre 1977:188, 198. On the continued Eurocentrism of the BIS in the 1960s, see the discussion of Toyoo Gyohten's experience in Volcker and Gyohten 1992:57.

48. Hirsch 1967:246–48, Strange 1976:84–86, Russell 1973, and Coombs 1976:24–41.

49. Horsefield 1969a:504.

to defend the dollar and the pound, it seemed to them that the financing was, as one French IMF delegate put it, simply "a trick of the Anglo-Saxon nations."[50] To prevent this, the French and West Germans insisted that financing be accompanied by "multilateral surveillance" of the receiving country's economic policies by the BIS, the IMF, and the newly created OECD's Working Party Three (whose members included officials from finance ministries and central banks). Even though this surveillance mechanism was established, the largely orthodox advice of these bodies was generally heeded only when a domestic "partner" also favored the policy—such as the Bank of England between 1964 and 1967 and the Bank of Italy in 1964.[51]

These various offsetting financing networks were important not just because they counteracted speculative pressures but also because they encouraged the building of closer international linkages between financial officials in finance ministries, central banks, and international organizations such as the OECD, IMF, the World Bank, and the BIS—mainly officials from the G-10 countries: the United States, Canada, Japan, the Federal Republic of Germany, France, Italy, the United Kingdom, Sweden, the Netherlands, and Belgium.[52] Moreover, such linkages encouraged a rekindling of the financial internationalism that had characterized the period before 1931 but was largely nonexistent during the early postwar years. Paul Volcker notes that in the 1940s and 1950s, the U.S. government "did not have many people with experience and expertise in international finance . . . few [policy officials] knew foreign financial officials at all well."[53] The meetings held in the 1960s, however, created "friendships of an enduring nature" among key financial policymakers in the G-10 countries and led to a common "sense of mission and camaraderie among the regulars."[54] Volcker recalls that in the OECD Working Party Three, for example, financial officials came to see themselves "as carrying a very special and important, if arcane, re-

50. Quoted in Jacobsson 1979:360. See also Strange 1976:99, 107, 109, 111 and Horsefield 1969a:504, 506.

51. Strange 1976:chap. 5; 1971:289–91; Russell 1973:461–62; and Hirsch 1967:254. For a history of multilateral surveillance, see Pauly 1992.

52. This was the membership of the OECD's Working Party Three and the Board of Directors of the BIS; the same countries were the founders of the General Arrangements to Borrow. Switzerland later joined the G-10, but the group's name remained unchanged.

53. Volcker and Gyohten 1992:24.

54. Quotations from Russell 1973:439 and Volcker and Gyohten 1992:30. See also Coombs 1976:26–28 and Strange 1976:971.

sponsibility to protect the stability of the international monetary system. Like high priests, or perhaps stateless princes, they were schooled in arts with which few were familiar, arts that required both a certain amount of secrecy and mutual confidence." Moreover, he notes that they "had an unusual sense of commitment and common purpose, and they built up a reserve of mutual trust that paid off later in an ability to reach quick decisions."[55]

The decade of the 1960s was one of transition in international finance. The widespread use of capital controls and the development of offsetting financing networks demonstrated that states throughout the advanced industrial world continued to be wary of speculative and disequilibrating capital movements and, more generally, of an open international financial order. In supporting the creation and growth of the Euromarket, however, the United States and Britain encouraged the first decisive shift away from the restrictive Bretton Woods financial order.

It is important to note that Britain and the United States promoted a more open financial order through *unilateral* action and that their unilateral liberalization moves proved effective in encouraging the rapid growth of international financial activity because of the unique mobility and fungibility of money. Resourceful market participants were able to take advantage of the small amounts of freedom allowed them by these two states. That unilateral liberalization could promote a more open order had already been demonstrated by British liberalization moves within the EPU in the 1950s. It would also become more apparent in the 1970s and 1980s.

Britain's leadership in supporting financial openness would also continue to characterize the politics of the globalization trend in the 1970s and 1980s. The British enthusiasm grew out of its historic commitment to maintain London's position as an international financial center. In the Euromarket, British financial officials had found a means by which to reconcile their status as a declined hegemonic power with this "lagging" commitment to London's internationalism.

American support for the Euromarket in this period also foreshadowed its growing enthusiasm for financial openness in the subsequent two decades. One reason for this support was that the New York financial community and multinational industrial firms de-

55. Volcker and Gyohten 1992:29, 30.

manded access to the Euromarket as compensation for the freedom they had lost as a result of the U.S. capital controls program. This alliance between industrialists and bankers represented an important change, for in the early postwar years the two groups had been divided over the issue of financial liberalism. Indeed, it signaled the beginning of the unraveling of the domestic coalition that had supported the Bretton Woods restrictive financial order and the emergence of a new one supportive of a more liberal approach. Another reason was that the United States found in the Euromarket an important tool for encouraging foreigners to help finance its external deficits. This tool would become more important in the next two decades as the United States would increasingly attempt to capitalize on its dominant position within the emerging open global financial order to preserve its policy autonomy in the face of growing internal and external constraints.

The creation of offsetting financing networks in the BIS also suggested the importance this body would assume in international financial politics in the next two decades, in contrast to its marginal role in the 1940s and 1950s. It also rekindled a spirit of central bank cooperation that had been sorely lacking since the 1931 crisis. In constructing the financing networks, G-10 central bankers laid the groundwork for their cooperative international lender-of-last-resort activities in the 1970s and 1980s, which are described in Chapter 8.

CHAPTER FIVE

Failed Cooperation in
the Early 1970s

JUST AS KEYNES AND WHITE HAD PREDICTED, THE GROWTH OF PRI-
vate international financial activity in the 1960s encouraged large
speculative capital flows that proved increasingly disruptive of the
Bretton Woods stable exchange rate system by the end of the decade. In the face of these growing speculative pressures, governments
in Western Europe and Japan made clear their preference for controlling capital flows in the interest of preserving the stable exchange
rate system. Like the Bretton Woods architects, they were also concerned about the way these flows might disrupt the international
trading system. As Belgium's Finance Minister Willy De Clerq put it,
"Is it reasonable that such speculative movements should influence
the flow of international trade, and hence the jobs of millions of
persons throughout the world? We are convinced that it is not."[1] In
order to control capital movements effectively, the Europeans and
Japanese focused their efforts on an initiative to introduce cooperative capital controls of the kind discussed at Bretton Woods. Considerable attention has been given to the politics surrounding the breakdown of the Bretton Woods exchange rate system, but this initiative
has largely been ignored, despite the importance attributed to it
by participants in the discussions at the time. Its failure, however,
helped to seal the fate of the Bretton Woods exchange rate system.

The first section of this chapter traces the emergence of the Euro-

1. Quoted in Hewson and Sakakibara 1975:72.

pean and Japanese initiative and describes how it was blocked by strong U.S. opposition. United States officials, departing from their commitment to maintain the restrictive Bretton Woods framework, not only opposed cooperative controls but began to press for the creation of a fully liberal international financial order for the first time since 1945–47. The second section of the chapter explains that this new financial liberalism in U.S. foreign economic policy stemmed from both a desire to use its dominant position in international financial markets to preserve policy autonomy and from a domestic political shift away from the postwar embedded liberal framework of thought.

Cooperative Controls and United States Opposition

Since the late 1940s, the use of offsetting financing and unilateral capital controls had enabled the policy autonomy of states, the Bretton Woods exchange rate system, and an open trading order to be reconciled with the existence of disequilibrating speculative capital flows. In the early 1970s, these mechanisms proved ineffective, however. As growing payments imbalances between the major economic powers eroded confidence in existing currency parities, there was a significant increase in international speculative capital flows that could no longer be offset with the current level of financing. This insufficiency of existing financial arrangements had first become evident in 1967 when an unprecedented level of financing from the IMF and the G-10 central banks failed to prevent the devaluation of the pound. It was confirmed in August 1971, when enormous flows of funds from the United States to Western Europe prompted the United States to suspend gold convertibility and forced the Europeans and Japanese to temporarily float their currencies. Although it might have been possible to increase the funds available for offsetting financing, the major powers had increasingly abandoned cooperative financing strategies by the early 1970s. As early as 1965–66, France had refused to participate in a central bankers' swap agreement with Britain, considering it a cover for Britain's failure to undertake appropriate adjustment measures.[2] By the late 1960s, West European governments had become increasingly unwilling to finance

2. Strange 1976:136.

growing U.S. deficits, whereas the United States hoped speculative flows would force these governments to undertake what it regarded to be appropriate revaluations of their currencies.

The crisis in the early 1970s was also caused by the increasing inability of unilateral capital controls to handle speculative flows. Their impotence was demonstrated most dramatically in 1971–73, when West European governments tightened their capital controls in an effort to prevent capital inflows from forcing a revaluation of their currencies and upsetting domestic economic policy.[3] Despite tighter controls, the European countries found it impossible to control speculative flows unilaterally, and by March 1973 they had been forced by market pressures to float their currencies. Even the Japanese, whose extensive controls proved more effective throughout this period, found speculative pressures too much to bear in early 1973 and adopted a floating exchange rate.[4] The ineffectiveness of capital controls reflected in part the inherent difficulties of controlling capital movements. In the early 1970s, these difficulties were compounded by the growth of international trade and multinational corporations, which had increased the opportunities to evade controls by means of leads and lags in trade payments and in intrafirm transactions.[5] The growth of international telecommunication links had also made enforcement of controls more difficult. At the height of one exchange crisis in the early 1970s, for example, the West Germans found that the only way they could curtail speculative flows was by prohibiting all international telephone calls.[6] Speculative activity now also took place in the offshore Euromarket, which could be effectively controlled only by cooperative regulation.

It had become increasingly apparent to West European and Japanese policymakers that their capital controls would have to be supplemented with one of the two options proposed by Keynes and

3. Even the West Germans, who had maintained a relatively liberal financial regime in the 1960s, moved toward an increasingly tight system of capital controls after 1971 in an effort to defend their currency parity and retain their monetary policy autonomy (Hewson and Sakakibara 1975:chap. 3).

4. Coombs 1976:220–21. Japanese controls had also been ineffective in the August 1971 crisis (Hewson and Sakakibara 1975:63; Strange 1976:338; Volcker and Gyohten 1992:94).

5. The Bundesbank estimated that two-thirds of West Germany's enormous capital inflow in the February 1973 currency crisis was caused by leads and lags in payments within multinational corporations (Haberler 1976a:73). See also Hawley 1987:5; Williamson 1977:3, 45–47; Hewson and Sakakibara 1975:39–40.

6. Hamilton 1986:203.

White at Bretton Woods if the stable exchange rate system was to be preserved. Between 1971 and 1973, however, they had demonstrated their unwillingness to consider the option of rigid, comprehensive exchange controls. In early 1973, a technical group of the IMF Committee of Twenty (C-20) said that such "brutal" controls were rejected because they "may involve a degree of administrative restrictions which could damage trade and beneficial capital flows."[7] In a world of growing interdependence, such draconian controls would have had enormous economic and political costs. Attention thus focused on the second option, cooperative controls.

Although the most important proposals in this respect were made after 1971, they derived from two initiatives taken that year. At the meetings held at the Smithsonian Institution in December, the West Europeans succeeded in convincing the United States to retain its controls on capital exports as part of an overall agreement to make effective the new par values agreed to at the meeting. This initiative, promoted by France (which had a particularly strong aversion to floating exchange rates), reflected the idea of Keynes and White that controls would be more effective if they were implemented "at both ends." Indeed, France had also sought to convince the United States to *tighten* its controls, as West Germany had agreed to do under French pressure during the exchange crisis in May 1971, but the United States had been unwilling to go this far.[8] The second cooperative initiative in 1971 was directed against the offshore Euromarket, which had been important in providing a base for the speculative activity of market operators. In June 1971, the G-10 central bankers agreed to limit their placements of funds in the euromarket in order to stem its growth. This decision called for a more limited move than the regulatory action against the offshore Euromarket proposed by officials such as Guido Carli, governor of the Italian central bank (and opposed by the Bank of England), but it was still important in that it was the first attempt to cooperate in curbing the expansion of this liberal financial market.[9]

These two routes to cooperative control—control "at both ends" and action against the Euromarket—became the focus of much dis-

7. IMF 1974:85.
8. Conybeare 1988:262; Hewson and Sakakibara 1975:43.
9. For Carli's ideas, see Ikle 1972:109, 119. On the Bank of England's opposition, see Strange 1976:193, Tsoukalis 1977:163, and BP, Box 34, "Eurodollar Problem—a Possible Action Program," May 21, 1971, p. 6.

cussion during the negotiations over the future structure of the international monetary system that began in 1972. The communiqué of the Smithsonian agreement had established the basis for these discussions: "Attention should be directed to . . . measures dealing with movements of liquid capital."[10] The importance of this issue was confirmed in early 1972, when the IMF staff, in the "sketch" it provided as the basis for the discussions, asserted that disequilibrating capital movements were "the main factor making it virtually impossible for officials of large industrial members to maintain par values for their currencies."[11] Margaret De Vries notes that "some of the Fund staff had been convinced for several years that disruptive capital movements were the single most important cause of the collapse of the Bretton Woods system and had been studying ways of controlling such capital movements in the reformed system."[12]

West European officials, particularly the French, argued the case for cooperative controls in preliminary discussions in early 1972. Indeed, the French attitude had been made public in March when Minister of Finance Valéry Giscard d'Estaing implored the United States to reverse its "indifference" to short-term capital outflows originating within its borders.[13] In these early discussions, the Europeans raised the issue of whether the powers of the Fund "should be extended in order to achieve improved coordination" in the area of capital controls. They also wondered whether Euromarket activity "should be subjected to some form of coordinated control" in order "to limit the extent to which disturbing short-term flows could be financed through these markets."[14] To prepare for future cooperative control initiatives, they insisted that all countries devise "a set of relatively simple and flexible instruments that could be activated promptly to obstruct at least the more important channels for disequilibrating short-term flows."[15]

Opposition by the U.S. representatives to any type of cooperative controls, however, prevented the issuance of a more firm recommendation. Indeed, the U.S. representatives hoped to discourage other countries from controlling capital movements altogether. According

10. Quoted in Strange 1976:344.
11. De Vries 1985a:125.
12. De Vries 1985a:192.
13. De Vries 1985a:18, 136–37; Brenner 1976:59.
14. Quotes from IMF "sketch" of different views in De Vries 1985c:50.
15. De Vries 1985c:50.

to U.S. representatives, a more fully liberal international financial order would permit international capital movements to encourage "the growth of international trade" and increase "the economic well-being of developed and developing countries."[16] They also challenged the view that disequilibrating capital movements were necessarily undesirable, asserting that such movements prompted countries to take appropriate adjustment measures. The U.S. disagreement with other countries on this question was reflected in the report submitted by the IMF executive directors to the Board of Governors in August 1972. They noted that such movements were harmful in that they interfered with policy autonomy, but also helpful in that they promoted appropriate policy change.[17]

Similar disagreements arose during the negotiations of the C-20 and of its important Committee of Deputies, which held its first meeting in November 1972. The issue of disequilibrating capital flows was one of the five topics on the agenda. The West European and Japanese representatives stressed the need to control such flows. The United States, however, continued to oppose controls, a position that was elaborated publicly for the first time by President Richard Nixon and Treasury Secretary George Shultz in late 1972. The position of the U.S. government, as stated in the *Economic Report of the President* to Congress in early 1973, was that "controls on capital transactions for balance-of-payments purposes should not be encouraged and certainly not be required in lieu of other measures of adjustment, nor should they become the means of maintaining an undervalued or overvalued exchange rate."[18] Moreover, the United States argued—explicitly challenging the Bretton Woods principle— that freedom of capital movements and freedom of trade in goods and services should be treated as equally important aspects of a liberal international economy. According to the president's 1973 report, the U.S. position was that

> restrictions have a distorting influence whether they are focused on trade in commodities, in services, or in assets (the capital account), and that this parallelism should be recognized in the rules governing the reformed international monetary system. In contrast, the provisions of the earlier [Bret-

16. Quotes from IMF "sketch" in De Vries 1985c:47. See also discussion on p. 48 there, and De Vries 1985a:137, 167.
17. De Vries 1985c:48–49.
18. U.S. Government 1973:128. See also the Shultz speech in IMF 1972:41.

ton Woods] system made a sharp distinction between controls on trade and other current transactions and controls on capital transactions.[19]

The breakdown of the stable exchange rate system in March 1973 only strengthened the case for cooperative capital controls in many people's minds.[20] The Japanese, who previously had favored only preserving the right of countries to control capital movements (they were confident of their ability to act unilaterally), now supported cooperative initiatives.[21] Similarly, IMF Managing Director Pierre-Paul Schweitzer exhorted countries—and the United States in particular—to cooperate in controlling capital movements as a way of defending the fixed exchange rate system. One IMF memo suggested that U.S. cooperation would be not only directly helpful but "psychologically useful."[22] Even some influential American policymakers (such as Paul Volcker), although they rejected Schweitzer's initiative, now conceded that it might be necessary for the United States at least to accept the right of countries to control capital movements.[23] Indeed, Shultz intimated in early March that he might be willing to help stem capital outflows from the United States if Europe would be more conciliatory in the ongoing GATT talks.[24]

In this atmosphere, the C-20's Committee of Deputies decided to create a Technical Group on Disequilibrating Capital Flows to study the problem more fully. The group met three times in April and May 1973 but remained deadlocked. There was widespread support among the Europeans and Japanese for cooperative measures involving countries sending and receiving capital flows as well as those serving as "throughflow" areas.[25] Some even favored amending the IMF's Articles of Agreement to give that body the power to force

19. U.S. Government 1973:128. Thomas Willett (1977:9), an influential U.S. official during this period, also argued that economic theorists in the Bretton Woods period had "exaggerated the distinction between the benefits of free trade and those of free capital flows."

20. De Vries 1985b:930–31.

21. De Vries 1985a:192–93. On Japan's new position, see also BP, Box 65, "IMF: C-20 Meeting, July 30–31, 1973," "Report on Japan's International Monetary and Trade Strategy," p. 2. Monroe (1973:5) notes earlier Japanese confidence in their controls.

22. BP, Box 55, "G-10 Meeting with EC, Paris, March 9–10, 1973," IMF memo dated March 2, 1973, p. 2. The memo proposed controls on Euromarket activity as well as on U.S. capital outflows. See also De Vries 1985a:77.

23. De Vries 1985a:193.

24. Brenner 1976:52.

25. IMF 1974:85.

members to adopt capital controls irrespective of whether they were drawing from the fund.[26] There were also proposals to introduce reserve requirements for Euromarket activity as well as to extend the 1971 G-10 agreement on central bank placements in the Euromarket so that it applied to all IMF members.[27]

The United States still strongly opposed cooperative initiatives, however. Moreover, it continued to press for a more liberal international financial order, again arguing that freedom of trade and freedom of capital movements should be treated as equally important aspects of a liberal international economy. It also continued to challenge the notion that disequilibrating capital movements were necessarily negative, noting that such flows often encouraged necessary adjustments in domestic economic policies. Indeed, the U.S. delegates argued that the term "disequilibrating" was misleading. They suggested that if such flows were in response to changes in relative inflation rates, they should be seen as restoring a basic "market equilibrium" (as opposed to an equilibrium of current account flows, which had been the focus of the early postwar economic thinking). The Technical Group explained that "there is no simple and straightforward definition of 'disequilibrating' capital flows. . . . Particular capital flows cannot be defined as disequilibrating simply because they increase a payments imbalance, since they may encourage a needed adjustment."[28]

When the Committee of Deputies resumed its discussion, Western Europe and Japan still strongly supported cooperative controls. In an internal Federal Reserve Board briefing paper prepared at the committee's September 1973 meeting, it was noted that a number of countries continued "to insist that the IMF should have authority to require countries to apply capital controls and that in some cases countries should be called up for IMF examination if they fail to impose controls."[29] A second internal memo pointed out that "the

26. Edwards 1985:455.

27. IMF 1974:89; Williamson 1977:156–58. The West Germans, the Dutch, and the Italians were especially keen on establishing reserve requirements for Euromarket activity; Britain, France, and Switzerland were less keen "because of the consequent shifting of business to tax havens" (BP, Box 55, Memo from J. Dewey Daane, p. 4; "Eurocurrency Problems and Policies," March 6, 1973). Developing countries were also wary of the initiative to extend the G-10 agreement on central bank placements in the Euromarket.

28. IMF 1974:78–79. See especially the discussion of Thomas Willett (1977:4).

29. BP, Box 65, "IMF: C-20 Meeting, September 23, 1973," "Summary of September Deputies Meeting, September 17, 1973."

United States is isolated in its opposition to controls. . . . We have acknowledged that volatile capital flows are a problem. Unwillingness to cooperate in limiting them makes us appear irresponsible."[30]

Despite its isolation, the United States continued to oppose cooperative controls and thereby effectively killed the initiative. Cooperative action could not succeed without U.S. support, given the central role of the New York financial markets, the dollar, and U.S. banks in the emerging international financial order. British Chancellor of the Exchequer Denis Healey concluded following his participation in the reform discussions that "no change could be made in structure of world finance without the consent of the United States."[31] The U.S. victory first became apparent with the publication of the report of the Committee of Deputies in June 1974. The committee noted that "cooperation in dealing with disequilibrating capital flows" would be one of the aspects of the new monetary system but proposed no overt obligations on members to control capital movements.[32] Rather than elaborating specific obligations, the committee simply listed a set of possible cooperative measures that included, in addition to controls, "arrangements to finance and offset [such flows], . . . harmonization of monetary policies, . . . prompt adjustment of inappropriate par values, use of wider margins, and the adoption of floating rates in particular situations."[33] The United States also continued to press for limitations on the right of other countries to control capital flows. It insisted, for example, on the inclusion of the following provisions:

> Countries will not use controls over capital transactions for the purpose of maintaining inappropriate exchange rates or, more generally, of avoiding appropriate adjustment action. Insofar as countries use capital controls, they should avoid an excessive degree of administrative restriction which could damage trade and beneficial capital flows and should not retain controls longer than needed.[34]

30. BP, Box 65, "IMF: C-20 Meeting, September 23, 1973," memo dated September 28, 1973, p. 7. See also De Vries 1985a:215.
31. Healey 1989:416.
32. De Vries 1985c:167. See also the discussion in Gold 1977:41–42. The United States had sought to confirm this point by the inclusion of a clause that read: "No country shall be directed or required to use controls." It was not accepted, however (BP, Box 65, "IMF: C-20 Meeting September 23, 1973," "Comments by U.S. Deputies on Draft Outline," p. 4).
33. De Vries 1985c:170.
34. De Vries 1985c:170; Dam 1982:248.

In the discussions in June 1974 concerning the issuance of the "Guideline" for the proper conduct of policy under the new floating exchange rate system, the United States also insisted that the IMF be given the authority to discourage countries from using capital controls to manipulate their balance of payments.[35] This proposal was, of course, the exact opposite of what the Europeans and the Japanese were pressing for. After considerable debate, a compromise (proposed by Otmar Emminger of the Bundesbank) was reached, whereby the IMF would be permitted to advocate both the imposition of controls and their liberalization. With regard to liberalization, however, the Europeans insisted that the IMF "bear in mind the distinction between capital controls applied for temporary balance of payments reasons and those applied for other economic and social reasons."[36]

By the time the results of the talks on the reform of the international monetary system were summarized in the 1976 second amendment to the IMF's Articles of Agreement, the success of the United States was clearly evident. The cooperative control obligations under Article 8-2b were not strengthened.[37] An important change was also made to the newly amended Article 4-1, which reflected the American effort to introduce a set of more liberal rules. As amended, the article stated that "the essential purpose of the international monetary system is to provide a framework that facilitates the exchange of goods, services, *and capital* among countries."[38] In suggesting support for a liberal international financial system, this clause seemed to raise the same difficulties that the promotion of

35. The United States had begun to press for this change in August 1973 talks. At that time, it had proposed a new clause: "Countries adopting or increasing trade or capital controls will become subject to consultation and examination." The U.S. deputy had justified this clause, saying that "it would not be appropriate to allow countries to avoid the examination process by suppressing an imbalance through a prolonged use of controls" (BP, Box 65, "IMF: C-20 Meeting, September 23, 1973," "Comments by U.S. Deputies on Draft Outline," p. 5).

36. De Vries 1985c:491; 1985a:215. This compromise was confirmed by an Executive Board decision in 1977 establishing the principles for enforcing the surveillance function set forth in the new Article 4, which permitted the fund to ask countries to liberalize capital restrictions being used for balance-of-payments reasons (Edwards 1985:456). Even so, the European countries and the United States continued to disagree over whether "fundamental" balance-of-payments equilibrium should refer to capital movements as well as to current account transactions (Dam 1982:264).

37. Gold 1982:438.

38. The text of the newly amended Article 4-1 can be found in De Vries 1985c:381–82 (emphasis added).

"productive" capital flows had during the Bretton Woods discussions. As the British had argued at Bretton Woods, such a clause might imply an obligation that was incompatible with the right to control capital movements included in Article 6-3. The primary drafter of the new wording, the fund's Joseph Gold, argued that no such conflict existed and that the right to control capital movements remained intact, but others questioned his interpretation.[39]

A New Financial Liberalism in the United States

The stance of the United States in the reform talks reflected a new liberal approach in American foreign economic policy with regard to international capital movements. The United States had not only opposed the cooperative controls proposals but, for the first time since 1945–47, had begun to press for a fully liberal international financial order. The new approach was also evident at the height of the currency crisis in February 1973, when the United States announced that in December 1974 it would abolish its own capital controls program, in place since the mid-1960s. This was a reversal of its commitment to maintain controls made at the Smithsonian meetings in late 1971.[40] In fact, the abolition took place even earlier, in January 1974.

Further evidence was the U.S. veto, in the wake of the 1973 oil price rise, of two proposals that would encourage the recycling of OPEC petrodollars through IMF channels on the grounds that such recycling should take place via international financial markets. The first such proposal had been put forward in January 1974 by the new IMF managing director, Johannes Witteveen, who had argued that public recycling of petrodollars would ensure that the process took place equitably and prudently. Although the idea was strongly supported by West European governments, the United States refused to give it serious consideration, and only a small facility within the IMF was created in June 1974. The U.S. opposition stemmed partly from its concern that a large facility would be seen as sanctioning the oil price rise that it opposed, but also from its goal of chang-

39. See Gold 1986:539–42 and Edwards 1985:483, 486.
40. Shultz had initially planned to abolish the controls at the time of the February announcement, but Paul Volcker persuaded him to defer the move to avoid causing further instability in foreign exchange markets (Volcker and Gyohten 1992:107, 110–11).

ing the international financial system from a controlled public system to a more market-based, liberal one. Indeed, the United States insisted that borrowing from the so-called Witteveen Fund should not be allowed if countries introduced capital controls or strengthened their existing controls.[41] A second proposal by Witteveen in 1975, to introduce a facility specifically for the developed world, was strongly supported by the West Europeans, Saudis, and Japanese, but also met strong opposition by the United States. Denis Healey remarked that "the Americans were bitterly opposed [to the proposal], because it would have meant interfering with the freedom of the financial markets."[42]

U.S. "Structural" Power in the Emerging International Financial Order

There were two sources of the new U.S. financial liberalism in the early 1970s. To begin with, administration officials realized that a more open, liberal international financial order would help preserve U.S. policy autonomy in the face of growing external and internal deficits.[43] In the short run, they perceived speculative capital movements as an important central tool in the U.S. strategy of encouraging foreigners to absorb the adjustment burden required to correct the country's large current account deficits. Market pressures would achieve what direct negotiations could not: both a revaluation of the currencies of Western Europe and Japan and an expansion of their economies. By deliberately neglecting its external deficit and "talking down" the dollar before and after 1971, the United States encouraged private financial operators to speculate against the dollar and in favor of other currencies. Foreign governments were then faced with two options. They could preserve their competitiveness vis-à-vis the enormous U.S. market by preventing the dollar's devaluation through dollar purchases that, in the end, would likely bring

41. De Vries 1985a:314–16, 336.

42. Healey 1989:423. See also De Vries 1985a:334 and Spiro 1989:471. The U.S. veto of Witteveen's proposals blunted opposition abroad to the emerging international capital markets, as states that sought to finance their sudden oil-related current account deficits were forced to borrow in those markets rather than from the IMF (Strange 1986:43–45). The French government, for example, once the most belligerent foe of international capital markets, became one of the largest borrowers in those markets (Cohen 1981:49).

43. This focus on the U.S. goal of policy autonomy accords with Gowa's (1983) analysis of U.S. policy during this period.

about an expansion in the domestic money supply as the dollar holdings proved difficult to sterilize. Alternatively, they could accept a revaluation of their currency, which also was likely to be followed by a domestic expansion as domestic exporters, hurt by their loss of competitiveness, would clamor for expansionary macroeconomic policies. The use of this "dollar weapon" by the United States was extremely successful. By 1973, the U.S. current account deficit had been largely eliminated, not as a result of changes in U.S. economic policy but rather by transferring to foreigners the bulk of the adjustment burden through a combination of these mechanisms. As U.S. policymakers were well aware, the continued openness of international capital markets was central to this strategy's success. Cooperative controls (or offsetting financing to defend currencies from speculative market pressures) would have been directly counterproductive to their strategy of, as John Odell put it, using "international markets to force a major adjustment in the system."[44]

A more liberal international financial system was also important because it would preserve U.S. policy autonomy in the long run. Although the West Europeans and Japanese were committed to using the international reform negotiations to create a more "symmetrical" international financial system, it was clear that a non-negotiated, market-oriented system would preserve America's dominant position in international finance. The dollar's position as a world currency, for example, would be preserved and reinforced in an open financial system because U.S. financial markets and the Eurodollar market would still be the most attractive international markets for private and public investors. No such markets existed to make the yen or the deutsche mark as attractive a reserve currency to hold because the Japanese and German financial markets were underdeveloped and overregulated.[45] The unique depth and liquidity

44. Odell 1982:194. See especially Odell 1982:191–99; Conybeare 1988:248–49; Dam and Shultz 1977:15. See also Calleo 1982, Parboni 1986, and Hudson 1977:chap. 8. As one U.S. official admitted in a briefing paper: "Many are suspicious that our position [on capital movements] and the planned removal of current controls is intended to force adjustment action which will improve our trade account" (BP, Box 65, "IMF: C-20 Meeting, September 23, 1973," memo dated September 28, 1973, p. 7).

45. See especially Hewson and Sakakibara 1975:9, 27, 73–75. During the C-20 discussions, the United States made it clear that one reason for its opposition to capital controls was a desire not to interfere with nonresident holdings of the dollar (IMF 1974:85). See Tavlas 1991 for the importance of well-developed, liberal domestic financial markets in facilitating the international use of a currency. Walter (1991:187) notes the increased international use of the dollar in the 1970s.

of U.S. financial markets also ensured that private investors, if given the freedom to invest globally, would continue to underwrite U.S. deficits through their holdings of attractive U.S. assets. In an influential internal U.S. government report of July 1974, for example, it was pointed out that the United States would benefit if OPEC funds could be recycled via the private markets because "the size and depth of the U.S. financial market" ensured that it would "receive the largest share of Arab investment, even if no special incentives are offered."[46] Arab funds would help to finance both external deficits and growing domestic budget deficits. The proposal to recycle funds through the IMF was opposed because, as David Spiro observed, that institution would be "in direct competition with the U.S. Treasury for Saudi funds."[47] In this way, OPEC investors would, and in fact did, join those of Western Europe and Japan in underwriting U.S. policy autonomy.[48]

The support of U.S. officials for a liberal international financial system thus reflected in part their attempt to develop a kind of market-based or "structural" power, to use Susan Strange's term, in global finance that would replace their declining influence in the publicly managed Bretton Woods order. In a deregulated system, the relative size of the U.S. economy, the continuing prominence of the dollar and U.S. financial institutions, and the attractiveness of U.S. financial markets all gave the United States indirect power via market pressure to, as Strange put it, "change the range of choices open to others."[49] Drawing on this structural power, the United States aimed to preserve its policy autonomy by encouraging foreign governments and private investors to finance and adjust to growing U.S. deficits. This strategy had roots in the administration's support for the Eurodollar market in the 1960s and represented a marked shift from the more benevolent hegemony of the early postwar years.

46. Quoted in Spiro 1989:402. Spiro notes that despite this confidence in a market-oriented result, the United States did in fact offer "special incentives" to encourage OPEC investment in U.S. financial instruments.

47. Spiro 1989:444. On worries about the need for foreign funds to help finance growing budget deficits, see Spiro 1989:350–54, 359, 375–76.

48. By the late 1970s, 83 percent of Saudi assets were dollar-denominated (Spiro 1989:464). See Mattione 1985 for additional statistics on OPEC's international investments.

49. Strange 1988:31. For a similar view, see Padoan 1986:56, Walter 1991, Spiro 1989:448, and Henning 1987:3.

The change was caused primarily by threats to U.S. policy autonomy that had not arisen in the early postwar period.

The Neoliberal Domestic Shift

The new financial liberalism of the United States in this period also reflected a domestic political shift. During the Nixon and Ford administrations, the making of international financial policy was largely influenced by advocates of neoliberal thought. Gottfried Haberler, who was an adviser to President Nixon on international financial issues, was a leading member of the Austrian neoliberal school. George Shultz, Treasury secretary after mid-1972, also gave prominence to the neoliberal position by virtue of his close affiliation with the University of Chicago and Milton Friedman. Friedman is said to have drafted Shultz's important 1972 IMF speech, in which the U.S. position on international monetary reform was first outlined.[50] Succeeding Shultz as Treasury secretary was William Simon who, according to Denis Healey, "was far to the right of Genghis Kahn and was totally devoted to the freedom of financial markets."[51] Another important supporter of neoliberal ideas was Thomas Willett, who served as senior staff economist to the Council of Economic Advisers in the Nixon administration and subsequently was director of international monetary research at the Treasury Department. Also important was Paul Volcker, whose views had been influenced by his education at Princeton under the "Austrians" Frederick Lutz and Oscar Morgenstern.[52]

Drawing on Hayek, Ropke, and other European neoliberals, these officials rejected the embedded liberal approach to capital movements that had inspired the restrictive Bretton Woods financial order.[53] A liberal international financial order, they argued, would

50. Dam 1982:224. See also Odell 1982:306, 310, De Vries 1985a:134, Volcker and Gyohten 1992:118, and Brenner 1976:52.

51. Healey 1989:419. See also Volcker and Gyohten 1992:140–41.

52. Neikirk 1989:78–80, 84–86. Lutz had been an early member of the Mont Pelerin Society and served as its president from 1964 to 1967.

53. For the views of these officials on capital movements, see, for example, Haberler 1976a, Willett 1977, Odell 1982:310, and Gowa 1983:81–86. Indeed, many neoliberals argued that the use of capital controls was antithetical to the liberal principles that they said were the basis of the Bretton Woods financial order (Gowa 1983:82, 86; Volcker and Gyohten 1992:32). Nixon, too, was apparently opposed to capital controls on ideological

promote a more efficient allocation of capital not only between countries but also within them by stimulating domestic financial competition. Like the U.S. bankers at Bretton Woods, the American neoliberals strongly opposed capital controls partly on the grounds that they represented a use of coercive "police power" by the state that was incompatible with individual liberty and a "free" form of government.[54] They were also highly skeptical of the Bretton Woods assumption that capital controls could be made effective without disrupting trade flows.[55] Moreover, American neoliberals took issue with the two reasons given at Bretton Woods for justifying capital controls. Unlike Keynes and White, they were not committed to the policy autonomy of the interventionist welfare state but instead applauded international financial markets because they would discipline government policy and prompt states to adopt more "sound" fiscal and monetary programs. They also dismissed the postwar concern that speculative capital flows would disrupt stable exchange rates by arguing strongly in favor of a floating exchange rate system. Such a system, they argued, would reconcile the desire of governments for policy autonomy (which they saw as partly a necessary evil and partly as important for pursuing an effective domestic monetary policy) with the absence of international economic controls. Whereas the West Europeans and Japanese were pressing for tighter capital controls in order to preserve policy autonomy and a stable system of exchange rates, the American neoliberals wanted to sacrifice stable exchange rates in order to preserve policy autonomy and a liberal international financial system.[56]

The advocacy of a floating exchange rate system was highly controversial, even within neoliberal circles.[57] Many feared that floating exchange rates would cause an increase in the kind of destabilizing speculative capital movements that existed in the 1930s. Friedman and others, however, argued that influential scholars of the period

grounds (Odell 1982:187). On the importance of European neoliberal thought to the revival of American conservatism, see Nash 1976:chap. 1.

54. Quoted terms are those of Fritz Machlup (1968:108), another American neoliberal prominent at the time.

55. Willett 1977:9.

56. This argument was first advanced in Friedman's (1953) article. Haberler (1945, 1954) had also been an early advocate of floating exchange rates on these grounds. Note, however, Volcker's more lukewarm support of floating rates (Brenner 1976:55).

57. Friedman notes that the question of fixed versus floating exchange rates had consistently divided the Mont Pelerin Society meetings (Nash 1976:356n169). See also Stigler 1988:145.

such as Ragnar Nurkse had misunderstood the 1930s experience.[58] In their opinion, the speculative capital movements of the 1930s had been logical responses to changes in the underlying financial and economic conditions in each country and they had exerted pressure on exchange rates accordingly. Therefore, as Friedman put it, "there is at least as much reason to call them 'stabilizing' as to call them 'destabilizing'." The instability of floating rates in the 1930s, in other words, had not been the fault of speculative movements but rather reflected the extreme instability of underlying economic and financial conditions.[59] This focus on the root cause of exchange rate instability directly paralleled that of orthodox financial thought after World War II. Indeed, Willett drew specifically on such thought to support his case that "the only way genuinely to enhance the stability of exchange rates is to reduce the instability of underlying economic and financial conditions."[60]

The argument that speculation under floating exchange rates would not be destabilizing was widely criticized in central banking circles. Many central bankers, closer to the realities of foreign exchange trading, argued that the small number of important banks and multinational corporations that dominated the markets were frequently prone to irrational, bandwagon behavior unrelated to changes in fundamental economic conditions. Friedman's followers predicted that floating exchange rates would smoothly adjust to changing underlying conditions, but most central bankers feared that such rates would prove volatile, disrupt trade patterns, and lead to widespread resource misallocation. On the whole, they favored stricter controls on speculative capital movements in the interest of preserving a stable exchange rate system and liberal trading order, for they viewed these as more important aspects of a liberal international economic order than a liberal financial system. Hans Kloss, the general manager of the Austrian National Bank counseled that "we should have the courage to say that the idea of liberalized capital movements cannot be upheld in all respects and at all times. Rather if monetary and economic damage is to be avoided, it is an ideal which can only be applied with extreme caution."[61]

58. Nurkse (1944). For criticisms of these scholars' views, see Friedman 1953:177, Willett 1977:6–9, Dam 1982:61–63, and Haberler 1976b.
59. Friedman 1953:177.
60. Willett 1977:35, 9.
61. Kloss 1972:107. See also the views of Guido Carli (1972:141–43). The IMF staff in 1972 also disagreed with Friedman's predictions (De Vries 1985a:16).

Many in the Federal Reserve System also supported this view.[62] The Federal Reserve had, in fact, been concerned since the late 1960s not only that international capital movements would disrupt the exchange rate system but also that speculative flows of funds would undermine its autonomy in formulating and implementing monetary policy. In 1969–70, when inflows of short-term speculative funds from the Euromarket disrupted its efforts to restrain domestic credit, the Federal Reserve restricted the Eurodollar borrowing of U.S. banks in order to ward off such inflows.[63] When the flow of capital suddenly reversed in the 1970–71 crisis, the Federal Reserve again attempted to persuade banks to reduce their capital outflows in order to provide "scope for greater monetary easing in this country."[64] These concerns, combined with the commitment of the Federal Reserve System to stable exchange rates, prompted many within it to support those calling for cooperative controls.[65] In 1972, a study was even commissioned within the Federal Reserve to study the technical possibilities of introducing an extensive system of controls on capital movements in and out of the United States.[66] The Federal Reserve System was thus the most sympathetic body in the federal bureaucracy to the West European and Japanese proposals. It was alone, however, and its influence on U.S. international monetary policy in this period was minimal.[67]

62. Coombs 1976:xiii–xiv, Conybeare 1988:253, and Gowa 1983:152.
63. In June 1969, U.S. banks were discreetly asked to stop this activity, and in August 1969 a 10 percent reserve requirement was placed on domestic borrowing from U.S. banks in the Euromarket.
64. BP, Box 33, Federal Reserve subject file, "Eurodollars: February–October, 1970," October 17, 1970.
65. Charles Coombs, in the Federal Reserve Bank of New York, called for restrictions on the placing of official reserves in the Euromarket. He advocated that the United States tighten its capital controls in the early 1970s and press the Europeans to tighten their own controls on Euromarket borrowing. In early March 1973, Alfred Hayes, president of the Federal Reserve Bank of New York, also tried to persuade Arthur Burns to tighten U.S. capital controls as well as to nearly double the existing swap network, from $11.7 billion to $20.0 billion, to defend existing parities (BP, Box 34, memo dated January 18, 1971; Box 34, "Eurodollar Problem—a Possible Action Program," May 21, 1971; Box 55, "Suggested Policy Package," March 6, 1973).
66. This may have been done in order to comply with the demands of other countries at this time that studies be made of the possibility of implementing such controls. See the paper entitled, "Can Controls Be Successfully Used to Prevent Speculative Capital Movements in the U.S. Balance of Payments?" marked "Strictly Confidential," in BP, Box 74, "International Monetary Reform—Issues Papers, August 1972." It was noted in the paper that "it would be technically feasible to design such a system of exchange controls" (p. 3).
67. Coombs 1976:204–5; Gowa 1983:111–17.

How do we explain the sudden prominence of neoliberal advocates in U.S. foreign economic policy circles in this period? One explanation is that their views on the desirability of a liberal international financial order were perfectly consistent with the more "nationalist" concerns about maintaining U.S. policy autonomy. Thus, a shift in personnel such as that in the Treasury Department, from the "nationalist" Secretary John Connally to the "neoliberal" Secretary George Shultz, led to no change in the administration's position on capital movements. There are, however, other important reasons. At the broadest level, growing inflation and slower growth in the early 1970s had produced increasing disillusionment with Keynesian economic strategies and New Deal regulatory policies.[68] In this more uncertain intellectual climate, neoliberal thinkers such as Milton Friedman vigorously promoted their alternative framework of thought and found a more receptive audience. Think tanks such as the American Enterprise Institute were also important in raising the profile of neoliberal ideas in this period.[69] There was also a broad unraveling of the coalition in U.S. politics that earlier had supported the embedded liberal approach to capital movements. New Deal industrial leaders who had previously been sympathetic to the need for capital controls had become frustrated in the 1960s with the increasing interference of such controls (both U.S. and foreign) on their growing multinational activities. Their frustration grew even stronger after 1968, when President Johnson imposed the first mandatory controls on foreign direct investment. Indeed, the U.S. capital controls program had also accelerated a change in the attitude of U.S. multinationals by encouraging them to move their financial operations offshore, thus acquiring a direct stake in the emerging international liberal financial order.[70] As early as 1966, the CED, the lobbying group of the "New Deal industrialists," began to support neoliberal thinkers and financial interests that had been promoting a more favorable view of financial liberalism throughout the postwar

68. Ferguson and Rogers 1986:68–105; Himmelstein 1990:chap. 5. See also Edsall 1984, 1989; Hawley 1987:107.

69. Indeed, the AEI is said to have "served as a research and recruitment base for the Nixon and Ford administrations." Peschek 1987:168. See also Peschek 1987:27–31, 229. Earlier, the AEI had published Haberler 1954 and Ropke 1952. On the efforts of neoliberal intellectuals to promote their ideas in this period, see Nash 1976:284–89, Parsons 1989:150, and Peschek 1987:229.

70. Hawley 1987:106.

period.[71] During the 1968 election campaign, the business community had also lobbied Nixon to promise to remove capital controls. By the early 1970s, multinational industrialists had joined bankers and many financial officials in strongly supporting the neoliberal message with regard to capital movements, and their voices were heard by many in the Nixon and Ford administrations.[72]

The new liberal approach to capital movements in U.S. foreign economic policy was thus a product of an alliance between neoliberal advocates and those concerned with maintaining the government's policy autonomy in the face of growing external and internal imbalances. Although the roots of this alliance could be seen in the U.S. support for the Euromarket during the 1960s, it was a dramatic departure from the early postwar alliance between cold war strategists and New Deal embedded liberals who were supportive of the restrictive Bretton Woods financial order. Only in the formation of the Trilateral Commission in the early 1970s did there seem to have been an effort to maintain the old alliance. The commission's advocacy of a more cooperative foreign economic policy with respect to West Europe and Japan appealed to the strategists, who hoped to reduce alliance tensions.[73] Many New Dealers were also attracted to the notion of a transfer of activist macroeconomic planning from the national level to the international level and an expansion of the resources and power of the IMF.[74] The commission's proposals in

71. A report by the CED (1966:18–19, 28, 44) stressed the importance of maintaining financial freedom (although note the objections of a few members, pp. 72–73). Its subcommittee studying international monetary issues was now chaired by Norris Johnson of First National City Bank, and the majority of its members were bankers. Its advisers included such neoliberals as Haberler and Machlup. See also Machlup's (1968:108) CED study and CED 1973:26, 53, 55.

72. Volcker and Gyohten 1992:107, Williamson 1977:82–83, and Gowa 1983:62. During the reform talks, it was noted in one internal briefing paper that the tightening of U.S. capital controls would be "politically unacceptable at home" and "disadvantageous to U.S. trade and financial interests" (BP, Box 65, "IMF: C-20 Meeting, September 23, 1973," memo dated September 28, 1973, p. 7). On the strong support of bankers for financial freedom and neoliberalism in this period, see Conybeare 1988:244, Odell 1982:180–81, Calleo 1982:75, Hawley 1987:100, Peschek 1987:27–31, and Aronson 1977:37–50.

73. See Gill 1990:chap. 6.

74. The CED's advisory board in the early 1970s included such prominent Trilateralists as Richard Cooper (for his link to the Trilateral Commission, see Gill 1990:137). Cooper (1971) was much more skeptical than the neoliberals of the benefits of financial integration. He was particularly keen on increasing the IMF's financial resources to offset speculative capital flows, a proposal that the CED (1973:27, 30, 69n3) supported. In December 1974, the Trilateral Commission also supported the creation of a bank to recycle OPEC funds (Gill 1990:175).

these areas found little support in Washington in this period, however. Not only was the old New Deal coalition disintegrating but Henry Kissinger, the most prominent strategist in the bureaucracy at this time, was a foreign policy specialist who was less interested in international economic issues. His limited efforts to challenge the Treasury Department's dominance of U.S. international financial policy between 1971 and 1973 and during the discussions concerning the establishment of the Witteveen facility were largely ineffective.[75]

The failure of the West European and Japanese initiative to move toward a more closed financial order in the early 1970s marked an important turning point in the globalization of financial markets. If cooperative controls had been introduced "at both ends" and imposed on Euromarket activity, the freedom of private financial operators to act at the international level would have been severely constrained. The decision not to implement such controls, however, signaled the beginning of the collapse of the Bretton Woods financial framework, for states abandoned the principle that liberalism in finance should be sacrificed in the interest of preserving a stable exchange rate system. Moreover, the floating exchange rate system, which emerged out of the events of the early 1970s, only stimulated international financial activity.

The failure of the European and Japanese initiative also revealed several key themes about the politics associated with the globalization process. First, the two mechanisms proposed by Keynes and White to make capital controls more effective proved politically difficult to implement. Tight exchange controls were economically and politically unattractive in the increasingly open world economy of the 1970s, whereas cooperative controls could be easily vetoed by a major state—in this case, the United States. These two problems, which had been encountered as early as the late 1940s, also help to explain state behavior in the late 1970s and early 1980s, as will be shown in Chapter 6. Second, the United States had a strong interest

75. Kissinger (1979949–62) often opposed those in the Nixon administration who advocated more aggressive foreign economic policies and he supported Healey's proposals for an increase in IMF resources in early 1975, in opposition to William Simon and Arthur Burns (Healey 1989:426). He also fought for an OECD "safety net" to recycle OPEC funds but was largely unsuccessful (Spiro 1989:427–28). See Dam and Shultz (1977:123) regarding the Treasury Department's domination of international monetary policy during the early 1970s.

in promoting a liberal financial order in this period in part because administration policymakers hoped to take advantage of U.S. dominance in international financial markets to encourage foreign governments and private investors to underwrite U.S. policy autonomy. Although the power of the United States in the publicly managed Bretton Woods monetary order diminished in this period, administration policymakers sought to draw on the "structural" power of the United States in the emerging open market-based global financial order. This motivation for supporting financial liberalism remained important for U.S. officials in the late 1970s and 1980s. Third, U.S. enthusiasm for a liberal financial order also reflected a policy shift from embedded liberal to neoliberal frameworks of thought in international finance during this period. The shift can be explained by the economic troubles of the period; the leadership of neoliberal intellectuals; and the emergence of a coalition of private financial interests, multinational industrialists, and financial officials that supported neoliberal ideas. The neoliberal shift foreshadowed a similar change that would take place throughout the advanced industrial world in the 1970s and 1980s, for essentially the same three reasons.

CHAPTER SIX

Four Turning Points in the Late 1970s and Early 1980s

ONE WIDELY PREDICTED BENEFIT OF THE FLOATING EXCHANGE rate system was that it would grant states a much higher degree of policy autonomy from external market pressures than had existed under the fixed exchange rate system. Floating exchange rates, it was said, would smoothly adjust the external account balance to reflect changes in a country's fundamental economic position. In fact, exchange rates after 1973 tended to move erratically and often with little relation to fundamentals. As central bankers had predicted, the source of the trouble was speculative capital flows which responded not just to economic fundamentals but also to the sometimes volatile and irrational judgments of currency traders and asset holders.[1] Such flows ensured that the system of floating exchange rates, far from insulating the domestic economy from external market pressures, often subjected it to new international constraints. Not only did the same problems of trying to retain domestic financial regulatory structures in an open global financial system remain, but also "vicious" circles of disequilibrium afflicted countries pursuing expansionary policies. A vicious circle began when overzealous global financial traders suddenly lost confidence in a country's economic policy, causing an exaggerated depreciation of its currency. This exchange rate "overshooting" exacerbated domestic inflation, leading to further loss of confidence and a self-reinforcing downward spiral

---

1. On predictions of central bankers, see note 61 in Chapter 5.

that could be stopped only by a tough austerity program designed to restore market confidence. The consequence was that, as Stephen Marris pointed out, "external discipline under the present exchange rate system is tougher than it was under the previous exchange rate system."[2] Economically conservative, low-inflation countries often experienced the opposite effect—a "virtuous" circle—leading Henry Wallich, among others, to conclude that the new floating exchange rate environment had created a world in which "the weak got weaker; the strong got stronger."[3]

The floating exchange rate system thus did little to resolve the continuing difficulties of preserving policy autonomy in an environment of financial openness. Rather, volatile exchange rates encouraged an ever-growing volume of speculative activity which only made problems worse. This set the stage for four important turning points in Western states that determined the future of the emerging open financial system—Britain in 1976, the United States in both 1978–79 and 1979–80, and France in 1983. In each case, policymakers in these countries considered restoring more effective controls on capital movements to preserve their policy autonomy, but such initiatives to restore a more controlled international financial order either were not acted upon or were unsuccessfully carried out. The importance of these attempts is often neglected in histories of the globalization process. Successful implementation of controls in any of these cases, however, would have been a considerable setback to the globalization trend. Three explanations are presented in this chapter for the failure of policymakers to implement more effective controls in this period: the growing interest in neoliberal frameworks of thought, the political difficulties of using either of the two mechanisms proposed at Bretton Woods for more effectively controlling capital movements, and, in the United States, its hegemonic interest in maintaining financial openness.

The End of National Keynesianism in Britain, 1976

Britain had borrowed extensively in international financial markets in 1974–75, but in 1976 British authorities suddenly found that

2. Marris quoted in Katz 1979:231.
3. Wallich quoted in Katz 1979:279. See the excellent discussions of vicious circles throughout Katz 1979.

operators in those markets, particularly those in London, began speculating heavily against the pound (even though Britain's current account situation was improving and inflation was decreasing[4]). As William Keegan and Rupert Pennant-Rea note, the pessimism of market operators in London with regard to the pound stemmed largely from their increasing disillusionment with the Labour government's Keynesian policies and the growing popularity of monetarism: "There was an interplay between the views of these [monetarist] commentators and the financial markets, which seemed to reinforce each other."[5] In a classic vicious circle, the pound's depreciating value reinforced domestic inflationary pressures, which only further undermined confidence in the pound.

Faced with this growing currency crisis, the Labour government initially sought offsetting financing from the IMF and foreign central bankers. Because the pound was subject to what IMF Managing Director Witteveen called "unreasonable exaggeration," a $5.3 billion credit was extended in June by the BIS, Switzerland, and most of the G-10 countries.[6] The crisis continued into the autumn, however, and it became apparent that more money would be required. At this point, the principal creditors changed their tune. In response to Prime Minister James Callaghan's further requests for financing, the United States and West Germany stated that they would extend more money only if Britain agreed to an IMF stabilization package that included strict monetary targets and spending cuts.

This tough stance was a considerable departure from the unconditional, accommodating extension of credit by creditor governments in the 1960s.[7] Some financial experts in the creditor countries argued that this new position was necessary because in the 1970s, international loans could not offset the enormous speculative pressures as readily as they had during the 1960s. Consequently, international support would have to be accompanied by austerity measures if the confidence of the markets was to be restored.[8] The advocacy of tough, conservative measures can also be explained by the increased political prominence in the creditor countries of officials sympathetic

---

4. Healey 1989:427; Cohen 1981:222.
5. Keegan and Pennant-Rea 1979:140. See also Keegan 1984:42, 88; Parsons 1989: chap. 6; and Healey 1989:412–13, 434.
6. Witteveen quoted in Callaghan 1987:419.
7. Kindleberger 1985:16; De Vries 1985a:478.
8. See especially Willett 1977:64–66.

to neoliberal ideas, such as, in the United States, Treasury Department Secretary Simon, his assistant Edwin Yeo, and Federal Reserve Board Chairman Burns. Although strategists, such as Kissinger, and representatives of the AFL-CIO and other New Deal forces advocated accommodating financing, they had little influence on U.S. policy.[9] In West Germany, the neoliberal approach was endorsed by prominent financial officials such as Otmar Emminger and Karl Otto Pohl, as well as by the economically conservative Chancellor Helmut Schmidt.[10]

The prominence of neoliberal thinking in the major creditor countries not only deprived Britain of unconditional financing but also eliminated the possibility of its using cooperative controls to handle speculative capital movements. Important Keynesian economists such as Fred Hirsch in Britain and Nobel Prize winner James Tobin in the United States had suggested such cooperative action in the mid-1970s. Hirsch advocated a "degree of controlled dis-integration in the world economy" and rejected the IMF's interference in domestic economic matters as "out of key with the needs of a loosened economic order that gives greater leeway to national preferences in domestic policies."[11] Tobin argued that the policy autonomy of states needed to be protected from the effects of speculative capital flows. He proposed a cooperative initiative in which all states would impose a transaction tax on spot foreign exchange transactions in order to "throw some sand in the wheels of our excessively efficient international money markets."[12] In the increasingly neoliberal intellectual climate of the 1970s, however, neither proposal found much political support. Tobin later acknowledged that his proposal, once recommended, "fell like a stone in a deep well."[13]

Without financing or cooperative controls, the Labour government faced a difficult choice. Winning back the confidence of global financial traders would require the adoption of the tough austerity program being advocated by the IMF and the foreign financial offi-

9. Fay and Young 1978:5, 7, 9, 15, 29, 30; Callaghan 1987:429, 431, 433, 437; Dell 1991:290n8; Burk and Cairncross 1992:62–63; Healey 1989:420, 430; and De Vries 1985a:469; 1985b:814.

10. De Vries 1985a:469; Fay and Young 1978:36. On Schmidt's economic conservatism, see Allen 1989:278 and Schmidt 1989:160, 162, 267.

11. Hirsch and Doyle 1977:55, 62. See also Hirsch 1978.

12. Tobin 1978:154. See also Tobin 1974:88–92. Keynes proposed a similar tax in 1930 (Flanders 1989:180–81).

13. Tobin 1978:155.

cials. This would signal the end of Britain's postwar commitment to national Keynesianism. Preserving policy autonomy, however, would require insulating the domestic economy from external financial pressures by imposing the kind of comprehensive exchange controls outlined by Keynes and White at Bretton Woods. Such controls would be extremely costly and would effectively shut down London as an international financial center.

Initially, there was considerable support in the Labour party for a strategy to impose exchange controls—a strategy that came to be called the "alternative economic strategy" (AES). At the September Labour party conference, the AES was in fact adopted as party policy, and a resolution was passed that called for an investigation into the "ways in which the buying and selling of sterling and foreign exchange can be taken out of the hands of private firms in the City of London."[14] There was also considerable support for the AES among a group of Cabinet ministers led by Tony Benn.[15] Although Prime Minister Callaghan and Chancellor Healey opposed the AES, they were forced to acknowledge that they would be defeated if an alliance were formed between Benn's supporters and the more moderate opponents of an IMF package, led by Tony Crosland. Indeed, at their November 23 meeting, the Cabinet members tentatively agreed to tell West Germany and the United States that Britain would not accept the IMF terms being discussed in secret negotiations.[16]

At this point, however, the dynamics within the Cabinet changed. Callaghan made it clear that in supporting the IMF package, he was willing to risk a rift in the government similar to that which had brought down the Labour government in 1931. The threat of such a breakdown, as well as friction between the Benn and Crosland camps, brought Crosland and his supporters behind the prime minister in the beginning of December.[17] Ironically, now that Callaghan had mustered enough Cabinet support for the IMF package the IMF toughened its stance, suddenly demanding on December 3 more

14. Labour Party 1976:308.
15. Benn had, for example, become extremely interested in a blueprint for exchange controls that the Treasury was supposed to have "locked away in a cupboard" (Benn 1989:657).
16. Crosland 1982:378, Callaghan 1987:435–37, and Dell 1991:261–62.
17. Crosland 1982:379–82, Fay and Young 1978:33, Callaghan 1987:439, and Benn 1989:649–50. Crosland 1982:379 notes that his decision to back Callaghan was also strongly influenced by Benn's rejection of his efforts to form an alliance on November 24.

spending cuts than had previously been agreed upon. Healey and Callaghan refused to discuss the new package and seemed prepared for the first time to consider the AES. Callaghan reports in his autobiography:

> [Healey] and I sat for some time in my bedroom talking over the various drastic policy changes that would be needed if a loan was not forthcoming. They would have meant a bumpy ride not just for the British people but also for the international community, with serious implications for our relations with the GATT, the European Community and NATO, as well as the United States. On that night anything seemed possible.[18]

The IMF quickly softened its position, however, and within two days presented a package that Callaghan and the Cabinet could accept. The measures were adopted with remarkably little opposition from the British public, and the pound's value soon stabilized, leaving a large part of the IMF loan unused.

The Cabinet's decision to accept the austerity package was a decisive moment in postwar British politics. Joel Krieger observed that it "destroyed the tenuous basis for cohesion within the [Labour] party and signified the end of Keynesian society in Britain. Thatcherism was soon to follow."[19] It was also an important turning point in the broader politics of financial relations between advanced industrial countries. Britain had played a vital role in the 1950s and 1960s in promoting a liberal international financial order, and it would continue to do so in the 1980s. Had Britain chosen to introduce tight exchange controls, the globalization trend would have suffered a serious setback. The following comments, made several years later by William P. Rodgers, who was then U.S. secretary of state, indicate the seriousness with which Britain's actions were viewed at the time: "As I saw it, it was a choice between Britain remaining in the liberal financial system of the West as opposed to a radical change of course, because we were concerned about Tony Benn precipitating a policy decision by Britain to turn its back on the IMF. I think, if that had happened the whole system would have come apart. . . . So we tended to see it in cosmic terms."[20] National Security Adviser Brent Scowcroft also remarked that "I spent more time on this matter

---

18. Callaghan 1987:441.

19. Krieger 1986:57–58. See also Keegan 1984:88.

20. Quoted in Fay and Young 1978:30. See also the comments of Edwin Yeo in Fay and Young 1978:12.

[Britain's financial crisis] during those weeks than anything else. It was considered by us to be the greatest single threat to the Western world."[21]

The Cabinet rejected the AES for two reasons. First, it recognized that tight exchange controls would have enormous costs, given the degree of Britain's economic integration in the world economy. Even supporters of the AES were forced to acknowledge that the economic costs—in terms of economic dislocation and possible foreign retaliation—would likely have been greater than those associated with the IMF package.[22] Moreover, they would have been especially difficult to sustain because of Labour's minority position in Parliament.[23] The international political costs would also have been great, as Callaghan noted in the passage just quoted.[24]

Second, the Cabinet's rejection reflected the government's growing dissatisfaction with embedded liberal frameworks of thought and its increasing acceptance of neoliberal ideas.[25] Chancellor Healey, for example, had become disillusioned with Keynesianism in the mid-1970s and had become a strong supporter of austerity measures prior to the 1976 crisis.[26] The same was true of many officials in the British Treasury and the Bank of England who had been strongly supportive of the position taken by the IMF and the U.S. Treasury Department during the crisis. Indeed, some were accused of having engineered the crisis to force more "sensible" policies on the Labour government.[27] Were it not for these domestic supporters of austerity measures, the international creditors might have been more accommodating in providing financing (as Crosland argued at the time).[28]

This shift toward a neoliberal framework of thought partly reflected a recognition of the growing difficulties of implementing na-

21. Quoted in Fay and Young 1978:30.
22. Healey 1989:431, Benn 1989:632, and Dell 1991:266.
23. Callaghan 1987:442.
24. Such costs probably weighed particularly heavily on Healey and Callaghan in view of their extensive international ties (Healey 1989:414, 419–21; Callaghan 1987:481; and Putnam 1984:73–74).
25. Burk and Cairncross 1992:chap. 5.
26. Healey 1989:378–79.
27. See especially Healey 1989:426–27, 430; 434; Ham 1981:21–22, 34–37; Benn 1989:551, 631; Fay and Young 1978:10, 14, 22, 24; Keegan 1984:88–89; Callaghan 1987:431; Dell 1991:219, 249; and Burk and Cairncross 1992:71–73, 244n51.
28. Crosland 1982:377–78. In fact, Callaghan (1987:431–32, 435) notes in his autobiography that Helmut Schmidt was willing to extend offsetting financing if the domestic political situation reached a breaking point, although Burk and Cairncross (1992: 65–66) question this conclusion.

tional Keynesian ideas in a globally integrated financial system. At one of the critical late November Cabinet meetings, Tony Benn reports that Healey argued: "We had to remember that the money-lenders did determine the value of our currency."[29] As in the United States, there were also other reasons for the ideological shift. The stagflationary environment of the 1970s had undermined confidence in embedded liberal ideas. This economic situation left Keynesians in what William Keegan called a "debilitated state of morale."[30] In this uncertain intellectual climate, neoliberal intellectuals—including Americans such as Milton Friedman—were, by contrast, full of confidence, and actively spread the neoliberal message through British think tanks such as the Institute of Economic Affairs (which had been established under Friedrich Hayek's leadership in the mid-1950s).[31] The neoliberal message found particularly strong support among private bankers and financial officials in the government. The latter group's neoliberal convictions were probably strengthened by their growing links with the high-level officials of foreign central banks, finance ministries, and public international financial institutions. The links had been forged in the 1960s with formation of the offsetting financing networks and were strengthened in forums such as the annual IMF-World Bank meetings. With many in this growing international network of financial officials holding neoliberal financial views, these links were likely an important channel through which these ideas were spread and reinforced. William Keegan reports, for example, that Healey's handling of the 1976 crisis led him to be "much feted in Washington at the [1977] IMF meeting," where he began "preaching to other countries the virtues of putting your financial house in order."[32] The influence of financial officials in the government was also enhanced by the growing power of the global markets themselves. Adrian Ham notes that officials in the British Treasury and the Bank of England could "take advantage of the 'uncontrollable' forces of international finance to obtain objectives which would not be possible with a cool and calm group of ministers in Cabinet."[33]

29. Healey quoted loosely in Benn 1989:659.
30. Keegan 1984:88–89.
31. On Friedman's role in spreading the neoliberal message in Britain, see Parsons 1989:173–75, Keegan 1984:42–44, and Burk and Cairncross 1992:143–45. On the Institute of Economic Affairs, see Hutton 1981:13 and Wood 1981.
32. Keegan 1984:108. Healey (1989:413) describes the growing international network. He also notes that in 1977 he was even approached to head the IMF (Healey 1989:438).
33. Ham 1981:34. See also Keegan and Pennant-Rea 1979:140.

The Volcker Shift: The United States Accepts
External Discipline, 1978–1979

In 1978–79, there was a crisis of confidence in the dollar of similar magnitude to that with regard to the British pound in 1976. The crisis was a result of the Carter administration's failed "locomotive" economic strategy. Carter's advisers favored a cooperative, managerial approach to the handling of the world's economic problems, in contrast to the more aggressive foreign economic policy of the United States in the early 1970s. They hoped to enlist the support of Japan and West Germany for a global reflationary strategy in which the three nations would act as "locomotives" pulling the world out of the 1973–75 recession by simultaneously pursuing expansionary policies. The strategy met considerable resistance from Japan and West Germany, however, and the Carter administration was forced to shift gears. Although the rhetoric retained a commitment to cooperation, the policy became one of pursuing a unilateral expansion.[34] As they had in the 1960s, foreign central banks stepped in to finance the large U.S. current account deficits that accompanied this unilateral expansion. The Japanese and West Europeans supported the dollar for the same reasons they had before: a dollar depreciation would be harmful to domestic exporters, for whom the United States was still the most important foreign market. The OPEC countries were also major defenders of the dollar in this period because both the revenue from oil exports and a large proportion of their assets were denominated in dollars. In mid-1977, the United States tried, as it had in the early 1970s, to reduce its external deficit by "talking down" the dollar in public pronouncements. This "dollar weapon" was particularly effective in prompting Japan to introduce a supplementary expansionist budget in January 1978. Although the West Germans were considerably angered by what they perceived as a U.S. attempt to export its inflation, they too agreed at the 1978 Bonn summit to a modest fiscal expansion.

In late 1978, however, the Carter strategy began to falter. With no sign that the United States was going to reduce its growing external deficit and curb domestic inflation, foreigners began to lose confidence in the dollar. Saudi Arabia began to sell its dollar reserves and warned of an oil price increase if the dollar's depreciation contin-

---

34. See Calleo 1982, Keohane 1979, and Ludlow 1982:69–77 concerning U.S. foreign economic policy in this period.

ued.[35] West European governments signaled their dissatisfaction with U.S. unilateralism by beginning negotiations that led to creation of the European Monetary System (EMS) in March 1979, resulting in the establishment of relatively stable European exchange rates and a new currency, the ecu. West German Chancellor Helmut Schmidt's strong support for the EMS, in particular, reflected his frustration with U.S. economic policy and his "diminishing confidence in American leadership."[36] Most important, there was enormous flight from the dollar in the increasingly powerful global financial markets.

With the dollar entering a free fall, the United States suddenly faced the most severe external constraint on its policy autonomy in the postwar period. The two options that Britain had considered in 1976 now presented themselves to American policymakers. One was to preserve U.S. policy autonomy by imposing external controls, thereby abandoning the strategy pursued in the early 1970s of promoting a more liberal international financial order. In late 1978, there was some discussion in U.S. policymaking circles of using capital controls to stem speculation against the dollar.[37] Indeed, only one year earlier, in response to concerns that the United States could become financially dependent on foreign creditors, Congress had passed the International Emergency Economic Power Act, granting the president the power to freeze the assets of any country that threatened "the national security, economy or foreign policy" of the United States.[38] Some in the Treasury Department at this time also began to consider abandoning efforts to preserve America's global financial preeminence. Indeed, a G-7 working committee was convened to consider mechanisms by which the dollar's global importance could be diminished by encouraging the international use of other currencies such as the deutsche mark and the yen. Toyoo Gyohten, the Japanese representative to the committee, later noted that, "it was amazing that the United States was for the first time officially exploring methods to reduce the dollar's role as a key currency."[39]

The second option, of adopting an austerity program in order to restore international financial confidence, proved more attractive to

35. *Economist*, April 1, 1978, pp. 25–26; Spiro 1989:464–66.
36. Ludlow 1982:69. See also Story 1988.
37. *Business Week*, August 6, 1979, p. 78; Hawley 1984:151.
38. Alerassool 1989. This power was first used in November 1979 to seize Iranian assets in American banks at home and abroad.
39. Volcker and Gyohten 1992:160.

the Carter administration, however. In November 1978, President Carter announced an anti-inflation program that included cutbacks in government spending and an increase in the interest rate. When these measures did not satisfy the financial markets or foreign governments, he became persuaded of the need for more decisive austerity measures to restore confidence in the dollar. In August 1979, to signal this determination, Carter appointed Paul Volcker—a renowned "hard money" man who had been vice-president of the Federal Reserve Bank of New York since 1975—to head the Federal Reserve Board. Vice-President Mondale said that this appointment was made "to reassure the financial markets, to buy back legitimacy and to reassure our major trading partners and our partners in the international financial institutions."[40] Volcker did not disappoint. The British experience in 1976 had convinced him of the need for decisive action to restore foreign confidence.[41] On September 29, 1979, he left for Europe, where he was lectured on the need for stern adjustment measures first by Helmut Schmidt and then by European central bankers and OPEC finance ministers at the IMF meeting in Belgrade. His resolve strengthened, on October 6, 1979, he announced a drastic tightening of monetary policy.[42]

The Volcker stabilization program was a key turning point in American politics. In the 1960s and early 1970s, the United States had found the emerging open international financial order extremely helpful in preserving its policy autonomy because of its "structural" power in that order. In the 1978–79 dollar crisis, however, foreign governments and private investors had suddenly attempted to impose an external discipline on U.S. economic policy. Facing this new external constraint, the United States was forced to choose between its goal of policy autonomy and its commitment to financial openness. Its decision to submit to the discipline of international financial pressures reflected the latter choice. Indeed, unlike the British Cabinet in 1976, Washington policymakers gave little consideration to the option of using capital controls after their brief discussions in late 1978. This decision was also crucial for the globalization pro-

40. Quoted in Neikirk 1989:11. See Greider 1987:chap. 1 on the appointment of Volcker.
41. Healey 1989:431 notes that Volcker "asked me to send him a detailed account" of Britain's stabilization program in late 1976.
42. Volcker and Gyohten 1992:168; Woolley 1984:82, 103–4; and Greider 1987: 106–7, 116–18, chap. 3.

cess as a whole. Given the centrality of the United States in the emerging open global financial system, a more antagonistic U.S. stance with regard to global financial markets in this period would have represented a challenge to the entire process.

In large part, the decision of the Carter administration not to consider capital controls reflected the neoliberal shift in domestic politics that had been begun in the late 1960s. Although some of Carter's advisers, particularly those on the Council of Economic Advisers, strongly opposed the severity of Volcker's policies, Carter himself recognized the new political atmosphere and refused to take a stand against Volcker. With the entire business community (and particularly the large U.S. banks) solidly behind Volcker, the chairman of the Council of Economic Advisers at the time Charles Schultze, was also forced to admit that "the White House had to be very careful about taking on the Fed."[43] In Congress, too, there had been a shift away from Keynesian ideas after the stagflationary 1970s, and there was a strong sentiment, even among Democrats, in favor of an austerity program.[44] As Peter Ludlow remarked, Volcker's stabilization plan signaled "the near total victory in the North Atlantic world of habits of the mind that may be termed post-Keynesian, Germanic, Friedmanite, even Thatcherite."[45]

The decision also reflected broader U.S. national interests, however. Although the dollar crisis appeared to indicate the erosion of the country's financial hegemony, several analysts pointed out that the financial power of the United States had not really declined with respect to other states but only vis-à-vis the growing global financial markets. If the confidence of private market operators could be restored, the United States would benefit once again from financial openness as a result of its enduring structural power in global finance. Anthony Solomon at the Treasury Department, for example, argued that the dollar's global position was not seriously challenged by developments such as the creation of the EMS because U.S. financial markets were still the most attractive to investors: "You must understand, though, that for other currencies to become meaningful reserve currencies, they have to open their capital markets the way

43. Quoted in Greider 1987:121. See also Greider 1987:114–19, 121, 152–53; Parsons 1989:chap. 5; and Volcker and Gyohten 1992:169.

44. Morris 1982:141; Greider 1987:96, 149–51. See also Edsall 1984 and Ferguson and Rogers 1986 for a discussion of the conservative swing in the Democratic party in the 1970s.

45. Ludlow 1982:250.

the United States has, and they have been reluctant to do that to the degree we have. There is no way of having a really important reserve function for a currency unless it has large capital markets to which the rest of the world can have access, can borrow."[46] In internal studies conducted at the time, others in the Treasury Department noted that the EMS would be a threat to the United States only if it resulted "in a closed currency block and restrictions on capital movements," which was seen as unlikely.[47] The global impact of Volcker's decisive action seemed to confirm such analyses. Susan Strange observed that Volcker's stabilization plan was "a monetary shot that echoed around the world," restoring confidence in the dollar and U.S. financial markets, and confirming America's centrality in the global financial system.[48]

The Federal Reserve's Initiative to Regulate the Euromarket, 1979–1980

Although Volcker had opposed any attempt to control international capital movements for the purpose of avoiding the discipline of the international market, he and other officials in the Federal Reserve and the Treasury Department were increasingly concerned in 1979–80 that Euromarket activity would have an adverse impact on the effectiveness of U.S. monetary policy.[49] As they had in 1969–70, international banks and multinational corporations were successfully evading the Federal Reserve's tight monetary policy by borrowing offshore in the Euromarket to satisfy domestic needs. By 1981, according to one estimate, the size of the Eurodollar market had increased to approximately 10 percent of the size of the U.S. M-3 money supply (up from 4 percent in 1974); consequently, such inflows of Eurodollars were potentially very disruptive to the Fed's efforts to control the domestic money supply.[50] Ironically, the triumph of "monetarism" seemed to be occurring at just the time that international linkages were reducing the Fed's ability to control the monetary base.

46. Quoted in Ludlow 1982:121.
47. Ludlow 1982:119. See also Ludlow 1982:192.
48. Strange 1990:268. See also Strange 1982 and Story 1986:266.
49. Hawley 1987:136.
50. Frydl 1982.

To prevent this disruption, the Federal Reserve had three options. First, it could isolate the domestic monetary system from international financial markets by instituting a system of controls, as it had begun to do in 1969–70. Several steps were in fact taken in this direction. When Volcker's stabilization program had been announced on October 6, 1979, the Fed also established new special marginal reserve requirements for offshore borrowing by U.S. banks to increase the cost of such borrowing. The Federal Reserve also issued interpretative statements and used moral suasion to discourage offshore borrowing by U.S. banks for domestic purposes in this period.[51] To many Federal Reserve officials, however, this overall strategy was unattractive because they favored an open international financial system.[52] Moreover, they realized that U.S. borrowers could simply seek funds from non-U.S. banks operating offshore. The Federal Reserve attempted to plug this "leak" by requesting, at a BIS meeting in April 1980, that foreign central banks impose restraints on the lending of their own banks to U.S. residents, but the request met with only token cooperation by the Bank of Japan and the Bank of Canada.[53] Even if this cooperative initiative had been more successful, it would not have prevented another form of "leakage"— offshore borrowing by U.S. transnational corporations and the subsequent transfer of such funds to the United States via intrafirm payments.[54]

The second option available to the Federal Reserve was to "overtighten" domestic monetary policy to compensate for the inflows from offshore. Although this was, in effect, the policy followed after October 1979, many in the Federal Reserve such as Henry Wallich, worried that in the long run, it would impose disproportionate domestic hardship. Indeed, Wallich thought that the maintenance of domestic interest rates at unduly high levels might increase political pressure to impose capital controls.[55]

To avoid this possibility, Federal Reserve officials chose to pursue the third option to reduce the disruptive impact of the Euromarket: the introduction of reserve requirements for all Eurodollar activity. Such regulations, it was predicted, would check the market's growth

51. Greider 1987:143; Dale 1984:25.
52. On Volcker's opposition to capital controls, see Volcker 1979. See also the views of Wallich 1985:37.
53. Dale 1984:25.
54. Greider 1987:144.
55. Greider 1987:143 and Hawley 1987:137.

and hence minimize its detrimental effects on domestic monetary policy.[56] Federal Reserve officials recognized, however, that to be effective, the strategy would require international cooperation. A unilateral imposition of reserve requirements on U.S. financial institutions operating offshore would only drive Eurodollar activity to foreign banks. Consequently, in April 1979, the United States pressed BIS members to establish a committee to consider the specific proposal that all member central banks be required to impose reserve requirements on their own banks' international activities.[57]

The Federal Reserve's proposal met with stiff opposition, both internationally and domestically. Most significant was that of the Bank of England and the Swiss National Bank. As hosts to important Euromarket centers, these institutions had a great deal to lose from any efforts that would reduce the attractiveness of this market. The strength of their opposition was bolstered considerably when the Bundesbank withdrew its initial support for the U.S. proposal after realizing that it did not have the legal authority to impose reserve requirements on German banks operating abroad. As a result, the proposal was overwhelmingly defeated at a BIS meeting in Basel in April 1980.[58]

The Federal Reserve's proposal also met with strong opposition from the U.S. banking community,[59] for it was in direct conflict with their own objectives in this period. Whereas the Federal Reserve sought to reregulate the Euromarket to conform with domestic bank regulations, large U.S. banks had begun to lobby in the late 1970s for domestic bank deregulation that would be consistent with the freedom of the Euromarket. Their stance reflected a desire to rid themselves of the burdensome New Deal regulations, as well as a desire to be able to compete more effectively with domestic unregulated, nonbank institutions that were increasingly moving into bank-related activities in the 1970s.[60] This competitive pressure resulted from the 1975 "May Day" decision to deregulate the New York Stock Exchange, a decision that had in turn been provoked by competition from off-floor trading systems and also by neoliberal deregulatory thinking. The move had encouraged domestic securities com-

56. Hawley 1987:137.
57. Dale 1984:24, 26; Frydl 1982:17–18.
58. Dale 1984:28, Hawley 1987, and Dam 1982:324–25.
59. Hawley 1987:138.
60. Hawley 1987:133. For an overview of the American financial "revolution," see Enkyo 1989:76–93 and Moran 1991:chap. 2.

panies to offer instruments such as cash management accounts that competed directly with the banks' interest-bearing demand deposits. In the inflationary 1970s, these unregulated instruments were more attractive than bank deposits, which were still constrained by New Deal interest rate ceilings. Other nonbank companies, such as Sears, Roebuck and American Express, had also moved into bank-related activities, offering market rates of interest and allowing the de facto taking of interstate deposits, which banks were prohibited from doing. To compete effectively, the banking community hoped to retain the Euromarket as a base in which to operate free of regulation. Moreover, banks sought to use competitive pressures of the Euromarket to force domestic deregulation.[61] They were successful in achieving both goals. In 1979, heavy bank lobbying persuaded Congress to reject the Eurocurrency Market Control Act, which would have provided support for the Fed's initiative.[62] Similar lobbying, combined with a feeling that regulations were preventing savers from protecting themselves from the ravages of inflation, prompted the Democratic-controlled Congress to pass the 1980 Depository Institutions Deregulation and Monetary Control Act and the 1982 Garn–St. Germain Depository Institutions Act, both of which dismantled many of the domestic financial regulations that had been established in the interwar period.[63]

The complete failure of the Federal Reserve's regulatory initiative was confirmed by its decision in 1981 to permit the establishment of tax-free, regulation-free international banking facilities (IBFs) on U.S. soil. The Federal Reserve had considered introducing IBFs in 1980 as part of a more confrontational strategy vis-à-vis foreign governments concerning Euromarket regulation. It had hoped that the possibility that IBFs would attract the bulk of Euromarket activity back to the United States would encourage Britain and others to listen more carefully to U.S. proposals.[64] Faced with broad foreign and domestic opposition to their overall objectives, however, policymakers in the Federal Reserve began in 1981 to tout IBFs as a way, in James Hawley's words, "to make the best of a bad Eurocurrency situation."[65] They argued that the United States might at least benefit

61. Hawley 1987:133.
62. Hawley 1984:155–56.
63. See, for example, Greider 1987:chap. 5.
64. Hawley 1987:139; Dale 1984:30–31.
65. Hawley 1987:139.

in terms of jobs and tax revenue from the rapidly growing Euromarket business. Moreover, by bringing Euromarket activity back to the United States, IBFs would allow U.S. banks to increase their participation in international finance, because smaller U.S. banks that could not go offshore would have a chance to enter the business.[66] The Federal Reserve policymakers had not only failed to curtail the growth of the Euromarket but by accepting the IBFs they had become totally resigned to its existence. Indeed, as Richard Dale pointed out, the IBFs would only further undermine domestic monetary policy by "creating additional opportunities for monetary leakage."[67]

The failure of the Federal Reserve's initiative was important for three reasons. First, it confirmed a lesson learned in the early 1970s: that cooperative mechanisms of restoring control over international financial markets were easily scuttled by the refusal of a major state or group of states to go along with them. Second, had the initiative succeeded, it would have considerably slowed the deregulation and liberalization trend throughout the advanced industrial world in the 1980s. Its failure ensured that competitive pressures from the Euromarket, as well as those resulting from the deregulation of the U.S. financial system, would promote financial deregulation and liberalization in the 1980s. Foreign governments would struggle to create markets that would match conditions in London and the United States in order to attract footloose global financial operators. As the Bank of England warned at the time, the establishment of IBFs in the United States "may prompt similar developments in other countries." The Bundesbank also spoke of the need to "retaliate" against the U.S. decision with deregulatory moves of its own.[68] Third, the initiative's failure demonstrated that the desire to preserve policy autonomy in a financially open environment was not restricted to those committed to the Keynesian welfare state. As was evident in the 1960s, conservative central bankers had emerged from the interwar experience committed to macroeconomic management (albeit of a more conservative type), making many of them also somewhat wary of financial openness.[69]

66. Dale 1984:30 and Hawley 1987:139.
67. Dale 1984:32.
68. Both quotations from Dale 1984:40, 32. See also the predictions of the Federal Reserve officials in Dale 1984:30.
69. This commitment of central bankers to monetary planning became increasingly controversial in neoliberal circles in the 1970s, however. In *Denationalisation of Money,*

The Mitterrand U-Turn: France in 1981–1983

The election of François Mitterrand in May 1981 brought to power a government that was committed to an expansionary Keynesian economic strategy to rescue France from the deflationary global economy of the early 1980s. From the outset, the new government found itself the target of speculators in international financial markets. As was true after Leon Blum's election in 1936, wealthy asset holders initially moved their funds abroad out of fear that they would be taxed by the new government. By the fall of 1981, however, the speculation had a different motivation. The government's expansionary program produced rapidly growing current account deficits as well as an inflation rate higher than that in other West European countries, both of which raised the possibility of a franc devaluation. Although a dramatic increase in the interest rate in May 1981 and a devaluation within the EMS in October had temporarily appeased the markets, speculation resumed in June 1982.

At this juncture, the government's choices became more difficult. France's West European partners would no longer accept a devaluation within the EMS unless it was accompanied by austerity measures that demonstrated the government's determination to decrease its external deficit. The Reagan administration also refused to extend offsetting financing unless the government changed its economic policies.[70] Indeed, Henry Nau, a senior member of the National Security Council who was responsible for international economic affairs, noted that the United States was intent in this period on using "international market pressures" to force countries

first published in 1976, Friedrich Hayek argued that monetary discipline could be best obtained by abolishing central banks and moving to a market-based system of competing currencies in which international markets, not governments, determined the supply of money. Under such a scheme, international movements of capital would not interfere with government attempts to control the money supply but rather would ensure the stable value of money throughout the world. "What we now need," Hayek (1990:133) concluded, "is a Free Money Movement comparable to the Free Trade Movement of the 19th century." The importance of Hayek's argument was not simply that it reconciled the neoliberal goals of monetary discipline and financial freedom. Also significant was his rejection of macroeconomic planning, which both left and right had accepted as necessary after the depression of the 1930s. Hawley (1987:134) notes that many U.S. business leaders also increasingly called into question the need for monetary management when opposing the Federal Reserve's reregulatory initiative in the late 1970s.

70. Singer 1988:133–34; Nau 1984–85:27.

such as France to pursue "common performance objectives of low inflation and market incentives."[71] Serious divisions began to emerge in the Mitterrand government concerning economic policy, mirroring those in the British Labour government in 1976. Whereas Finance Minister Jacques Delors and Prime Minister Pierre Mauroy argued strongly in favor of an austerity package, others (such as Laurent Fabius, Pierre Bérégovoy, and Jean-Pierre Chevènement) advocated a strategy similar to the AES—France would leave the EMS and increase trade and exchange restrictions in order to preserve its domestic expansionary program.

Because of his strong commitment to his pro-European policy, Mitterrand was unprepared initially to consider the latter course. Instead, he favored a compromise, whereby European Community members would be asked (as France had asked them in 1971[72]) to introduce Community-wide capital controls that, by uncoupling European interest rates from those of the United States, would permit a Community-wide recovery. Although other Europeans were also frustrated by Volcker's high interest rate policy, the French proposal found little support when it was put forward in early 1982. The British were unprepared to consider closer European monetary cooperation or accepting restrictions on London's financial activities, both of which would have been necessary if they endorsed the plan. The West Germans were suspicious that under the plan, they would simply end up bailing out the inflationary French economy.[73] Rebuffed, Mitterrand agreed to a package in which France would begin an austerity plan in return for a 10 percent devaluation of the franc within the EMS.

These measures did little to reassure the markets, however, and speculation against the franc continued through the fall of 1982 and into early 1983. Although the Mitterrand government was able to replenish its reserves by borrowing funds from a consortium of international banks in September 1982 and from Saudi Arabia in January 1983, these funds were rapidly depleted.[74] By the time municipal elections were held in March 1983, Mitterrand was forced to

71. Nau 1984–85:27. See also Nau 1990:204.
72. Hewson and Sakakibara 1975:43.
73. Henning 1987:18; Kaufmann 1985:85. In 1981–82, however, West Germany had shown some interest in the idea of uncoupling European interest rates from those of the United States and pursuing more reflationary policies (Kennedy 1991:40–55; Goodman 1992:94–95).
74. Bauchard 1986:121, 124.

make a decision on the government's future economic policy. After receiving a considerable setback in the first round of the elections on March 6, and with the strong support of many of his advisers, Mitterrand suddenly endorsed the plan to pursue an independent expansion—that is, leaving the EMS and tightening exchange controls. But the refusal of Prime Minister Mauroy to agree to the new policy precipitated a governmental crisis.[75] Whereas Bérégovoy and other advisers continued to press for "a more industrial, more daring, more expansionist policy," Delors went on the offensive, stressing the enormous risks of such a course.[76] He argued that leaving the EMS would cause the franc to fall by 20 percent, or perhaps 30 percent, which would not only reinforce domestic inflationary pressures but also increase France's debt service costs.

A meeting on March 16 between Mitterrand's advisers and Michel Camdessus, head of the Treasury and future managing director of the IMF, changed the government's direction. Camdessus emphasized that France's foreign exchange reserves had fallen to a very low level; they would last "several days, but not weeks" in the event of a serious exchange crisis.[77] Moreover, he argued that leaving the EMS would prevent any further borrowing by the French government and that interest rates would have to be raised from the existing 14 percent to more than 20 percent to defend the franc. There was general agreement that only draconian exchange controls would prevent speculation. Faced with the prospect of widespread unemployment and business failures, Fabius threw his support behind the austerity plan, as did Bérégovoy and others.[78] This shift convinced Mitterrand to rejoin the Delors camp the same day. By the end of the week, Delors had negotiated an 8 percent devaluation of the franc within the EMS as well as a loan of 4 billion ECUs from the European Community in return for a promise to implement an austerity program at home. The plan finally convinced the markets that France was seriously tackling its economic difficulties. It also marked the final collapse of the French government's effort to pursue "Keynesianism in one country."

The dramatic decision of the Mitterrand government to give up its expansionary fiscal policy because of international financial pres-

75. Bauchard 1986:142–45; Giesbert 1990:169–78.
76. Bérégovoy quoted in Bauchard 1986:140–41 [my translation].
77. Camdessus quoted in Bauchard 1986:144 [my translation].
78. Bauchard 1986:145; Giesbert 1990:178–79.

sures had important ramifications both at home and abroad. In France, the embedded liberal framework of thought that the Mitterrand government had endorsed on taking office was rejected overnight in favor of a neoliberal focus on monetary discipline and market liberalization.[79] Indeed, in 1984, Bérégovoy initiated a program to liberalize and deregulate France's financial markets—changes that, as John Goodman points out, "would make it even more difficult for France to pursue in the future any monetary policy that diverged from world trends."[80] The French experience also resonated beyond its borders. France soon became an important advocate of the pan-European neoliberal 1992 project that, after January 1985, was led by Delors in his new capacity as European Commission president. Equally important, the French experience encouraged a rethinking by left-of-center intellectuals and politicians in other advanced industrialized countries who had closely followed the Mitterrand government's progress. For them, the government's forced acceptance of international market discipline was an indication of the enormous difficulties of attempting to preserve the "old world" of national Keynesianism in the new global financial environment.

The decision of the Socialist government not to resort to a system of tight exchange controls was made for similar reasons as that of the Labour government in 1976. Most important were the costs of pursuing the alternative strategy. Even its supporters were forced to acknowledge that there would have been enormous economic disruption as well as the possibility of foreign economic retaliation.[81] In terms of international politics, the introduction of exchange controls would have represented a radical step away from the pro-European strategy that had been the basis of French foreign policy in the postwar period. The French choice also reflected the growing influence of neoliberal thinking. Delors and others in the French financial bureaucracy had become increasingly convinced of the need to make a policy shift, replacing Keynesian theories with a neoliberal focus on monetary discipline and market liberalization. In addition to reflecting a pragmatic recognition of difficulties of preserving embedded liberal ideas in an environment of global finance, the shift was also encouraged by the stagflation of the previous decade. In France, as in Britain and the United States, the influence of neoliberal advo-

79. Hall 1986:201, Bauchard 1986:139, and Singer 1988:151–52.
80. Goodman 1992:139.
81. Hall 1986:196; 1987:56; Giesbert 1990:172–73; and Bauchard 1986:148.

cates in the government was enhanced by the power of the global financial markets. The appointment of Delors as finance minister in 1981, for example, like the appointment of Volcker in the United States in 1979, was made to reassure the markets of the Mitterrand government's intention to pursue sound economic policies.

Although other advanced industrial countries experienced similar crises in this period, the four turning points that occurred in Britain, the United States, and France are the most significant in a political history of the reemergence of global finance. Had controls been introduced in any of these cases, the globalization trend would have been set back considerably. The British and U.S. experiences were crucial because of the central position of these countries in the emerging open global financial order. The French experience was important not only in a symbolic sense but also in terms of the politics within the European Community. More broadly, these turning points were important because they marked the further collapse of the Bretton Woods financial framework. Having already sacrificed in the early 1970s the commitment to control finance in the interests of exchange rate stability, states had now abandoned the commitment to policy autonomy. The stage was set for the liberalization trend of the 1980s.

Three explanations can be given for the failure of these initiatives to reverse the globalization trend. First, as was also apparent in the early 1970s, serious political difficulties were encountered in attempting to implement either of the two mechanisms that Keynes and White had argued could effectively control capital movements. In the integrated world economy of the 1970s and 1980s, the introduction of tight exchange controls would impose enormous political and economic costs that policymakers were not willing to consider. Cooperative controls would be easily vetoed by states with a stake in the new open global financial system, such as those that were home to Euromarket financial activity.

A second explanation was the growing disillusionment throughout the advanced industrial world with the embedded liberal framework of thought that had sustained the Bretton Woods order and the concomitant shift toward neoliberalism. This change was partly a product of a practical acknowledgment by many policymakers of the problems of pursuing Keynesian policies in the new environment of global financial markets. The change also resulted from the stagflation of the 1970s, which undermined support for embedded liberal ideas. Like Keynes and his followers in the 1930s, neoliberal intellectuals worked actively—and often transnationally, as the British case revealed—to fill the ideological vacuum that had emerged. Neoliberal ideas also found strong support among private financial interests and financial officials whose governmental influence was enhanced by the growing power of the global financial markets. The U.S. experience in 1979–80 demonstrated, however, that central bankers remained more wary of the globalization process than other financial officials because of concerns for monetary policy autonomy. Their caution also stemmed from worries about financial crises, a subject that will be discussed in Chapter 8.

The third explanation, relating to the U.S. experience in 1978–79, was the continuing recognition by some U.S. policymakers that the United States could benefit from the emerging open international financial order because of its dominant position in that order. It was true that international financial markets during the 1978–79 dollar crisis had undermined U.S. policy autonomy. For this reason some scholars have argued that the crisis signaled the decline of American financial hegemony.[82] Although the United States had lost power to the growing global financial markets, these policymakers argued, correctly, that it had not lost financial power with respect to other states. They noted that the preeminence of the dollar and of U.S. financial markets in the open global financial order continued to give the United States a dominant position in global finance that it could use to its advantage. This power was effectively demonstrated by the global impact of Volcker's stabilization plan and even more strikingly by that of the economic policy of the Reagan administration, which is a subject of Chapter 7.

82. Gilpin 1987:332. See also Hawley 1984:149.

CHAPTER SEVEN

The Liberalization Trend
in the 1980s

THE FAILED INITIATIVES TO REVERSE THE GLOBALIZATION OF FI-
nance in the 1970s and early 1980s were followed by a dramatic
liberalization trend as advanced industrial states began to abolish
capital controls that had been in place for almost a half-century. Indeed, by the early 1990s, the restrictive Bretton Woods financial order had been completely overturned and an almost fully liberal pattern of financial relations had emerged between advanced industrial
states, giving market operators a degree of freedom unparalleled
since the 1920s. The trend began when Britain abolished its forty-
year-old system of capital controls in 1979. The British move was
copied in Australia and New Zealand in 1984–85. Many continental European countries also initiated financial liberalization programs in the mid-1980s and by 1988, all the member countries of
the European Community had committed themselves to the complete abolition of their capital controls within two years (an extended deadline was granted to Greece, Portugal, Spain, and Ireland). The Scandinavian countries made similar announcements in
1989–90. Throughout the 1980s, Japan also progressively liberalized its rigid capital controls, which had been in place since the
early 1930s. The first section of this chapter provides an analysis of
the support for financial liberalism in the three states in which were
located the financial centers that came to dominate global finance in
the 1980s: the United States (New York), Britain (London), and Japan (Tokyo). The second section focuses on the politics behind the

liberalization moves elsewhere in the European Community and in New Zealand, Australia, and the Scandinavian countries. In general, three political considerations explain the liberalization trend in the 1980s: the specific "hegemonic" interests of the United States, Britain, and Japan as existing, fallen, and rising financial powers; the growing strength of the neoliberal movement; and the prominence of competitive deregulation strategies.

Politics in the Three Major Financial Centers

A precondition for the dominant position of New York, London, and Tokyo in the open global financial system of the 1980s was the liberal policy stance that their respective states adopted toward capital movements. Whereas the United States had already abolished its capital controls in 1974 and thus had only to maintain its stance, both Britain and Japan had to undertake some significant liberalization moves in order to make London and Tokyo more liberal international financial centers. The political conditions underlying the behavior of these three states are summarized in this section.

Reaganomics and Global Finance

Although U.S. policymakers had become somewhat wary of the emerging open international financial order in 1978–80, they abandoned their caution in the early 1980s. This change was first signaled by the decision to introduce IBFs in 1981, a move designed to capture offshore Euromarket business (as described in the preceding chapter). By 1983, the United States began to show the same enthusiasm for financial liberalism that it had demonstrated in the early 1970s. This stance reflected a second motivation: international financial markets once again helped the United States to retain policy autonomy in the face of large domestic and external economic imbalances.

The newly elected administration of President Ronald Reagan succeeded in convincing Congress both to increase military spending and to approve a program of extensive tax cuts, as detailed in the 1981 budget. This combination spelled fiscal trouble, for the government deficit rose from $9 billion in 1981 to $207 billion in 1983.[1]

1. Henning 1987.

Had the United States been a closed economy, its growing fiscal deficit would have "crowded out" domestic financial markets, thus pushing up interest rates and inducing a recession. This set of developments never occurred, however, because the deficits were financed by enormous inflows of foreign private capital. According to some estimates, as much as one-half of the U.S. budget deficit was being financed (indirectly and directly) with foreign capital by 1985, keeping interest rates as much as 5 percent lower than they otherwise would have been.[2] Foreign capital inflows also financed the growing external current account deficit that accompanied the rapid expansion in the U.S. economy after 1982. In fact, so great was the enthusiasm of foreign private investors for making investments in the United States that the current account deficit was actually "overfinanced." The dollar, far from falling as a result of that deficit, actually rose, thereby exacerbating the imbalance on the current account.

The United States relied to a much greater extent in this period than in the past on *private* foreign financial support rather than the support of foreign central banks, which had proved so fickle in the late 1970s. The basis of America's ability to attract the world's private capital in this period was its continuing structural power in global finance, a power that derived from the unique depth and liquidity of U.S. financial markets and the global importance of the dollar. Japanese investors, the largest single source of foreign financing in the 1980s, found U.S. financial markets to be the only ones deep enough to absorb their enormous pool of surplus savings. Latin America investors, another important source of capital, were attracted by the stability of the dollar and the security of U.S. financial markets compared with the instability and uncertainty of their own debt-plagued economies. The desirability of making U.S. investments was also reinforced by high U.S. interest rates, which emerged from the mix of loose fiscal and tight monetary policy that had facilitated the country's economic recovery. By contrast, the economic expansion after 1976 had been initiated by a loose monetary policy that had only driven foreign private capital away from the U.S. economy.

It is unclear whether U.S. policymakers were initially aware of the role that international financial markets would play in underwriting the country's policy autonomy in this period.[3] By 1983–84, how-

2. Hamada and Patrick 1988; Marris 1985:44.
3. Cohen (1983:116) points out that U.S. economic policy in the first Reagan administration was initially made "in almost total disregard for the outside world." But Henry

ever, the contribution of the open international financial order was difficult to miss. As during the 1960s and 1970s, the benefits that the United States derived from its dominant position in that order in the early 1980s led Washington officials to become enthusiastic supporters of financial openness. The Treasury Department, in particular, became a strong advocate of financial liberalization at home and abroad for this reason.[4] At home, to increase the attractiveness of U.S. financial assets and financial markets to foreign investors, it convinced Congress to abolish the 30 percent withholding tax on interest payments to foreign holders of U.S. bonds in 1984. Like the 1981 decision to permit the establishment of IBFs, the move was also intended to return Eurobond business to New York markets.[5] The department also issued a special set of "targeted" Treasury bonds directly into the Eurobond market for the first time in 1984; the following year, it allowed foreigners to purchase Treasury bonds anonymously, an opportunity that was especially attractive to those involved in Latin American capital flight.[6] Abroad, special efforts were made to encourage financial liberalization, including the yen-dollar agreement of May 1984, which set forth a detailed timetable for Japanese financial liberalization. The Under Secretary of the U.S. Treasury for monetary affairs, Beryl Sprinkel, explained that the U.S. government hoped that such liberalization would "result in greater access by foreigners to Japanese capital."[7]

The End of British Exchange Controls and the Big Bang

London was still the second major center of international financial activity in the 1980s, as it had been in the 1960s and 1970s. But whereas it had previously served as an offshore Euromarket center, in the 1980s, its domestic and offshore financial markets were integrated for the first time. Two decisions made such integration possi-

---

Nau (1984–85:22), a National Security Council adviser in those years, suggests that U.S. officials recognized that "U.S. power in the international marketplace, exploited effectively and enhanced through noninflationary policies, remains much greater than its power at the bargaining table."

    4. See especially Destler and Henning 1989:29–30.
    5. See the comments of Robert Hormats in Kaushik 1987:50.
    6. Destler and Henning 1989:29, Levich 1988:222, and Walter 1989:232–34.
    7. Quoted in Frankel 1984:27. In taking this initiative, the Treasury Department was also motivated by the desire of U.S. financial institutions to operate in Japanese markets as well as by a hope that Japanese liberalization would increase the value of the yen and stem the dollar's rise (Frankel 1984:3–4, 44; Hamilton 1986:155–56).

ble. The first was the new Thatcher government's dramatic abolition of Britain's forty-year-old system of exchange controls in October 1979. The move released from employment one-quarter of the Bank of England's staff who had been monitoring the controls and greatly surprised financial officials at home and abroad.[8] As an OECD official in charge of enforcing the organization's Code of Liberalization of Capital Movements noted: "Nothing like this had ever happened before in the history of the Code. At one stroke, all United Kingdom reservations were removed, all controls wiped out."[9] Geoffrey Howe, the government minister responsible for the decision, later recalled that it had felt like "going over a cliff" and that "it was the only decision of my political life that ever has given me a sleepless night".[10]

Although the move had been foreshadowed by a loosening of capital controls in 1977–78 following the December 1976 stabilization program, the key explanation for it was the neoliberal orientation of the new Thatcher government, which perceived exchange controls as preserving outdated Keynesian strategies.[11] As Howe explained in a speech at the time, controls had "now outlived their usefulness. . . . The essential condition for maintaining confidence in our currency is a government determined to maintain the right monetary and fiscal policies."[12] The abolition of controls was also favored by neoliberal advocates at the time on the grounds that it would "remove what is a substantial restriction on, and could become a threat to, individual liberty."[13] Indeed, the government is reported to have destroyed the British Treasury's files on exchange controls to prevent any future government from reimposing them.[14] Hayek had argued in 1976 that from a neoliberal standpoint, capital controls would "remain a threat so long as governments have the physical power to enforce such controls."[15]

8. Williamson 1991:143.

9. Bertrand 1981:20.

10. Quoted in Peter Norman, "Going over the Cliff," *Financial Times*, October 23, 1989.

11. On the policy shift of the British Conservative party to neoliberalism in the mid-1970s, see Keegan 1984:chaps. 2–3.

12. Howe quoted in Norman, "Going over the Cliff."

13. Quotation is from a 1979 pamphlet published by the Institute of Economic Affairs, which had close ties to the new government (Miller and Wood 1979:68).

14. Glyn 1986:38.

15. Hayek 1990:125 (first published in 1976). Hayek had also hoped that the prohibition of capital controls would be made "an entrenched constitutional provision."

The abolition of exchange controls was also promoted by London's business and financial leaders. British pension funds and insurance companies, for example, wanted the opportunity to expand their international activities as well as to diversify their portfolios in the new floating exchange rate system. More important, the Bank of England saw the abolition of exchange controls as a way of attracting more financial business to London. Because London's emergence as an offshore Euromarket center in the 1960s had depended in part on the U.S. capital controls program, the U.S. decision to abolish these controls in 1974 had threatened London's competitiveness as an international financial center. Unless it abolished its exchange controls, London would lose its reputation as the most liberal and deregulated of such centers, which was key to maintaining and attracting footloose global financial business.[16]

The second key decision that integrated British domestic financial markets with global markets was the opening up of the London Stock Exchange to foreign securities firms in October 1986 (a move known as the "Big Bang").[17] At the same time, the exchange's fixed commissions were abolished in order to increase the London market's attractiveness to outsiders and to make it more competitive with other financial centers. The government's pressure on the stock exchange to introduce these reforms stemmed in part from a neoliberal desire to eliminate restrictive practices in London. More important, however, was the goal of preserving London's position as an international financial center at a time when global financial business was shifting from banking to securities activity. The abolition of exchange controls had pointedly demonstrated the lack of competitiveness of the London Stock Exchange, for it prompted British investors to shift their trading activity to New York securities markets, which had been deregulated in 1975. Unless it could match New York's conditions, the London Stock Exchange would increasingly risk being used as a center for the trading only of low-grade British securities. Once again, the mobility of financial activity encouraged a competitive deregulation dynamic: British authorities felt compelled to join the U.S. deregulation movement. As Bank of England governor Robin Leigh-Pemberton put it in 1984, "Change in

---

16. Coakley and Harris 1992:40–41, 44; Newton and Porter 1988:200–201; and Moran 1991:74.

17. For an overview, see Moran 1991:chap. 3 and Hamilton 1986:chap. 6.

the United States has already gone further, leading and requiring change here."[18]

Japanese Liberalization: A Financial Power on the Rise

The emergence of Tokyo as the third leading global financial center in the 1980s was one of the most remarkable developments of the decade. Since 1931, Japan's domestic financial markets had been tightly sealed off from external influence by a set of strict capital controls. Although some liberalization moves had been made in the mid-1960s, the Japanese government had assumed a more cautious stance in the 1970s because of large balance-of-payments fluctuations. In the late 1970s, however, the Japanese government initiated a process of liberalization that gathered momentum in the 1980s.

Some analysts have attributed Japanese financial liberalization since the late 1970s to U.S. pressure,[19] which is said to have resulted in two policy decisions: the 1980 revision of the 1949 Foreign Exchange and Foreign Trade Control Law and the May 1984 yen-dollar agreement between the U.S. Treasury Department and the Japanese Ministry of Finance. There are important reasons to qualify this interpretation. Although U.S. pressure was central to the 1980 decision, the revision simply confirmed informal liberalization moves that had already been initiated in the late 1970s. Moreover, the reform did little to dismantle the basic tool of the Japanese government's administrative guidance system: foreign exchange monopoly of the special foreign exchange banks. It was, as Louis Pauly observed, "a symbol largely for foreign consumption."[20] The 1984 agreement was undoubtedly of greater importance because it established a detailed timetable of liberalization moves, committing Japan to develop a Euroyen market, institute capital market deregulation and liberalization, and allow foreign financial institutions access to Japanese financial markets. Although they do not deny the importance of these moves, most analysts note that, with the exception of permitting the entry of foreign firms, all were initiatives that the Japanese government was set to embark upon anyway.[21]

Pressure by the United States clearly was a catalyst in promoting

18. Leigh-Pemberton quoted in Enkyo 1989:198.
19. See, for example, Calder 1988:537.
20. Pauly 1987b:14. See also Lincoln 1986:250–52, Hollerman 1988, and Rosenbluth 1989:57 on the relative insignificance of the 1980 move.
21. See, for example, Lincoln 1986:252 and Rosenbluth 1989:chap. 3.

liberalization, but several domestic developments that accompanied Japan's rapid rise as an economic and financial power were the main reason for this change in Japanese policy. As the leaders of Tokyo's private financial community became increasingly prominent in international financial markets in the 1970s, they began to favor the liberalization of Japan's restrictive capital controls. Indeed, the eagerness of Japanese bankers to play a prominent international role had been apparent as far back as the late 1960s, when they had begun calling for the development of Tokyo as an international financial center. By that time, Japanese banks constituted the second largest foreign group (after the American banks) in London.[22] In the 1970s, the bankers' frustrations only increased, for the extensive capital controls intended to offset Japan's balance-of-payments troubles interfered with their efforts to improve their international standing and expand their profitable international business.

Another domestic development was the shift in political power in the late 1970s within the important Ministry of Finance in favor of internationalists who saw financial liberalization as a key to the continuation of Japan's increasing global economic and financial importance.[23] Their influence first became apparent following the 1979 oil shock. Those within the ministry who favored closing the yen bond market to foreigners, as had been done in 1973, were successfully opposed by "a group more conscious of Japan's growing role in international affairs, and the need to be sensitive to the requirements of foreign borrowers."[24] The ministry also responded favorably at this time to a request by Japanese banks that controls on their international lending not be extended to foreign currency loans in the Euromarkets in order that their new international standing might be preserved. In July 1980, the ministry announced for the first time that international banking would be classified as one of Japan's predominant industries.[25] Further evidence of the growing strength of the internationalist position within the ministry was the increased influence of the International Finance Bureau, a strong supporter of liberalization, in key intraministry battles.[26]

22. Adams and Hoshii 1972:459, 469. See Iwasa 1970, an article by the then president of the Fuji Bank.
23. See especially Horne 1985:181; 1988:187, 190, 199; and Rosenbluth 1989:62–67; also Fujioka 1979:63–67.
24. Horne 1985:181.
25. Duser 1990:100.
26. Horne 1988:177; Hollerman 1988:57.

This change within the bureaucracy was reinforced by the emergence of a group of younger leaders in the ruling Liberal Democratic Party—most prominently Prime Minister Yasuhiro Nakasone (in office from 1982 to 1987)—who favored a more prominent international political role for Japan to match its growing economic clout. They were strongly committed to a program of liberalization as a means of transforming Japan into an "international state" suitable for global leadership.[27] Nakasone depended on leading bankers (such as Goro Koyama of Mitsui) to press for such policies in the financial sector. When the bureaucracy resisted change, for example, he created informal advisory groups on which leading bankers held important positions.[28] The large Japanese banks also supported the proposal to establish IBFs, which the Nakasone-appointed Hosomi commission had recommended in the early 1980s.[29]

Japan's emergence as a major creditor to the world after 1981 also encouraged liberalization. From the end of World War II until the 1980s, Japan had been a net borrower of funds from the world. After 1981, excess savings—resulting primarily from the slowdown in Japanese growth in the early 1970s and cutbacks in government deficits after the late 1970s—began to flow abroad in search of higher returns.[30] By 1985 Japan had become the world's largest creditor, and at the end of 1990 its external assets were valued at $328 billion.[31] Japan's new creditor status eliminated concerns about the vulnerability of Japan's external balance of payments, concerns that provided a key justification for capital controls in the postwar period. It also gave Japanese financial institutions a much more prominent international position because they were the chief intermediaries exporting Japanese funds. This position was strengthened by the yen's rise after 1985. By the late 1980s, Japanese banks were controlling the largest share of international bank assets, and the four largest Japanese securities houses consistently found themselves among the top six Eurobond underwriters.[32] This new global prominence led Japanese financial institutions to become even more vocal in their calls for Tokyo to become a fully liberalized global financial

27. Pyle 1987:256–57.
28. Funabashi 1988:89.
29. Sakakibara 1986:243.
30. For an overview, see Lincoln 1988.
31. *Globe and Mail* (Toronto), May 22, 1991.
32. Helleiner 1992c:41–42.

center.[33] Indeed, liberalization at home was especially necessary to avoid foreign retaliation for overly restrictive Japanese controls.[34] Japan's new creditor status also gave a boost to those within the bureaucracy and in political circles who favored liberalization on grounds of "national interest." In becoming the world's largest creditor, Japan increasingly had a direct stake in a stable and open global financial system as a source of future income.[35] The government's well-publicized 1986 Maekawa plan, for example, stressed the importance of international financial services in the future Japanese economy and seemed to predict that Japan would be an international "rentier state" living off its creditor earnings. A stable and open international financial system was also important because it was the basis of smooth relations with the United States, which had become Japan's major debtor. A proposal in 1985 to put controls on capital outflows to curtail the yen's fall was turned down by the Ministry of Finance out of fear of the American reaction.[36] Japan's sudden creditor position thus encouraged the Japanese government to endorse financial liberalization more quickly that it otherwise might have. Its liberalization program can be said to have represented the "leading" behavior (in contrast to Britain's lagging hegemonic behavior) of a financial power on the rise, behavior which was also encouraged by Japan's desire to maintain stable relations with the United States (in terms of both agreeing to U.S. demands for liberalization and not restricting capital outflows to the United States).

The Japanese liberalization process was also encouraged by the increasing spiral of competition, innovation, and deregulation that began to grip the Japanese domestic financial system after the mid-1970s. Although competitive pressures from the United States and the Euromarket played a part in causing this upheaval, its principal cause was the growth of the government deficit in the 1970s. As corporations and financial institutions accumulated government bonds, they demanded and received in 1977 the right to trade them

33. See, for example, discussion of a 1986 Nomura Research Institute report in Gilpin 1987:337–38.

34. Pauly 1988:89; Rosenbluth 1989:14.

35. See Frieden 1988 for this general argument.

36. Funabashi 1988:87. Interestingly, Liberal Democratic politicians were also persuaded against controls at this time by arguments that such controls would damage the emerging international reputation of Japanese markets in the same way that the U.S. markets were harmed by the U.S. capital controls program in the 1960s (Volcker and Gyohten 1992:53–54).

in a secondary market for portfolio management purposes. The establishment of this freely functioning open market not only forced the government to offer more competitive market rates for its new issues but also greatly increased the competition between banks and securities firms, which spurred innovation, leading to demands for further deregulation, which only heightened competition. This growing spiral led to a profound change in Japan's financial system; the "bank credit-control paradigm" that had characterized it since the 1930s was increasingly replaced by a "market-determining open money market paradigm" more characteristic of the Anglo-American systems.[37] As the Japanese authorities lost regulatory control over domestic financial activity, they became more receptive to the loss of financial control that would come with external liberalization. The Bank of Japan, for example, had initially strongly opposed the establishment of IBFs in Japan, fearing that such a development would bring a loss of control over domestic interest rates. By mid-1983, however, it had acknowledged that the proposal might soon be acceptable because interest rate controls were being removed anyway.[38] Moreover, as was true in the United States and elsewhere, increased domestic competition gave Japanese financial institutions a strong interest in operating internationally, both to supplement their declining domestic profits and to escape domestic regulations. As James Horne put it, international activity "was an outlet for tensions which were building up in the domestic markets."[39] As holders of increasing levels of government debt, financial institutions also had greater leverage over the government in pressing for liberalization.[40]

Liberalization outside the Major Financial Centers

Extensive liberalization moves were also initiated elsewhere in the advanced industrial world in the 1980s. The most important were those in the European Community.

37. Yoshitomi (1985:12) uses these terms. For an overview of the change, see Feldman 1986, Suzuki 1987, and Rosenbluth 1989.

38. Dale 1984:44. The IBFs were finally established in Japan in 1986, for many of the same reasons as in the United States: to allow small banks to do business in the offshore markets, to achieve greater surveillance over Euromarket activity, and to recapture lost business (Lincoln 1988:240–41; Hamilton 1986:171).

39. Horne 1988:196. See also Horne 1988:176–78 and Duser 1990:75.

40. Crum and Meerschwam 1986:289.

Liberalization in the European Community

Although the liberalization of capital movements was one of the formal objectives of the Treaty of Rome (1957), it received little attention from West European governments in the 1960s and 1970s.[41] The British decision to abolish its controls in 1979 was the first sign of change, as we have already seen. By the mid-1980s, other European governments had also initiated comprehensive financial liberalization and deregulation programs. In France, the Mitterrand government launched a financial reform program in 1984.[42] The West German government began a program to liberalize and deregulate its financial system in the mid-1980s, reversing its previous practice of defending German monetary autonomy by means of controls and regulatory constraints on the international use of the deutsche mark.[43] In 1984 and 1986, respectively, Denmark and the Netherlands eliminated the bulk of their external capital controls in one quick move.[44]

At the same time that individual governments began to liberalize, the European Commission started to promote financial liberalization. Its 1985 White Paper, which established the framework for the 1986 Single European Act, emphasized the importance of liberalizing capital movements as part of its goal of completing the creation of the single market. Moreover, Bank of Italy official Tommaso Padoa-Schioppa points out that after SEA was agreed upon by Community member governments, "a decision was taken separately in 1986 by the Commission, and by Jacques Delors in particular, to give the freedom of capital transfers absolute priority in the goals the Commission was pursuing."[45] In particular, Delors (as the Commission's new president) pushed Community member governments to liberalize capital movements well in advance of the 1992 deadline for the creation of the single market outlined in the SEA. In October

41. Prior to the 1980s, there had been only two European Community directives on liberalizing capital movements, in 1960 and in 1962. The Community's 1962 Program of Action had stressed that financial liberalization would be necessary, but even at this time the issue was "treated lightly" and in a "superficial" manner (Cohen 1963:618). See also Tsoukalis 1977:80.

42. See Loriaux 1991:223–27 and Cerny 1989.

43. See Tavlas 1991; Hamilton 1986:181, 194–95; and Goodman and Pauly 1990: 21–22.

44. On Denmark, see Hoffmeyer 1986. Its last capital controls were removed in October 1988.

45. Padoa-Schioppa 1988:437. On Delors's key role in promoting financial freedom, see also *Financial Times*, September 16, 1987.

1985, European governments were persuaded to permit unit trusts and other collective investment trusts to operate freely across borders within the European Community. This decision was followed in late 1986 by an agreement to scrap all controls on capital movements directly related to trade and investments.[46] In late October 1987, the Commission proposed a draft directive under which states belonging to the Community would permit freedom for *all* capital movements. The European Community's Council of Ministers approved it on June 24, 1988, thus committing member governments to abolish all capital controls by mid-1990 (a slight extension was given to Greece, Spain, Portugal, and Ireland).[47]

The directive's acceptance was sealed by two important decisions. First, Delors had made it clear that the issue of capital controls could be raised only after European central bank governors agreed in September 1987 to strengthen intervention measures within the EMS. Without the promise of expanded credit facilities, many countries for which capital controls had been necessary to maintain the parity of their currencies within the EMS would have been wary of accepting a commitment to the freedom of capital movements.[48] The second decision concerned the question of tax evasion, which had also worried Keynes and White. French Finance Minister Bérégovoy, supported by Denmark, had threatened to obstruct the approval of the capital movement liberalization directive unless other members agreed to introduce a Community-wide withholding tax aimed at preventing tax evasion.[49] Only after the Community agreed in June 1988 to study the withholding tax proposal did he back down. In the resulting discussions, strong opposition by Britain and Luxembourg (and eventually West Germany) prevented agreement on a withholding tax, and the French were forced to accept a more limited scheme in which national tax authorities would cooperate in antifraud investigations.[50]

These decisions facilitated the 1988 agreement, but the determina-

---

46. Italy, Spain, Portugal, Greece, and Ireland were exempt from this obligation.

47. Spain, Portugal, and Ireland abolished their capital controls by December 1992.

48. French Finance Minister Edouard Balladur had pressed for such intervention measures (*Financial Times*, September 14, 1987). For Delors's view on their importance in permitting capital liberalization discussions to begin, see *Financial Times*, May 13, 1989.

49. *Financial Times*, June 13, 1988; Walter 1989:294.

50. On the opposition of Britain, Luxembourg, and West Germany, see *Financial Times*, February 8, 9, 14 and May 9, 22, 1989. Belgium, Italy, and Spain agreed with the position of France and Denmark. The Commission strongly supported the French position.

tion of Western European governments to liberalize capital movements after the mid-1980s stemmed from other factors. In one respect, it was simply part of the broader drive to achieve closer European economic integration in this period. Indeed, Delors made it clear that one reason he pushed especially strongly for the liberalization of capital movements was that he saw it as a means of accelerating the move towards economic and monetary union (EMU). As he put it, "in terms of synergy and dynamism, this is the central decision. . . . It is this that allows us to envisage passing from the EMS to enlarged economic and monetary union."[51] He hoped that the removal of capital controls would force European governments to move to closer monetary cooperation if they wanted to preserve stable exchange rates and regain some degree of control over monetary policy in the new open financial environnment.[52] Indeed, only two weeks after Council of Ministers approved the capital liberalization directive, it set up the Delors Committee to study "concrete steps" to achieve economic and monetary union. Delors also hoped that financial liberalization might encourage Germany and Britain, both of which favored the removal of capital controls, to become more enthusiastic about EMU. Germany had in fact refused to discuss EMU until France and other Community members abolished their controls.[53]

Even without these regional objectives, the Commission and many continental European governments still would have pursued financial liberalization in this period because of competitive pressures from the Euromarket and the U.S. financial system.[54] As early as the 1960s, the Euromarket had posed a competitive threat to continental European financial systems as West European citizens and multinational corporations had shifted their financial activities to the more attractive market offshore.[55] Faced with this challenge, European financial authorities had worried not only about losing financial business but about whether domestic industrial firms without access to the international financial market would be disadvantaged

51. Quoted in *Financial Times*, March 14, 1989.

52. *Financial Times*, March 14, 1989. See also Goodman 1992:202, and Padoa-Schioppa 1988:440.

53. *Financial Times*, March 14, 1989; Goodman and Pauly 1990:35–36, 42; and Padoa-Schioppa 1988:438.

54. Moran 1991:3, Strange 1990:264–65, and De Cecco 1987a:8.

55. Pringle 1989:17–18, Hirsch and Oppenheimer 1976:667, and Altman 1969:11.

in international competition by their country's relatively inefficient domestic financial system.

The deregulation and liberalization of the U.S. financial system in the 1970s and 1980s (described in the preceding chapter) greatly increased this competitive pressure because they enhanced the attractiveness of U.S. financial markets and firms vis-à-vis their West European counterparts. As many observers had predicted in 1981 when the United States permitted establishment of IBFs, West European governments felt increasingly compelled to match U.S. deregulation and liberalization moves in order not to lose both international and domestic footloose financial business. West Germany's first liberalization move in the 1980s, the abolition of its withholding tax on foreign holdings of German securities in 1984, was a direct response to a similar move by the United States the same year.[56] Britain's Big Bang—itself also a response to U.S. deregulation—further increased pressure on West European authorities as they saw their chief financial firms, such as West Germany's Deutsche Bank, shift the European base of their capital market operations to Britain. Indeed, Robert Pringle notes that "the German government was informed by its central bank that unless it relaxed restrictions on capital market business in Germany, its big banks would migrate to London."[57] Japanese liberalization and deregulation only reinforced the fears of national authorities in smaller countries that financial activity would come to be concentrated in London, New York, and Tokyo.

These competitive pressures from abroad gave rise to the idea that the financial sector required an "industrial policy" to retain its competitiveness. Such a policy would include liberalization and deregulation in order to maintain or attract mobile financial business in the face of competition from abroad.[58] The increasing use of the term "financial services" was an indication that finance was increasingly seen as a "business"; indeed, in the 1970s and 1980s, finance was one of the fastest growing sectors of the world economy. West European governments sought to construct more competitive financial markets not just to create a comparative advantage in financial ser-

56. Hamilton 1986:181, 195. See also Tavlas 1991:19.
57. Pringle 1989:27. See also Hamilton 1986:192 and Goodman and Pauly 1990:24. On the importance of competitive pressures from Britain and the United States in prompting French financial reform, see Cerny 1989, Lebegue 1985:23, 29, and Plender 1986–87:40–41.
58. For the views of the European Commission on this subject, see Underhill 1991: 205, 207–8, and Vipond 1991:229.

vices but also to attract footloose private capital. The United States in the Reagan years effectively demonstrated that financial power in the world economy derived in large part from the "pulling power" of a country's markets with regard to internationally mobile funds. Only by emulating the liquidity, complexity, and openness of U.S. financial markets would West European governments be able to compete with the United States for international capital with which to finance budget or current account deficits. The European Commission officials, for example, made clear that one of the objectives of European financial reform was to augment European financial power within the world economy. As Delors put it, the creation of a single European financial market would give "our financial centres the opportunity to be among the most important in the world," and "it is this that gives us our say in the world with the Americans and Japanese on debt, on financial flows."[59] In a similar vein, it was also hoped that financial liberalization and deregulation would increase the international attractiveness of European currencies in relation to the dollar, particularly when they could be held in a unified European money market that the European Commission argued would be "the largest in the world."[60]

In addition to these competitive pressures, European financial liberalization was encouraged by the increasing prominence of neoliberal conceptions of finance throughout the Community in the 1980s.[61] Capital controls had been a central element in national Keynesian and corporatist planning strategies throughout Western Europe; now they were suddenly viewed as a component of outdated economic policies, constraining individual freedom, and, in particular, inhibiting the efficiency of the financial intermediation process both domestically and internationally. The European Commission's 1985 White Paper, for example, took up the last criticism, stressing that "the decompartmentalization of financial markets should boost the economic development of the Community by promoting the optimum allocation of European savings."[62] Similarly, the 1988 Cecchini Report, which provided the economic justification for the sin-

59. Quoted in David Buchan and Geoffrey Owen, "Undimmed Ambitions for Unity in Europe," *Financial Times*, March 14, 1989.

60. European Commission 1990:182.

61. Many observers have commented on the general "neoliberal" orientation of the overall single market project (Sandholtz and Zysman 1989; Grahl and Teague 1989; Moravcsik 1991). On the financial sector specifically, see Vipond 1991:230–31.

62. Underhill 1991:205–6.

gle market project, emphasized the neoclassical economic benefits of financial market integration.[63] As one observer noted in 1988, "the link between overall economic performance and vigorous financial markets is more widely accepted in Europe than ever before."[64]

This ideological shift had been encouraged by a growing recognition of the difficulties of defending embedded liberal ideas in a world of global finance after the French U-turn in policy in 1983. There was also a general disillusionment with postwar regulatory frameworks as a result of the economic slowdown of the 1970s and 1980s. Moreover, neoliberal thinking was promoted especially strongly by a coalition of social groups similar to that which had supported neoliberal ideas in the United States in the 1970s. European financial interests and multinational businesses, for example, were important advocates of the neoliberal argument for financial freedom in this period.[65] The former had generally favored financial liberalism throughout the postwar period, but they advocated it even more strongly in the 1980s as a means of coping with growing competitive pressures both domestic and international.[66] The latter had been sympathetic to the principles of the Bretton Woods financial order in the early postwar period but had become increasingly frustrated with cumbersome capital controls as their interests had become more internationalized. Officials in European central banks and finance ministries were also strong proponents of neoliberal approaches to finance in the 1980s. Phil Cerny notes that in France, financial liberalization and deregulation were encouraged by the growing power of financial officials within the bureaucracy after the 1983 U-turn in economic policy.[67] In Denmark, the initiative to abolish capital controls "originated from the Central Bank."[68] Financial officials in international institutions such as the OECD also pressed for financial liberalization in this period, as they had since the

---

63. Underhill 1991:205, 222n1; Vipond 1991:229–30.

64. Guy de Jonquières, "1992: Countdown to Reality," *Financial Times*, February 19, 1988.

65. For example, see Goodman and Pauly 1990:16–18, 22–24, 42–43; Frieden 1991:440–42. Sandholtz and Zysman (1989) also emphasize the importance of the support of European multinational firms for the overall single market project.

66. Pringle 1989:26.

67. Cerny 1989. Top civil servants in the French Treasury—Daniel Lebegue and Jean-Charles Naouri, in particular—are said to have strongly promoted financial reform. For Lebegue's views, see Lebegue 1985.

68. Hoffmeyer 1986:96.

1960s.[69] Indeed, the frequent international meetings of financial officials in such institutions as the OECD appeared to be important forums in which neoliberal ideas were expressed. As one OECD official noted in 1981, "Time and again, one hears at international meetings of finance people that governments, especially in the industrialised countries, should begin to dismantle exchange controls or at least co-operate to make them less arbitrary and harmful to business."[70]

Abolition of Controls in New Zealand, Australia, and Scandinavia

Because capital controls in New Zealand, Australia, and the Scandinavia countries had been among the most comprehensive in the advanced industrial world since 1945, the decisions of governments in these countries to fully liberalize them in the 1980s marked a significant change in policy. The liberalization decisions in New Zealand and Australia can generally be explained by an ideological shift in favor of a neoliberal conception of finance within newly elected Labour governments in each country in the mid-1980s.[71] As in other countries, this shift stemmed in part from a recognition of the difficulties of preserving embedded liberal ideas in an increasingly integrated global financial order—a recognition prompted in both countries by a major currency crisis. Neoliberal ideas also found their greatest support among officials in the Finance Ministry and the central bank whose views were often influenced by their links to the international financial community. The neoliberal framework was also strongly supported by private financial interests and by the multinational business community, both of which sought to free themselves from restrictive capital controls, as had their counterparts in the United States in the 1970s and in the European Community in the 1980s.

---

69. The OECD's Committee for Capital Movements and Invisible Transactions (which was composed of ex-Treasury Department and central bank officials) exerted an especially strong push for financial liberalization in the 1980s (see OECD 1981a, 1982, 1987b), as did the OECD's Committee on Financial Markets, established in 1971 (see OECD 1978, 1984, 1981b, 1987a). For their enthusiasm for this policy in the 1960s and 1970s, see Bertrand 1981:7, 14, 15, 20, and Kindleberger 1987b:79.

70. Bertrand 1981:3.

71. The OECD (1991:46) stresses "philosophical" considerations in explaining the moves to liberalize capital controls, as do Pauly (1987a:89, 66) in the Australian case, and Jesson (1987:chap. 7) and Easton (1989:105) in the New Zealand case.

This combination of developments was most visible in New Zealand. Although the Labour government elected in 1984 had not campaigned on a neoliberal platform with regard to finance, capital controls were abolished during its first year in office and a broad domestic financial deregulation program was initiated. Leading these initiatives was Finance Minister Roger Douglas, whose neoliberal views had been influenced by officials in New Zealand's Treasury and Reserve Bank as well as by IMF advice.[72] From Douglas's perspective, the abolition of capital controls (which he later called "one of the three or four most important decisions we made") was necessary partly to facilitate the international expansion of New Zealand business. Indeed, representatives of business and the financial sector in New Zealand were strong advocates of the move, as well as of neoliberal approaches to economic policy more broadly in this period.[73] Douglas also argued that the issue of removing capital controls "was really about whether New Zealanders should be allowed to join the rest of the free world."[74] Concerning the broader domestic financial deregulation, he concluded: "At last we had left behind the long outdated idea that the government was the only agent capable of managing the financial market and economy for its citizens."[75] Douglas's proposals met with relatively little resistance in the Cabinet and the Labour party as a whole, largely because he was able to utilize the uncertain atmosphere created by a currency crisis that occurred shortly after election of the new government to define the policy agenda. As Bruce Jesson notes, the Cabinet was "overwhelmed by the daring, the sense of certainty and the sheer volume of Treasury and Reserve Bank policy" in the wake of the currency crisis.[76]

There were many similarities between the New Zealand and Australian cases. Australia's new Labour government elected in 1983

72. Jesson 1987:123. Jesson notes (p. 120): "The international shift from Keynesianism to neo-classical economics and monetarism had its most important effect in New Zealand inside the Treasury and the Reserve Bank." See also Boston 1989:76, Oliver 1989:18–27, and Schwartz 1991:250–52 on Treasury and Reserve Bank influence. See Douglas (1987:48) on the IMF's support for neoliberal policies in New Zealand in the early 1980s.

73. Jesson 1987:122, chap. 7; Schwartz 1991:250–52. Douglas quote from Douglas 1987:143.

74. Douglas 1987:143.

75. Douglas 1987:150. For an overview of New Zealand's domestic financial reforms in this period, see Harper and Karacaoglu 1987.

76. Jesson 1987:123. See also Easton 1989.

did not have a neoliberal mandate from the electorate with regard to finance. Indeed, the Labour party's electoral platform emphasized the importance of "carefully regulating foreign investment and short term financial flows."[77] As in New Zealand, the new government was welcomed into office by a major currency crisis brought about by speculators who feared the economic consequences of the change of government. In this context, Louis Pauly notes that the government's leaders "immediately realized that long term stability depended upon reassuring a wary business community."[78] The new finance minister, Paul Keating, visited New York financial leaders soon after the election "to put to rest any fears of the Mitterrand factor," then moved rapidly to float the Australian dollar and abolish exchange controls.[79] These moves were part of a broader domestic financial deregulation that Keating hoped would "simultaneously break a perceived roadblock to growth and appeal to the business community."[80] The abolition of exchange controls was also strongly advocated by officials of Australia's Treasury and central bank in this period. Andrew Glyn speculates that they were motivated in part by a hope that "the greater openness of financial markets would weaken the ability of a Labour Government to behave in an 'irresponsible way'."[81] Louis Pauly also notes that Keating's views had been influenced by his association with international bankers; his liberalization decisions certainly received their accolades: "Those same banks welcomed him to [the next IMF meeting in] Washington like a conquering hero."[82]

The financial deregulation and liberalization programs in Sweden, Norway, and Finland were just as dramatic as those in New Zealand and Australia. In each country, controls on finance, both internal and external, had been a central element of postwar planning strategies.[83] In the mid-1980s, however, the Scandinavian countries initiated financial reforms and, in 1989–90, announced their intention to abolish their postwar capital controls completely.[84] One explana-

77. Quoted in Pauly 1987a:60.
78. Pauly 1987a:66. See also Glyn 1992:119.
79. Quote from the *Australian Financial Review* in Glyn 1992:123.
80. Pauly 1987a:66.
81. Glyn 1992:120.
82. Pauly 1987a:81–82. See also Glyn 1992:123, 135n6.
83. Bertrand 1981:18–19.
84. The Swedish government announced in January 1989 that it planned shortly to abolish all foreign exchange controls, which it did in July 1989. Soon thereafter, the

tion for the decisions was the growing desire of these countries to join the European Community. Competitive pressures and ideological shifts were equally important explanations, however. Concerning the former, financial deregulation and liberalization had become necessary to prevent financial business from moving abroad—particularly to London after the Big Bang.[85] Concerning the latter, the movements for financial reform were often spearheaded by advocates of neoliberal ideas. In Sweden, for example, the financial deregulation and liberalization program was designed and promoted by Finance Minister Kjell-Olof Feldt and the country's central bank governor, Bengt Dennis, both of whom were free-market advocates who explicitly rejected the country's earlier endorsement of planning.[86] Both were strongly supported by their international financial colleagues and by domestic bankers.[87] Strong backing for financial liberalization throughout Scandivania also came from large industrial firms whose interests had rapidly become internationalized in the 1980s.[88]

The extensive liberalization initiatives throughout the advanced industrial world in the 1980s granted international financial market operators more freedom than had been allowed in the preceding half-century. Indeed, for the first time since the 1920s, there was a high degree of consensus in favor of a liberal international financial system. As Rimmer De Vries noted, "Capital flow freedom has won the hearts and minds of policymakers, contrary to earlier instincts."[89] In a reflection of this new consensus, the OECD countries agreed in May 1989 to extend the OECD Code of Liberalization of Capital Movements to cover *all* international capital movements, including short-term financial transactions.[90]

Three political explanations can be given for the financial liberal-

---

government of Norway made a similar announcement as did the Finnish government, in November 1990.

85. Enkyo 1989; Hamilton 1986:191.

86. On their close relationship and important role, see *Financial Times*, January 18 and June 29, 1989. For Feldt's views, see the interview in the *Financial Times*, April 17, 1989, in which he notes: "I have never believed in planned economies. I have seen the results and I saw them earlier than some of my colleagues in the party."

87. On Feldt's prominence in international financial circles, see the *Financial Times*, April 17, 1989. On Swedish bankers' support, see *Financial Times*, January 11, 1988.

88. Pringle 1989:34. See also Pauly 1988:177.

89. De Vries 1990:1.

90. Ley 1989; OECD 1991.

ization trend in the 1980s. First were the special "hegemonic" interests of the three states that housed the major financial centers of the 1980s—the United States, Britain, and Japan—whose support for financial liberalism partly reflected their respective positions as existing, fallen, and rising financial powers. American officials recognized in the early 1980s, as they had in the 1960s and 1970s, that an open, liberal international financial order would help them gain foreign support to finance internal and external deficits because of the dominant structural power of the United States within such an order. Britain supported liberalization in part because of its "lagging" hegemonic commitment to London's position as an international financial center, a commitment derived from its past as a financial hegemon in the nineteenth century. In contrast, Japan's financial liberalization reflected the "leading" behavior of a financial power on the rise, a lead that was encouraged by Japan's sudden emergence as the world's largest creditor, its special relationship with the United States, and a domestic cycle of financial deregulation, innovation and competition.

Second, a competitive deregulation dynamic also explains liberalization in Britain, the other European Community countries, and Scandinavia. It had also driven the U.S. decision in 1981 to permit the establishment of IBFs, as was discussed in the preceding chapter. The mobility of financial capital was behind the dynamic. When one state began to deregulate and liberalize its financial markets, other states were forced to follow its lead if they hoped to remain competitive in attracting footloose funds and financial business. The United States and Britain were the leaders of the competitive deregulation movement. Their unilateral moves to support the Euromarket and their liberalization and deregulation decisions in the 1970s and 1980s prompted other states to "retaliate" with similar deregulatory decisions in the 1980s, which led to the unraveling of the restrictive Bretton Woods financial order.

The third political explanation was the policy shift from embedded liberal to neoliberal frameworks of thought. Although the shift took place at different rates of speed in different advanced industrial countries, it had common roots. In part, it reflected a growing skepticism about the practicality of embedded liberal ideas in a world of global finance, particularly after the economic crises described in Chapter 6. The neoliberal focus on efficient financial intermediation appealed to those concerned with issues of competitive deregulation. The shift was also the result of two broader trends: the economic slowdown of the 1970s and 1980s, which undermined confidence in embedded liberal ideas; and the growing strength of a coalition of private financial interests, multinational industrial firms, and financial officials who supported financial openness.[91]

91. Pringle (1989:17) argues that financial liberalization was also encouraged by the emergence of "a new class of internationally mobile individuals" in professions, businesses and international organizations—a group similar to the "transnational managerial class" that Cox (1987:359–68) argues became an important social force in the advanced industrial countries in the 1970s and 1980s. See also Moran 1991:130.

CHAPTER EIGHT

Weathering International
Financial Crises

As has been demonstrated in Chapters 4–7, states proved important to the globalization of financial markets by providing market operators a greater degree of freedom and by refraining from the introduction of more effective controls. Equally important, however, is the role that states have played in preventing major international financial crises. Crises such as that in 1931 can quickly bring about the collapse of an open international financial system, for in their wake, private financial operators tend to retreat to the safety of more familiar domestic markets to avoid the currency risks involved in international investment and the uncertainties of predicting how states will treat foreign assets.[1] States may also be tempted to introduce stringent controls during and after a major crisis, thus reinforcing this market behavior. If the crisis provokes severe capital flight, for example, states might suddenly decide that the benefits of introducing a system of tight exchange controls are larger than the costs, as did Japan and many central European countries in 1931. Because it brings economic disruption and instability *simultaneously* to each state, a major international financial crisis can also encourage collective action aimed at controlling capital movements.

This combination of likely market and state responses to major international financial crises makes their prevention a central task for those hoping to preserve an open, liberal international financial

1. See, for example, Spero 1989:129.

order.[2] There is considerable agreement among academic specialists that financial systems are endogenously prone to periodic crises as a result of imperfect information and the mobile, liquid nature of capital.[3] States can, however, minimize the likelihood of crises by initiating regulatory and supervisory activities to discourage overly risky financial practices in the private markets. More important, small financial panics can be prevented from turning into major crises through the existence of a lender of last resort who preserves confidence by extending emergency credit.[4]

Before the 1930s, there had been little discussion among central bankers or financial analysts of the need for these activities at the international level. Financial regulation and supervision was still regarded as a primarily national activity. Similarly, Charles Kindleberger notes that as late as the 1920s, "the doctrine [of lender of last resort] as developed from Henry Thorton (1802) and Walter Bagehot (1873) was thought of exclusively in national terms."[5] The 1931 crisis caused a dramatic change of attitude, however. Its international dimension led financial analysts to conclude that the maintenance of financial stability in the future would require international action—in particular, there was a need for an international lender of last resort.[6]

Despite this new thinking, there was little discussion of the need for international financial regulation, supervision, or lender-of-last-resort activities at the 1944 Bretton Woods Conference. This reflected the general skepticism of the participants concerning global financial markets. Except for capital controls, the IMF's Articles of Agreement did not establish any mechanisms for handling international financial crises.[7] Indeed, the fear of international financial crises was one reason the authors of the Bretton Woods Agreement discouraged the reemergence of global financial markets. Only in the proposals of the American bankers had attention been given to the task of preventing such crises. The bankers emphasized the need to

2. See also Bryant 1987:153 and Spero 1980.
3. Baltensperger and Dermine 1987:70–71; Guttentag and Herring 1983:5–6; 1986, and Goodhart 1985. See Minsky 1982 for a more elaborate thesis concerning why financial systems are prone to crisis.
4. See, for example, Dale 1984, Eichengreen and Portes 1987, Guttentag and Herring 1983, Kindleberger 1978, and Minsky 1982.
5. Kindleberger 1988:44.
6. Kindleberger 1989:215.
7. Kindleberger 1987b:57.

preserve global financial stability through close central bank cooperation within the BIS. The statutes of the BIS, however, because they were a product of the pre-1931 era, did not include mechanisms by which lender-of-last-resort action, regulation, and supervision might be conducted at the international level. Although the bankers prevented the implementation of the Bretton Woods resolution calling for the abolition of this institution, its statutes thus did not provide specific guidelines for action.

When international financial markets began to reemerge after the late 1950s, policymakers were thus forced to innovate in response to crises that erupted in the markets. This chapter examines how states successfully handled three major international financial crises: the 1974 banking crisis, the 1982 debt crisis, and the 1987 stock market crash. Several of the points raised in the preceding four chapters help to explain states' willingness to play this key role in the globalization process. The discussion also focuses on another development that proved to be important: the consolidation of an increasingly sophisticated regime among BIS central bankers to handle international financial crises.

The 1974 International Banking Crisis

The first major test of the resolve of states to prevent an international financial crisis came in May 1974 with the threatened collapse of the Franklin National Bank in the United States. Although the Franklin was a small bank, its troubles—which stemmed largely from imprudent foreign exchange speculation—sent shock waves throughout the nascent international banking system.[8] Banks that held deposits in or had outstanding foreign exchange contracts with the Franklin bank could not be sure that they would see their money again; others worried that the Franklin's troubles might trigger further collapses in associated banks. Compounding the crisis initially was uncertainty concerning whether American authorities would be prepared to bail out foreign creditors of the U.S. bank and, more broadly, whether any state's lender-of-last-resort functions would be extended to the new offshore Eurodollar market.

The threatened collapse was prevented from becoming a full-

8. Guttentag and Herring 1986:19.

fledged international financial crisis by (1) decisive action by the Federal Reserve; and (2) the close cooperation of foreign central banks in G-10 countries. First, the Federal Reserve acted quickly to assume the role of international lender of last resort. It arranged a large loan for the Franklin National Bank but put no restrictions on the use of these funds for the Franklin's foreign branches in London and Nassau, the Bahamas.[9] The Federal Reserve also bought the Franklin's book of foreign exchange contracts, thus guaranteeing that they would be fulfilled, and it initiated extensive efforts to find a buyer for the bank, which culminated in its sale in October. The Fed was concerned that the collapse of the Franklin Bank would, as the vice-president of the Federal Reserve Bank of New York put it, "tarnish the reputation of United States banks in general."[10] In a period when U.S. officials were hoping that American banks would assume a major role in recycling OPEC financial surpluses, the maintenance of their sound reputation was essential. The Fed also worried that the crisis would undermine confidence in the dollar and in the American financial system, a confidence that was crucial given the increasing reliance of the United States on international financial support to fund its economic imbalances.[11]

In addition to sharing crucial information with the Federal Reserve, foreign central banks in G-10 countries agreed at a May 1974 BIS meeting to defend the dollar collectively against speculation. They also cooperated with the Federal Reserve to try to find a purchaser for the Franklin National Bank. The Bank of England was also central in arranging collateral for the Federal Reserve loan to the Franklin's London branch and helped to close the branch as part of the October sale.[12] Just as American bankers had hoped in the 1940s, cooperation among central banks was greatly facilitated by the BIS. Its monthly meetings, along with the cooperation developed under its auspices during the 1960s in the management of offsetting financing networks, had resulted in what Joan Spero has described as "a close personal network and high degree of consultation among central bankers" that proved to be key to their actions in this period.[13]

9. Spero 1980:129.
10. Richard Debs quoted in Spero 1980:114.
11. Spero (1980:114) notes the concerns of U.S. officials about confidence in the dollar.
12. Spero 1980:147–49, 150–52.
13. Spero 1980:153.

After the 1974 crisis, the BIS also served as a forum for discussions concerning the creation of more formal arrangements aimed at preventing future crises. In September 1974, the BIS central bankers issued a communiqué declaring, "The governors had an exchange of views on the problem of lender of last resort in the Euromarket. . . . They were satisfied that means are available for that purpose and will be used if and when necessary," thus implying that they had reached a specific agreement on the allocation of lender-of-last-resort responsibilities to banks operating in international markets.[14] The statement in fact represented only a fairly general agreement, but Jack Guttentag and Richard Herring note that it did much to restore confidence in the international markets.[15] Indeed, for months after the Franklin crisis, foreign exchange trading and Euromarket activity remained sharply below their precrisis levels and smaller banks were squeezed out of the crucial international interbank market.[16] The need for some clarification of lender-of-last-resort responsibilities had also been made apparent by the collapse of the German Herstatt Bank in June 1974, when the Bundesbank had chosen not to repay the bank's international creditors immediately. The decision almost caused the U.S. bank-clearing system to collapse. Guttentag and Herring note that the Bundesbank's action in closing the bank "seemed to have been taken without regard for international transactions."[17]

In addition to discussing international lender-of-last-resort responsibilities, the BIS central bankers—prompted by the Bank of England—established a committee in the autumn of 1974 to study jurisdictional responsibilities concerning international bank supervision. The Standing Committee on Banking Regulations and Supervisory Practices was chaired by an official of the Bank of England and given a secretariat in the BIS. It brought together bank supervisory officials from the G-10 countries, Luxembourg, and Switzerland for the first time since World War II. By December 1975, these

14. Quoted in Spero 1980:155.
15. Guttentag and Herring 1985:31. For a discussion of the exact contents of the agreement, see Dale 1984:178–79 and Spero 1980:154, 156–58, 168–69.
16. Spero 1980:112–16.
17. Guttentag and Herring 1985:26. West German authorities closed the bank at the end of the business day, after deutsche mark payments had been made *to* Herstatt but before corresponding dollar payments had been received *from* Herstatt. The bank's international creditors were finally paid off after they had taken complicated legal action (Spero 1980:112). For a discussion of the problems the decision caused for the U.S. bank-clearing system, see Lepetit 1982:252.

officials had reached an agreement, the Basel Concordat, which included a set of jurisdictional rules governing regulatory and supervisory activities in international banking markets. Host countries were given supervisory responsibility for the liquidity of foreign branches of banks and the solvency of foreign subsidiaries and joint ventures, on the assumption that they would likely have better information on such operations. Home governments were given responsibility for the solvency of their banks' foreign branches since this was linked so closely to the solvency of the head office.[18] Spero notes that in addition to establishing these specific guidelines, the bank supervisors' committee created "an international network of high-level supervisory authorities who know each other well, trust each other, and are able to communicate confidentially with each other." This network constituted "an informal but important international early warning system for international banking."[19]

These various initiatives arising out of the 1974 crisis represented important steps in the consolidation of a regime designed to minimize the collective action problems arising from international lender-of-last-resort activity and bank supervision.[20] The origin of the regime could be said to have dated back to the creation of the BIS in 1930. The bank's statutes set forth the basic principle that would guide the regime: encouragement of central bank cooperation for the purpose of maintaining global financial stability.[21] They also established important decision-making procedures and rules of the regime, such as the requirements that the BIS Board of Directors meet at least ten times a year and that no government officials except central bank governors serve as directors, thus enhancing the board's independence.[22] Like the initiatives taken in 1974–75, the BIS itself was the product of an atmosphere of crisis in the late

18. Guttentag and Herring 1983:15, Spero 1980:159–66, and Dale 1984:172–73.

19. Spero 1980:164. See also the comments of Robert Gemmill in Eichengreen and Portes (1987:61).

20. For discussions concerning the collective action problems involved in maintaining global financial stability, see Dale 1984, Guttentag and Herring 1983:11–16, Kapstein 1989, Bryant 1987:chap. 8, and Spero 1980:185.

21. For the statutes, see Schloss 1958:146–60. Article 3 states that a key object of the bank is "to promote the cooperation of central banks." The Experts' Plan of 1929, which recommended the establishment of the bank, stated that this cooperation "was essential to the continuing stability of the world's credit structure" (quoted in Schloss 1958:58). The body had, of course, also been established for the specific task of handling German reparations payments.

22. Articles 32 and 31, respectively.

1920s. As one of its founders, American banker Owen Young, noted in 1929, "Either it [the international financial order] must break down or it must be improved, and drastically."[23] Although the BIS lost influence after 1931 and was almost abolished after the Bretton Woods Conference, it regained international prominence in the wake of the dollar crisis of 1960, which prompted European central banks to invite officials of the Federal Reserve System to attend BIS meetings and led to the central bank swap arrangements. The 1974 crisis encouraged a consolidation of this nascent regime with the establishment of the Basel committee and the rules concerning international regulation, supervision, and lender-of-last-resort activities.

The 1982 International Debt Crisis

An international debt crisis was triggered by the Mexican government's declaration of its imminent default in August 1982. The root of the crisis was the large lending by Western banks to developing countries, especially in Latin America, after the oil shock in the 1970s. From the borrowing countries' standpoint, these loans were attractive because they provided a cheap means of external financing with little conditionality. From the banks' standpoint, loans to countries such as Argentina, Mexico, and Brazil were a useful means of rapidly turning over their petrodollar deposits; they also looked likely to be repaid because these countries were rapidly industrializing. The immediate cause of crisis was a global macroeconomic shock that could not have been foreseen by either the banks or the borrowers: Volcker's deflationary policy in 1979–82. The effect of the sudden shift in U.S. economic policy was that real interest rates on bank loans suddenly jumped from an average of 0.8 percent in 1971–80 to 11.0 percent in 1982. At the same time, the recession in the advanced industrial countries caused commodity prices to collapse and severely reduced export markets for manufacturers from the developing countries. The ability of debtors to service their debts was also diminished because banks suddenly became more hesitant to make new loans in order to roll over past debts. The debtor countries' foreign exchange reserves were further eroded by the flight of capital from uncertain economic prospects, high tax burdens, and overvalued currencies in this period.

23. Quoted in Costigliola 1972:604.

The debt crisis broke when Mexico's finance minister, Jesus Silva Herzog, telephoned officials in the Reagan administration and the IMF on August 12, 1982, to inform them that Mexico was no longer able to service its debts. With more than $80 billion owed to major banks around the world, Mexico was in a financially vulnerable position that had the potential of triggering a major crisis in international financial markets. As one Mexican official correctly pointed out, the crisis was not just a problem for Mexico—it "was everybody's problem."[24] International financial officials realized that a default by Mexico might soon be repeated by other major Latin American debtors such as Brazil and Argentina. Because many of the largest Western private banks had extended loans to Latin American countries worth well over 100 percent of their total capital, these combined defaults would be catastrophic. As stated in a Federal Reserve Bank of New York study published later, "International bankers and policymakers faced a threat of financial disorder on a global scale not seen since the Depression."[25]

The Mexican crisis—like the crisis in 1974—was handled by a combination of U.S. leadership and BIS central bank action. Within two days of Silva Herzog's distress call, the United States had organized a $1 billion loan to Mexico in the form of an advance payment for oil destined for the U.S. strategic oil reserve. This money was supplemented by a $1.85 billion bridging loan from BIS central banks to the Bank of Mexico, of which the United States contributed approximately half. Federal Reserve Chairman Paul Volcker led the effort to organize both stabilization packages; Bank of England governor Gordon Richardson played a pivotal role in coordinating the actions of BIS central bankers.[26] With the immediate liquidity crisis solved, Federal Reserve officials organized a meeting on August 20 between representatives of the major private banks and Mexican financial officials, at which the latter demanded and were granted a temporary suspension of further payments. Again, Volcker provided leadership in encouraging the private banks to accept this decision and to organize their rescheduling negotiations with Mexico. The U.S. government also made clear to the Mexican government that no rescheduling agreement could be reached with the banks unless it

24. Angel Gurria quoted in Kraft 1984:3.
25. Quoted in Spero 1990:181.
26. Kraft 1984:10. See also Volcker's comments in Volcker and Gyohten 1992:201, 203.

first accepted a tough IMF austerity and restructuring program designed to restore the confidence of foreign creditors. By late August, it looked as though such an agreement would be reached in time for the meetings of the IMF and World Bank in Toronto in early September.[27]

The crisis seemed temporarily under control. But on September 1, in his valedictory address to the Mexican Parliament before handing over power to the newly elected president, Miguel De La Madrid, Mexican President José López Portillo dropped a bombshell. With very little warning even to his own advisers, he launched a harsh attack on the entire international financial order including, by inference, the IMF:

> The financing plague is wreaking greater and greater havoc throughout the world. As in Medieval times, it is scourging country after country. It is transmitted by rats and its consequences are unemployment and poverty, industrial bankruptcy and speculative enrichment. The remedy of the witch doctors is to deprive the patient of food and subject him to compulsory rest. Those who protest must be purged, and those who survive bear witness to their virtue before the doctors of obsolete and prepotent dogma and of blind hegemoniacal egoism.[28]

At the same time, López Portillo announced his decision to, in effect, ignore the IMF's orthodox advice by nationalizing the banking system and introducing a system of exchange controls in order to prevent capital flight, which totaled approximately $30 billion between 1978 and 1982.[29] He argued that controls were needed on "a group of Mexicans . . . led and advised and supported by the private banks who have taken more money out of the country than the empires that exploited us since the beginning of time."[30]

Because it raised the possibility of default, López Portillo's speech created an atmosphere of panic at the meetings of the IMF and World Bank a few days later. As Walter Wriston later described it, "We had 150-odd finance ministers, 50-odd central bankers, 1000 journalists, 1000 commercial bankers, a large supply of whiskey and a reasonably small city that produced an enormous head of steam

27. Kraft 1984:21, 23, 28–29.
28. Quoted in Kraft 1984:39.
29. Maxfield 1990:111.
30. Quoted in Kraft 1984:39.

driving the engine called 'the end of the world is coming'."[31] López Portillo's moves also frightened Mexican asset holders, stimulating more capital flight. Indeed, the size of this flight capital was so great that it threatened the stability of Mexican banks and, as Volcker pointed out, "brought the complex and automated international clearing machinery to the edge of breakdown, threatening confidence in the entire system."[32] Collapse was prevented only by Volcker's release of large amounts of the BIS bridging loan to Mexican banks on the condition that they require their depositors—mostly other banks—to pledge not to withdraw additional funds.[33]

López Portillo's sudden moves were the product of an internal struggle within the Mexican government. As Sylvia Maxfield points out, Mexican economic policymaking had long been divided into two competing "policy alliances" of government and societal groups.[34] These were similar to the neoliberal and embedded liberal coalitions existing throughout the advanced industrial world, as described in previous chapters. A "bankers' alliance" consisted of private bankers, large corporations, and financial officials who favored more orthodox and laissez-faire policies. Opposed to them was the "Cárdenas alliance" comprising labor, peasants, and their allies in the Mexican government who favored the nationalist, interventionist policies propounded by "structuralist" economists throughout Latin America who had in fact been strongly influenced by Keynesian thought.[35] Each group had held considerable power throughout the 1970s, but the 1982 crisis forced López Portillo to side decisively with one or the other, a choice not unlike that faced by Mitterrand in 1982–83 and Callaghan in 1976. López Portillo's own views leaned toward those of the Cárdenas camp. Earlier in the year, for example, he had appointed a group to study more radical approaches to handling the impending crisis. The group had concluded that exchange controls and bank nationalization were needed to restore a degree of national autonomy from international financial market forces; attention had been given in particular to Mitterrand's 1981 bank nationalization program. After López Portillo had been "infuriated" by reports of businesses and banks withdrawing enor-

31. Quoted in Kraft 1984:40.
32. Volcker and Gyohten 1992:204.
33. Volcker and Gyohten 1992:204–5; Kraft 1984:41.
34. Maxfield 1990.
35. Palma 1978:906.

mous sums from Mexico in August, he threw his weight behind this radical strategy and appointed one of its authors, Carlos Tello, as central bank governor in charge of implementing it.[36]

López Portillo's decision plunged the government into chaos. When De La Madrid, a more conservative thinker whose career had begun in the central bank, made clear that he would reverse the strategy on assuming office, the presidential succession was suddenly brought into question and rumors circulated of "troop movements and assassinations" and even a coup d'état.[37] Bankers, business leaders, and conservative leaders within the government strongly opposed the new measures, arguing persuasively that it would be very difficult to make capital controls effective given Mexico's 2,000-mile border with the United States.[38] On September 11, López Portillo backed down, having become "resigned to an IMF accord," and he approved the reopening of negotiations with the IMF.[39] Although Tello continued to fight the "neoliberals" to obtain "an anti-IMF agreement," a deal was struck with the IMF in early November.[40] When the De La Madrid administration took office on December 1, Tello was replaced by his conservative predecessor as head of the central bank and exchange controls were quickly dropped.

With the Mexican government finally onside, the U.S. government and the IMF focused on pressuring the private banks to commit new funds to Mexico as part of the stabilization packages. These funds were forthcoming from the large banks that were heavily exposed to the debtors, but Federal Reserve officials and U.S. bank regulators had to pressure the hundreds of smaller banks that were less inclined to throw good money after bad. Volcker also convinced foreign central bankers and bank regulators to push their banks to participate in the loan payment rescheduling and new lending activity.[41] When the banks had advanced enough funds, the IMF loan was finally approved and the funds were released.[42] The Mexican packages served as the model for other debtor countries after 1982. When

36. Maxfield 1990:143–46.
37. Kraft 1984:40. For De La Madrid's views, see Maxfield 1990:152.
38. Maxfield 1990:75, 146–48; Kraft 1984:38. Interestingly, President Lázaro Cárdenas had chosen not to introduce exchange controls in the early 1930s partly for this reason (Maxfield 1990:72, 75).
39. Kraft 1984:44.
40. Tello quoted in Maxfield 1990:11 and Kraft 1984:45.
41. Lissakers 1991:206–7; Kraft 1984:48–50.
42. Volcker and Gyohten 1992:206.

short-term liquidity crises struck Brazil, Argentina, and some of the other Latin American debtors in 1983–84, the United States and the BIS central banks offered these countries short-term bridging loans in return for an agreement to participate in rescheduling and adjustment programs backed by the private banks and the IMF.

Although many bankers and policymakers initially compared the 1982 debt crisis with the financial crisis of 1931, it was clear by the mid-1980s that the debt crisis would not produce a major international financial collapse. Four explanations can be given for the different outcomes of these two crises. First, creditor governments were able to act much more effectively in the early 1980s than in 1931 in part because they were able to call upon existing institutions—the IMF and the BIS—to facilitate their cooperation.[43] Second, the United States also provided leadership in the early 1980s, whereas in 1931 it showed little interest in doing so, despite holding a dominant international financial position in both eras. The most important reason for the decisive U.S. action in the early 1980s was the extreme vulnerability of the American financial system to the crisis, given that American banks held by far the largest proportion of the debt. By contrast, in the early 1930s, thousands of individual American bondholders held European and Latin American debt, and their losses did not threaten the collapse of the U.S. financial system.[44]

Third, whereas in 1931 the major debtors in central Europe, Japan, and Latin America chose default over adjustment, in the early 1980s Latin American governments perceived the costs of default to be much higher. The strong stance of Western governments suggested to Mexico that default might be met with Western trade sanctions and seizure of assets. Moreover, in the early 1980s (but not in 1931), debtors owed money to the same banks that had provided them with short-term trade credits; they thus risked serious financial disruption of foreign trade if they defaulted.[45] Faced with the prospect of being cut off from the world economy, the debtors balked, as

43. An institutional approach that also proved helpful was the case-by-case rescheduling method developed by Western governments belonging to the Paris Club during the 1960s and 1970s (Griffith-Jones 1988). For a broader argument about the importance of institutionalization, see Pfister and Suter 1987.

44. Lipson 1986:224–25, Fishlow 1986:83, and Eichengreen 1991:163–64. For the importance of the failure of U.S. leadership in triggering the 1931 financial crisis, see Kindleberger 1973.

45. Eichengreen 1991:163. Kaletsky (1985) argues, however, that the debtors exaggerated the costs of default.

had British and French policymakers in 1976 and 1982–83 when they had contemplated the repercussions of tight exchange controls. As Silva Herzog pointed out, "it [default] didn't make any sense. We're part of the world. We import 30 per cent of our food. We can't just say 'Go to Hell'."[46]

A fourth explanation for the different outcomes of the two crises is the ascendancy of neoliberal frameworks of thought in both creditor and debtor countries in the early 1980s. The neoliberal orientation of the Reagan administration, as reflected in its enthusiasm for orthodox stabilization programs,[47] can be contrasted with President Franklin Roosevelt's rejection of liberal orthodoxy in the early 1930s. Similarly, the growing interest in neoliberal ideas among Latin American policymakers in the 1980s made them more willing to accept IMF austerity and liberalization programs after 1982 than were debtors in the 1930s, who were rapidly abandoning the orthodoxy of the pre-1931 period. In Latin America, as in the advanced industrial world, this neoliberal shift was encouraged by the economic crisis of the 1980s, which undermined support for prevailing structuralist theories. Neoliberalism also found particular support among bankers, internationally oriented business leaders, and financial officials who strongly influenced government policy during the debt crisis.[48]

The ascendancy of neoliberalism in both creditor and debtor countries was also important in that it precluded alternative mechanisms for resolving the debt crisis. López Portillo's left-wing advisers had hoped that Mexico's debt crisis could be eased by regulatory action to curtail and repatriate capital flight, much as West European governments had hoped to do during the exchange crisis of 1947. The private assets of many Latin American countries were almost equal to and in some cases exceeded their respective external debts; therefore, a compulsory repatriation of capital flight, aided by the cooperation of creditor countries, represented a possible alternative mechanism for resolving the crisis to some. American economist David Felix, one of the more active proponents of such a strategy,

46. Kraft 1984:4. Some observers have said that in the early 1980s (but not in 1931), the major debtors perceived the crisis as temporary for the first few years and believed that they might return to international financial markets if they behaved as "good" debtors (Griffith-Jones 1988; Fishlow 1986:83; Kaufman 1990; Felix 1990:759).

47. Kahler 1990 and Fishlow 1986.

48. On the importance and dynamics of the ascendancy of neoliberalism in Latin America, see Biersteker 1992, Kahler 1990, Ocampo 1990, and Nelson 1990:12.

explained that "foreign asset mobilization would distribute the burden of adjustment to the debt crisis over the rich and the poor more
equitably than the IMF-imposed programs."[49] With neoliberal ideas
in the ascendancy, however, this interventionist approach stood little
chance of being implemented. More orthodox economists than Felix
stressed, as they had in 1947, that "capital flight ought to be viewed
as a symptom of underlying economic problems, rather than as the
source of the problem," and debtors were advised by bodies such as
the BIS "to put their house in order" if they wanted to repatriate
capital flight.[50] Debtor governments, with the exception of the López
Portillo government in 1982 and the Alan García administration in
Peru in 1987, did not strongly challenge this interpretation.[51] As
Susan Strange notes, the refusal of creditors and debtors to consider
regulatory action to halt and reverse Latin American capital flight
can be seen as an important "non-decision" in the history of the
debt crisis and of the globalization of finance.[52]

The 1982 debt crisis, like the 1974 crisis, was a catalyst for the
further strengthening of the emerging supervisory and regulatory regime in international banking. In particular, the crisis focused the
attention of bank regulators on the need for healthy capital-asset
ratios in international banking. Following the crisis, Volcker was
instrumental in encouraging the Basel-based bank supervisors' committee to initiate discussions on international standards for bank
capital adequacy.[53] When discussions in the BIS ended in disagreement over the question of how to measure capital, it fell to the
United States and Britain to push for an agreement. In September
1986, representatives of the Federal Reserve and the Bank of England began talks that resulted in a bilateral agreement on bank capital adequacy standards in January 1987. Other BIS central bankers
worried that they might be excluded from the important New York
and London markets unless they adopted the new standard, and by
December an agreement had been reached within the Basel committee (and formally signed in July 1988) that committed all banks su-

49. Felix 1985:51. For other discussions of regulatory action that could have been
taken against capital flight, see Diaz-Alejandro 1984; Henry 1986; Williamson and Lessard 1987:139, 143, 196, 238–42; and Naylor 1987. For a comparison with the period
1947–48, see Helleiner 1992a.
    50. Quotations from Cumby and Levich 1987:51 and BIS 1984:171.
    51. See Maxfield 1992 for the Peruvian case.
    52. Strange 1990:264.
    53. Kapstein 1989:333.

pervised by BIS central banks to move toward a common 8 percent risk-adjusted capital-asset ratio by the end of 1992.[54] Even before its formal implementation, this agreement is said to have had "a rapid and profound effect on the psychology of senior bankers"; it served as "an important instrument in forcing more discipline into the banking markets."[55]

The 1982 debt crisis also encouraged a trend toward securitization in international financial markets. Banks sought to supplement their declining profits with off-balance-sheet activity in securities markets, and corporations found borrowing in capital markets to be less expensive than borrowing from the troubled banks. The securitization trend in the 1980s was strengthened by technological changes, the volatility of interest rates and exchange rates, and the emergence of Japanese creditors who preferred to deal in securities markets. The growth of international securities trading had important implications for international financial stability. In the 1970s and early 1980s, efforts to contain and prevent international financial crises had concentrated only on international banking markets. The new securities markets were equally vulnerable to crises, however.

The 1987 Stock Market Crash

The vulnerability of securities markets was brought home by the 1987 global stock market crash. The crisis stemmed largely from a loss of market confidence in the sustainability of the large economic imbalances between advanced industrial states that had become evident by the late 1980s. As described in Chapter 7, America's unilateral economic expansion after 1982 and the dollar's rise produced large American current account deficits. Although they were financed by foreign private capital, by the mid-1980s, the deficits had begun to worry U.S. policymakers, as well as those in Western Europe and Japan, because protectionist sentiment was growing in the United States. In September 1985, the major industrialist countries signed the Plaza Agreement, in which they agreed to try to reduce the U.S. current account deficit by encouraging the dollar to fall.[56]

54. See Kapstein 1989:1992.
55. Quotes from R. Preston and R. Waters, "Banks Aim for Stability and a Level Playing Field," *Financial Times*, December 31, 1992; and from the IMF's 1992 edition of *International Capital Markets*, reprinted in *IMF Survey*, November 9, 1992, pp. 345–46.
56. On the importance of protectionist pressure in leading to the Plaza Agreement, see Funabashi 1988:15–16.

Policymakers in the Reagan administration hoped that, as in the past, a falling dollar would not only improve the U.S. trade position but would also encourage foreigners to bear the main burden of adjusting to the U.S. external deficit. By "talking down the dollar," they hoped both to devalue the U.S. external debt and indirectly to prompt foreign governments to begin expansionary policies that would help reduce the U.S. deficit without requiring the United States to arrest its growth.[57]

Although the U.S. strategy was initially successful, it began to run into trouble in early 1987 as private investors, anxious about their growing losses and the lack of improvement in the U.S. current account position, began to pull out of U.S. investments. Fearing an uncontrollable collapse of the dollar, the United States agreed in February 1987, under the Louvre Accord, to defend the dollar jointly with foreign central banks and to reduce its budget deficit, which was seen abroad as the key source of the U.S. trade deficit.[58] This did little to calm the markets, however. Japanese investors, in particular, continued to make sharp reductions in their U.S. investments. By August and September 1987, Japan was in fact a net importer of capital for the first time since the early 1980s.[59] Although central bankers filled the financing gap by making enormous purchases of dollars, both they and the market operators became increasingly nervous, for the United States had shown little sign of acting to reduce its budget deficit.

In mid-October, stock markets around the world collapsed. The immediate catalyst for the collapse was a very public disagreement over the optimal course of global adjustment between the West German finance minister and the U.S. Treasury Department secretary. The publication of an unexpectedly high U.S. trade deficit figure also contributed to the collapse. It began in Tokyo and rapidly spread around the world, demonstrating the new interconnectedness of global securities markets. The stock market crash also eroded confidence in other international financial markets, as evidenced by the considerable retreat from the Euromarket and other cross-border investment positions.[60] The immediate crisis, however, proved tempo-

57. Kawasaki 1993; Funabashi 1988:4; Henning 1987:35; Destler and Henning 1989:51.
58. Funabashi 1988:180; Destler and Henning 1989:59.
59. Helleiner 1989:347.
60. Davis 1989:App. 1; B. Riley, "Home Looked Safest," *Financial Times*, October 14, 1988.

rary because BIS central banks acted quickly to pump liquidity into the securities markets to prevent the collapse of any major securities houses. In addition, the Japanese Ministry of Finance instructed the four principal Japanese securities firms to halt the Tokyo stock market's fall. This appeared to help stabilize markets worldwide. One observer commented that the global crash had both "started and stopped in Tokyo."[61] The markets were still jittery, but two actions calmed them somewhat in the following months. In late 1987, the Reagan administration and Congress (having been prodded by the crash) agreed to reduce the budget deficit by $23 billion. In January 1988, aggressive central bank action in defense of the dollar convinced market operators that the major economic powers were once again serious about cooperation.

The crash demonstrated Japan's growing financial power. Japan's new creditor status made the United States and other countries highly dependent on Japanese capital exports. The liberalization and deregulation of Japan's financial system had also increased the international prominence of its financial markets and institutions. Because Tokyo's stock market had become increasingly incorporated in world markets and because of its growing size, foreign financial analysts were forced to follow its movements more closely; by the late 1980s, it accounted for a larger share of world stock market capitalization than the New York stock market. The growing international importance of Japan's financial institutions had been demonstrated only two months before the crash, when a syndicate of Japanese banks helped the Bank of America out of its financial difficulties by purchasing a significant share of its subordinated debt. In 1988, Japanese financial institutions occupied the top twenty-five positions in one ranking of the size of the world's financial institutions measured by market capitalization.[62]

Japan could not be said to have replaced the United States as the hegemonic financial power in the world economy in the late 1980s, however. The dollar was still the world's dominant currency, and U.S. financial markets (in particular the Treasury bill market) were still the most attractive to international investors because of their unique deregulated, liquid, and sophisticated nature.[63] But the 1987

61. Murphy 1989:73.
62. The ranking was compiled by the magazine *Euromoney*. Helleiner 1992c:41–42.
63. For a broader discussion of the limitations of Japan's financial power, see Helleiner 1992c, b.

crash did demonstrate Japan's willingness to act as a financial leader. As was true of its sudden interest in financial liberalization in the 1980s, this "leading" hegemonic behavior partly reflected its creditor position, which gave it a strong interest in global financial stability. Japan's broader economic and security dependence on the United States also encouraged it to take a special interest in restoring that country's financial stability following the crash.[64]

Whereas the 1974 and 1982 crises had been catalysts for the establishment of a regime of supervision and regulation to prevent future international banking crises, the 1987 stock market crash also focused attention on the need to extend that regime to international securities markets. Some action had been taken on this front before the crash. The U.S. Securities and Exchange Commission had begun to press in the mid-1980s for coordinated international securities regulation in order to reduce the opportunities for fraud and to prevent the lack of regulation abroad from decreasing the competitiveness of U.S. markets.[65] One body through which it pursued this goal was the International Organization of Securities Commissions (IOSCO), created in 1974 (under a different name) to bring together securities regulators from the Americas to encourage the development of securities markets in Latin America. In 1984, however, the United States pressed successfully for it to be transformed into a global forum of securities regulators with a permanent secretariat in Montreal.[66] In 1986, the body adopted a U.S.-sponsored declaration committing members to the sharing of information. Two months before the crash, its technical committee, comprised of top-level officials of the world's most important securities regulatory bodies, met for the first time to discuss international regulatory cooperation.[67] The crash was a key catalyst for further action. One IOSCO document states that it "highlighted the potential capital exposure of securities firms to developments in those markets and the need for all markets to have an adequate regulatory structure for the prudential supervision of securities firms."[68] As their banking counterparts had

64. Kazuhide 1991:24. In this sense, Japan's "reactive" style of foreign economic policymaking (Calder 1988) encouraged it to exercise leadership behavior during the 1987 crash.

65. Porter 1992b:11.

66. For a discussion of its organizational structure, see Guy 1992:292. By 1990, it had members from at least fifty countries.

67. Guy 1992:294; Porter 1992b:10–12. The membership consisted of the G-7 countries plus Sweden, the Netherlands, Switzerland, Hong Kong, and Australia.

68. IOSCO 1989:8.

in the banking field, American and British securities regulators took the lead in pressing for regulatory action. Both signed bilateral memorandums of understanding to encourage the sharing of information and the enforcement of securities regulations in cooperation with other West European countries, Canada, and Japan.[69] Tony Porter notes that Britain and the United States were parties to almost all of the thirty-one bilateral agreements that by 1991 had been signed between securities regulators around the world.[70] In addition to monitoring these agreements, in 1988 IOSCO initiated discussions on the need to impose minimum capital-asset ratios on all securities companies to match those agreed to by the banking community in December 1987. The BIS bank supervisors' committee pressed for and helped guide these discussions because it worried that market operators might try to use securities markets to evade the new banking standards. Beginning in 1988, it convened joint meetings with G-10 securities regulators and urged the creation of a new global forum for consultation and cooperation among securities and banking supervisors.[71]

The regime supportive of global financial stability was also strengthened by several other initiatives in the 1980s. The Basel Concordat was revised one year after the 1982 Banco Ambrosiano crisis, in which the Italian government had refused to come to the rescue of an Italian bank's subsidiary in Luxembourg. Supervisory responsibility for the solvency of foreign subsidiaries was given to both host and home governments (instead of only the former) by the adoption of a principle of consolidated supervision. Supervisory responsibilities were also expanded to cover bank holding companies. Porter notes that these changes strengthened and expanded internal reporting mechanisms at bank head offices after 1983.[72] The weaknesses in this supervisory system were exposed by the closing of the Bank of Credit and Commerce International in July 1991, however, prompting the bank supervisors' committee to issue in July 1992 a set of new "minimum standards" for supervision. International

---

69. *Financial Times*, February 8 and November 15, 16, 1988. Several of these bilateral memorandums were signed before the crash.

70. Porter 1992b:13.

71. Porter 1992a:6; 1992b:14. The 1988 BIS annual report called for such a global forum. See also *Financial Times*, April 5 and October 5, 1991; *Economist*, October 26, 1991, p. 95. Such a forum had not been created by mid-1993. The negotiations concerning a common capital-asset ratio for securities companies had also not been successfully completed by this date.

72. Porter 1992a:9. On these changes, see also Hart 1989:99 and Dale 1984:174–78.

banks would now be supervised on a consolidated basis by their home authority, which would have the right to obtain information on the banks' operations from foreign authorities. Banks wishing to operate abroad would also be required to receive the prior consent of both the home and host countries.[73] Throughout the 1980s, an effort was also made to encourage non-BIS members (in particular the loosely regulated offshore financial centers) to adopt the Basel Concordat. A clause was inserted in the revised 1983 Concordat permitting BIS bank supervisors to prevent their banks from operating in jurisdictions considered to be improperly supervised. This clause, as well as more direct pressure from the BIS, encouraged supervisors from seventy-five countries outside the G-10 to endorse the Basel Concordat in 1984.[74] When the "minimum standards" were issued by the BIS committee in July 1992, non-BIS members were also strongly encouraged to adopt them by the fact that under the standards, host governments were permitted to prohibit foreign banks from operating in their markets if the banks' home supervisors did not uphold them.[75]

Those who discount the importance of states in the globalization of finance ignore the extent to which international financial markets have proven vulnerable to major crises that could have quickly brought about a collapse of the emerging open international financial order. States have prevented such crises through international lender-of-last-resort activities as well as international regulation and supervision. A number of the explanations for state behavior that have appeared in the four previous chapters were also important in explaining the willingness of states to perform these functions.

To begin with, the U.S. leadership during the 1974 and 1982 crises, as well as in encouraging the building of the BIS-centered regime, provides further evidence of its enthusiasm for the globalization process and once again stemmed largely from its dominant position in the emerging open financial order. This position gave it both the power and the desire to prevent major international financial crises. The power of the United States to act as international lender-

73. *Financial Times*, October 23, 1992.
74. Porter 1992a:7–8; Bryant 1987:146. Pressure to adopt the concordat was exerted at several international conferences convened by the BIS committee in the late 1970s and early 1980s, to which were invited bank supervisory authorities from countries outside the G-10.
75. *Economist*, July 11, 1992, pp. 72–74.

of-last-resort during the 1974 and 1982 crises stemmed primarily from its authority over U.S. banks, which remained the most important private financial institutions in international markets well into the 1980s.[76] Its leadership in international regulatory and supervisory discussions also reflected the global importance of U.S. private financial institutions, in addition to that of U.S. financial markets (as was evident in the capital-adequacy negotiations in the 1980s). This central position of U.S. banks and financial markets in the emerging international financial order, as well as the importance of the dollar, also provided the United States with a strong interest in maintaining the stability of that order.

The leadership exercised by Britain and Japan in attempting to preserve global financial stability in this period reflected a similar pattern of "hegemonic" behavior by these two states as that outlined in previous chapters. In assuming a leadership role in consolidating the BIS regime (as well as in assisting the United States during the first two crises), the Bank of England demonstrated the same "lagging" hegemonic behavior that had characterized Britain's promotion of globalization since the 1960s. The bank sought not only to stabilize the global markets on which London's position as an international financial center depended, but also to continue the tradition of British financial leadership that dated back to the late nineteenth century. As one of the bank's key negotiators of the capital adequacy standards agreement noted in 1990, "Britain's reputation in many areas has declined. But the two things in which we have not lost our international prestige are the monarch and the Bank of England."[77] Japan's key role during the 1987 stock crash illustrated its "leading" hegemonic behavior as a rising financial power in the 1980s. As was true of its rapid liberalization in that decade, this "lead" was encouraged both by its rapid acquisition of overseas assets and by its special relationship with the United States.

The behavior of the U.S. and Latin American states during the debt crisis was also influenced by the ascendance of neoliberal frameworks of thought in finance. Neoliberal ideas became prominent in Latin American countries for many of the same reasons that they had in advanced industrial countries in this period: the economic slowdown undermined support for existing economic para-

76. See Spero 1980 for the 1974 crisis and Strange 1987:569 for the 1982 crisis.
77. Sir George Blunden quoted in David Lascelles, "Discreet Charm of the Bank," *Financial Times*, March 5, 1990.

digms and neoliberal thinking found strong support among bankers, internationally oriented business leaders, and financial officials. The political difficulties associated with following alternative policies, such as regulating capital movements more effectively or defaulting on loans, in the increasingly integrated world economy and open international financial order also persuaded many Latin American policymakers of the need to follow the advice of neoliberal advocates.

Finally, the important role played by the central banks of the major advanced industrial states in cooperating to prevent financial crises in this period was facilitated by the growing strength and sophistication of the BIS-centered regime. The construction of this regime was a long process that had its roots in developments described in previous chapters, such as the creation of the BIS in 1930 and the emergence of offsetting financing networks in the 1960s. In the wake of the three major crises in the 1970s and 1980s, increasingly specific norms, rules, and decision-making procedures were established concerning lender-of-last-resort, regulatory, and supervisory activities in order to prevent further crises. These provisions greatly assisted central banks in cooperating by altering expectations, making information available, and institutionalizing patterns of cooperation. Equally important, they did much to alter market behavior and instill confidence among private operators by demonstrating the seriousness with which financial officials were attempting to handle potential problems. Still, the regime's strength should not be overstated. It was focused only on the narrow task of preserving global financial stability through lender-of-last-resort, regulatory, and supervisory activities. A more comprehensive regime attempting to prevent financial crises would also have dealt with key issues such as international macroeconomic and exchange rate coordination. Certain provisions established by the regime, such as the rules governing lender-of-last-resort activities, also remained fairly general, and potentially quite unclear.[78]

Although the BIS regime was designed to maintain the increasingly open, liberal international financial order, it did so by means of a limited reregulation of global financial markets. The capital adequacy standards, for example, effectively halted one aspect of the competitive deregulation dynamic by imposing a set of harmonized

78. Kapstein 1989:330.

regulations on international bankers. Whereas the Bretton Woods financial order represented an "anti-market" type of regulation, the regulations of the BIS regime were a "pro-market" type of regulation designed to prevent financial crises.[79] Indeed, the central bankers who built the regime had always been more skeptical than other neoliberal supporters of claims that the international financial markets would operate smoothly and efficiently without any regulation. This replacement of anti-market regulation with pro-market regulation was not the only way in which the world of Bretton Woods had been turned upside down. The very institution around which the regime was centered, the BIS, was supposed to have been liquidated under the Bretton Woods Agreement. Its prominence in the 1970s and 1980s certainly proved wrong those at Bretton Woods who had argued that "the day of central banks was gone and any cooperation based on these banks could not lead to anything."[80]

79. Phil Cerny made this helpful distinction in discussions at the two panels on international finance at the meetings of the International Studies Association in Atlanta, Georgia, April 1992.
80. Schloss 1958:120.

PART III

CONCLUSION

CHAPTER NINE

Explaining Differing State
Behavior in Trade and Finance

CHAPTERS 2–8 SUMMARIZED THE POLITICAL HISTORY OF THE globalization process. An important question remains and is addressed here: Why have states embraced an open, liberal financial order in a period when they have retained numerous restrictive trade practices? The different state behavior in trade and finance in recent years could be presented as evidence that the globalization phenomenon in finance is in fact "beyond politics." Given protectionist tendencies with regard to trade, the globalization of finance might seem to have taken place only because states have been unable to resist it when faced with market and technological pressures. Since one objective of this book has been to refute this argument, it is necessary to provide some convincing explanations of why state behavior in finance has been so different from that in trade. These explanations should also have broader theoretical relevance for the field of international political economy. As Roger Tooze and Craig Murphy have recently argued, the study of international trade has to date been relatively "privileged" in that field, for many of its theoretical models and concepts have been developed for the specific purpose of explaining developments in the trade sector in the 1970s and 1980s.[1] But because state behavior in finance has been different from that in trade, some of these theoretical models and concepts may need to be reevaluated. In particular, the explanations of this difference may

1. Tooze and Murphy 1991:15–16, 25–26.

prove helpful to wider IPE debates concerning the ability of states to create and maintain open, liberal international economic orders.

Of the five explanations for the differing state behavior in trade and finance which are given here, four point to contrasts between the two sectors; the fifth concerns their interrelationship.

Differing Collective Action Dynamics

The first explanation is that the collective action problems involved in creating and maintaining an open, liberal international economic order in trade were much less significant in finance because of the unique mobility and fungibility of money. To begin with, for an open financial order to emerge, it was not necessary for states collectively to obey liberal rules, as is assumed to be the case in the trade sector. An open order could be created if a single state or group of states unilaterally provided resourceful financial market operators with a degree of freedom. By supporting the Euromarket in the 1960s, for example, Britain and the United States were able unilaterally to tilt what Susan Strange calls the "balance of power" between state and market in international finance in favor of the market.[2]

States also did not experience collective action problems in liberalizing capital controls because a primary benefit of financial openness was the ability of a state to attract footloose global capital and financial business to its own territory. This benefit was "consumed" through unilateral rather than collective action. Therefore, few risks were associated with unilateral liberalization, nor were many specific relative gains to be obtained by retaining controls. By contrast, in trade, the "consumption" of the primary benefit of an open order—access to foreign markets—requires that foreign states reduce or eliminate their trade barriers. Trade liberalization thus lends itself naturally to "free-riding" behavior and "prisoner's dilemma" problems that did not arise in the process of financial liberalization. Indeed, unilateral financial liberalization and deregulation constituted what John Plender has called a state's "mercantilist" strategy to maximize its own benefits from the open system at other

2. Strange 1986:26.

states' expense.[3] As markets became increasingly globalized and liberalization took place in the major centers, states found themselves pitched in a war of competitive deregulation in which they sought, as one observer put it, "to dismantle protectionist financial regimes in order to secure a stake in the emerging global financial marketplace."[4] Such policies not only would bring employment, tax revenue, and foreign exchange benefits that accrue to global financial centers but would enhance the "pulling power" of a state's own markets to attract global funds that could finance national budget and current account deficits. Moreover, as Michael Moran notes, there were also "benefits of prestige" in the international arena for states that housed global financial centers.[5] Whereas heightened competition for market share encouraged interventionist policies in trade, it thus fostered liberalization in finance because states had to respond to what Richard Dale calls the "unusual sensitivity to regulatory differentials between financial centers" of market operators.[6]

This competitive deregulation dynamic in fact made the gradual unraveling of the restrictive Bretton Woods financial order very likely. If one major state or group of states unilaterally departed from the order and initiated a process of liberalization and deregulation, the others would feel obliged to follow. In the postwar period, the United States and Britain demonstrated the power of such unilateral action. Their liberalization moves also promoted an open financial order more directly by providing resourceful market operators an extra degree of freedom. With individual states able to promote the emergence of an open financial order unilaterally in these direct and indirect ways, it was difficult to prevent the eventual erosion of the restrictive Bretton Woods financial order unless some means could be devised to guard against such unilateral liberalization moves. The collective action problems in finance were thus the opposite of those in trade. They concerned the maintenance of a closed financial order rather than the creation of an open one. In particular, states would be tempted to derive the benefits of a closed financial order (such as increased policy autonomy and more stable exchange rates), while "free riding" by unilaterally liberalizing their markets to gain advantages for their national financial systems.

3. Plender 1986–87:41.
4. Dale 1992. See also Dale 1984:21.
5. Moran 1991:6. See also Pauly 1988:176.
6. Dale 1984:40.

If policymakers did not encounter collective action problems in *creating* an open, liberal financial order, they also did not encounter them in *maintaining* an open system in finance in the same way as in trade. To maintain an open trading order, it is necessary to find some way to prevent states from moving toward closure by increasing their tariff barriers. Because of the difficulties of controlling finance, however, regulatory moves to achieve closure could hope to be successful only if states used either total exchange controls or cooperative controls. The postwar experience showed that neither option was likely to be chosen. As became clear in the late 1970s and early 1980s, states were unlikely to move *unilaterally* toward closure because of the enormous economic and political costs associated with the imposition of tight exchange controls.[7] More effective *cooperative* strategies for controlling finance could be easily vetoed by a major state or group of states, as the United States demonstrated in the late 1940s and the early 1970s, and Britain and Switzerland did in 1980. Indeed, because cooperative initiatives were the most effective means to achieve closure, the collective action dynamics in finance were once again the reverse of those in trade. Rather than making it difficult to maintain an open order, they made it difficult to create a closed one in finance. This dynamic suggests that openness, not closure, is more likely to be the normal condition in international finance.

Central Bankers as a Nascent Transnational Epistemic Community

Although collective action problems did not exist in the same way in finance as in trade, they were still present with respect to the activities necessary to prevent financial crises, such as lender-of-last-resort, supervisory, and regulatory action.[8] As was discussed in the preceding chapter, one way these problems were overcome in the 1970s and 1980s was through the consolidation of a regime centered around the Bank for International Settlements. Why was con-

---

7. Even supporters of such a strategy, such as Glyn (1986:45), acknowledge that such controls would be "draconian." Duvall and Wendt (1987:45) also emphasize these costs in explaining why states have not controlled international finance to the same extent as international trade.

8. See references in note 33 in Chapter 1.

solidation of such a regime possible, and in a period when the post-war trading regime appeared to be less strong? One key reason is that as a group, central bankers, unlike trade officials, have much in common with what Peter Haas has called "transnational epistemic communities."[9]

As Haas has argued, members of such communities hold in common "a set of principled and causal beliefs" as well as "shared notions of validity and a shared policy enterprise," which foster cooperative action in the international political arena.[10] Although central bankers do not fit this description entirely, they do so to a greater extent than do trade officials. With respect to principled beliefs, trade officials do not always agree on the need for free trade, but there has rarely been any controversy among central bankers concerning the need to preserve international financial stability. Indeed, even the general population has viewed international financial stability as a relatively uncontroversial public good. In terms of causal beliefs, central bankers have also long agreed that cooperation among themselves is essential to maintaining this stability.[11] Fred Hirsch has observed that central bankers see themselves as "joined in a kind of international fraternity" committed to this task.[12] As a result of these common principled and causal beliefs, central bankers have a long history of common policy projects.[13] Indeed, the BIS was created by central bankers in 1930 with the goal of fostering such cooperative projects. The BIS annual report in 1935 explained that the institution was designed to encourage "frequent meetings, visits, incessant exchange of information, common consultation and joint discussion" of international financial problems.[14] Almost invariably, common policy projects among central bankers have been prompted by a major financial crisis.[15] The BIS was created in response to the financial chaos of the late 1920s. Similarly, its revival in the 1960s was prompted by the 1960 dollar crisis. Each of the initiatives to

9. Indeed, Haas (1992:7n6) cites Robert Russell's (1973) study of central bank cooperation in the 1960s in support of his general argument concerning the importance of transnational epistemic communities.

10. Haas 1992:16.

11. Kapstein 1992:284.

12. Hirsch 1967:219.

13. Kapstein 1992:267.

14. Quoted in Schloss 1958:68.

15. Kapstein (1989:328; 1992:268) also points to the importance of crises in this respect.

strengthen the BIS regime came in the wake of three major crises—
in 1974, 1982, and 1987.

If members of a community do not share "notions of validity,"
common policy projects will flounder. In the 1920s, although central
bankers agreed in principle on the need for cooperation, the absence
of what Barry Eichengreen calls a "common conceptual framework"
undermined their ability to cooperate effectively.[16] Indeed, one of
the most important early goals of the BIS was "to evolve a common body of monetary doctrine and assure the widest possible measure of common agreement on monetary theory, problems and practice."[17] Central bankers found this goal easier to attain than did
trade officials for three reasons. First, because the issues of international finance were seemingly more complex, there were higher
"barriers to entry" into the field, and central bankers around the
world had a somewhat similar education and background.[18] Second,
the accrual of shared notions of validity was facilitated by the long
tenure of central bankers compared with that of trade officials.
Third, the collective experience of past international financial crises
emphasized common lessons for central bankers around the world.
The crisis of 1931, in particular, convinced central bankers almost
everywhere of the need for lender-of-last-resort action. Ethan Kapstein also notes that the 1974 crises produced a "paradigmatic
change" in the attitude of banking officials throughout the advanced
industrial world.[19] In sum, as Paul Volcker puts it, central bankers
"are almost uniquely able to deal with each other on a basis of close
understanding and frankness" because of their common "experience, tenure, and training." In explaining the role of central bankers
during the debt crisis, he recalls that "certainly, we didn't have to
spend a lot of time explaining to each other the nature of this emergency."[20]

The epistemic community model does not fully explain central
bank behavior. Kapstein has pointed out that for central bankers to
constitute a fully functioning transitional epistemic community, they
would have to develop a more "substantial body of consensual theo-

16. Eichengreen 1992:263. See also Clarke 1967.
17. The BIS annual report of 1935 is quoted in Schloss 1958:64.
18. The BIS annual report noted in 1935 that "central banks (like national public
health services) have a community of similar technical interests" (quoted in Schloss, 1958:
63).
19. Kapstein 1989:328.
20. Volcker and Gyohten 1992:201.

retical and empirical knowledge on international banking" and would have to be guaranteed that they could act independently of domestic political pressures.[21] The argument made here is simply that central bankers interact in a more cooperative manner than do trade officials in part because they resemble a transnational epistemic community more closely than do trade officials. Moreover, as Kapstein argues, "if central bankers are not yet an epistemic community, they are becoming increasingly like one."[22]

Differing State Power and Interests in Trade and Finance

Of equal importance to the unique nature of central bank interaction in explaining the strength and influence of the BIS regime was (as Kapstein has emphasized) the leadership of the United States and Britain in encouraging its consolidation.[23] These two states also compensated for the regime's weaknesses by acting as lenders of last resort during the 1974 and 1982 crises. More broadly, they have promoted the globalization phenomenon through regulatory action since the 1960s. In the 1980s, these two states were joined by Japan, which has increasingly exercised leadership in preserving global financial stability. The special leadership of these three states had little equivalent in the trade sector in this period.

The leadership of the United States is best understood as a product of its hegemonic position in global finance. In contrast to its declining position in world trade, the United States retained a central position in global finance well into the 1980s as a result of its structural power within the emerging open global financial order. This power derived from the size of its economy, the relative attractiveness of its financial markets, and the prominence of its financial institutions and the dollar within this order. As proponents of the hegemonic stability theory predict, this dominant position gave the United States not only the capability but the desire to promote an open, liberal international financial order.[24] Its desire to act as a financial leader, however, stemmed not so much from a goal of wanting to provide an international public good as from the objective of

21. Kapstein 1992:268.
22. Kapstein 1992:267–68.
23. Kapstein 1992.
24. See, for example, Krasner 1976.

using the open financial order to maintain its policy autonomy in the face of growing internal and external constraints. From the 1960s to the 1980s, American officials recognized that the United States could utilize its dominant position in the open, liberal international financial system to encourage foreigners both to finance and to bear the burden of adjustment to its growing current account and fiscal deficits. That America has been more willing to promote an open, liberal order in finance than in trade in recent years is thus a reflection of the fact that its hegemonic position in finance has lasted longer than that in trade.[25] Indeed, the former was used to compensate for difficulties arising from the decline of the latter.

The leadership of Britain and Japan in finance can also be understood by applying a slightly modified version of the hegemonic stability theory. The British interest in financial openness can be viewed as an extreme example of what Stephen Krasner has called "lagging" hegemonic behavior. A declining hegemonic power may continue, in the absence of a severe crisis, to be locked into a policy of promoting openness that dates from its hegemonic days.[26] In Britain's case, the lag was attributable to the continuing strength in British politics of a nexus consisting of the Bank of England, the Treasury, and the City of London stemming from Britain's past as a financial power in the late nineteenth century.[27] Although the crisis of 1931 and the Great Depression forced these groups to reorient their interests in accordance with a protected sterling bloc, they remained committed to maintaining London's position as an international financial center.[28] When the viability of a closed sterling bloc was seriously threatened in the late 1940s, they once again became champions of an open, liberal international financial order. Although a similar lag existed in British trade policy in the early twentieth century, the lag in finance proved politically sustainable after 1945 because the Euromarket provided London with a mechanism by which to regain its leading position in international finance.

25. This pattern repeats the experience of formerly hegemonic states, such as Britain in the late nineteenth century and the Netherlands in the eighteenth century (Wallerstein 1980).

26. Krasner 1976:341–43. See also Moran 1991:6.

27. Ingham 1984.

28. Even Labour's 1945 nationalization of the Bank of England was what Strange (1971:231–32) has referred to as "an act of almost total irrelevance to policy. It did not affect the working of the Bank nor its relation to the government; the role of the City in the national economy was unchanged."

Japan's leadership in the 1987 stock market crash, as well as its sudden financial liberalization drive in the 1980s, is an example of the opposite phenomenon. As a rising financial power, it was demonstrating hegemonic behavior in advance of having attained a hegemonic position in finance. A somewhat similar dynamic might be said to have existed in Japanese trade policy, but it was more pronounced in finance for three reasons. First, Japan quickly acquired an interest in global financial stability because its financial rise was accompanied by a rapid and enormous accumulation of external financial assets. Second, Japan's economic and security-related dependence on the United States gave it a strong incentive to support global financial openness and stability to ensure smooth bilateral relations, especially after the United States began to press strongly for Japanese financial liberalization in the 1980s. Finally, the domestic cycle of financial deregulation, competition, and innovation that began in the late 1970s encouraged liberalization to proceed more rapidly than it otherwise might have.

The Low Domestic Political Visibility of Financial Liberalization

The fourth explanation for the difference between state behavior in trade and finance is the low domestic political visibility of the issue of financial liberalization relative to that of trade liberalization. None of the decisions made to liberalize capital movements in the 1970s and 1980s were subjects of significant domestic debate among politicians and the general public, whereas such debate regularly takes place concerning trade liberalization decisions. This difference permitted advocates of neoliberal approaches to economic policy more autonomy to encourage liberalization in finance than in trade.

The issue of financial liberalization had a low domestic political visibility in part because of the highly technical and seemingly complex nature of international financial issues. International financial matters, unlike trade issues, rarely attract the attention of the general public and politicians except in the event of a major crisis such as that in the early 1930s.[29] Policymaking in this area is thus dominated to a large degree by financial specialists in government. As we

29. Krause 1971:535; Bertrand 1981:15, 17–18, 21; Bryant 1987:152–53; Kapstein 1989:332; Krasner 1978:65; and Duvall and Wendt 1987:46.

have seen, many of these specialists became increasingly enthusiastic proponents of neoliberal approaches to finance in the 1970s and 1980s. Some embraced neoliberal ideas when confronted with the political difficulties involved in maintaining the embedded liberal policy framework in an era of globalization. Others found their faith in embedded liberal ideas shaken by the stagflationary environment of the 1970s and 1980s, and they were attracted to the new framework of thought being actively put forward by important neoliberal intellectuals such as Hayek and Friedman in this period.[30] The growing international links between financial officials in this period also provided an important channel through which neoliberal ideas were spread.

The ability of financial officials to influence the policy agenda in the international financial arena without significant domestic constraints has been remarked upon by several observers. Kenneth Dam and George Shultz learned during their own experience in the U.S. government during the international monetary reform talks in the early 1970s that "even businessmen and economists in government defer to international monetary specialists in a way they would never defer on issues of fiscal policy or domestic monetary policy."[31] Similarly, Louis Pauly has observed that when the liberalization of capital controls was taking place in Australia, the traditional left of the Labour party, who might have been expected to oppose the move, "remained preoccupied with other issues" and "never really fully mastered the technical details of an arcane subject matter."[32] In Sweden, Robert Taylor also has reported that Bengt Dennis, the central bank governor who pushed strongly for the abolition of capital controls, was surprised that the move did not cause much domestic controversy.[33]

A second reason for the low domestic political visibility of the issue of financial liberalization is that no specific popular social group was directly affected in a negative way by the liberalization of capital movements, as is true of the liberalization of trade. Although

30. Indeed, Friedman (1953:179–80) had predicted back in 1953 that a "a few modern inflations" might "establish a climate" in which the neoliberal message might be received more sympathetically. See also Hall 1989:390–91.

31. Dam and Shultz 1977:109. See also Odell 1982:347.

32. Pauly 1987a:83, 94.

33. Robert Taylor, "Riksbank Governor Turns Revolutionary," *Financial Times*, June 29, 1989.

financial liberalization had important effects on the general public (as Keynes and White had made clear), its potentially negative impacts were at the macroeconomic level and were therefore less visible. As Raymond Bertrand has observed, "It is obvious that the pursuit of the liberalisation of capital movements generates less conflict and less ardour than the maintenance of free trade. The reason is that trade restrictions have quick and visible effects on jobs and profits, whereas the impact of restrictions on capital flows is invisible to the public, and quite often a matter of great uncertainty for the specialists."[34]

Indeed, the domestic political dynamics associated with financial liberalization were the reverse of those associated with the liberalization of trade. Trade liberalization is generally controversial because the costs in terms of lost jobs are readily visible and they are borne by concentrated populations, whereas the benefits in terms of lower consumer prices are less tangible and more dispersed. Financial liberalization arouses less controversy because the kinds of costs discussed at Bretton Woods are dispersed at the macroeconomic level, whereas it provides direct benefits to specific individuals or groups operating at the international level. Indeed, we have seen that representatives of multinational corporations and large financial institutions did in fact strongly promote financial liberalization in this period in order to remove cumbersome controls on the cross-border movement of money as their operations became increasingly international. A 1990 report from the United Nations Conference on Trade and Development summed up these differing domestic political dynamics associated with liberalization in finance and trade:

> [The] costs of financial openness (loss of policy autonomy, increased financial instability, etc.) being collective are anonymous in their incidence, whereas the benefits accrue to particular economic agents (especially international financial and non-financial enterprises, and rentiers). Political pressure by the latter for financial opening therefore does not meet significant resistance. By contrast, in the field of trade, it is the costs of restrictiveness that are borne collectively, and the benefits accrue to particular groups.[35]

34. Bertrand 1981:21.
35. UNCTAD 1990:112.

Liberal Trade and Liberal Finance: Uneasy Bedfellows

Although the first four explanations of the differing state behavior in trade and finance have focused on distinctions between the two sectors, the final explanation points to a direct relationship between the two phenomena. It is important to remember that the postwar commitment to capital controls stemmed not just from an embedded liberal ideology but also from a desire to defend the postwar liberal trading order and the stable exchange rate system from speculative capital movements. Perceiving an inherent conflict between liberalism in finance and the Bretton Woods trading and monetary orders, policymakers in the early postwar years chose to sacrifice liberalism in finance. But when policymakers began to encourage an open, liberal financial order in the 1970s and 1980s, this set of priorities was increasingly turned upside down. In the early 1970s, they found that financial openness was becoming incompatible with the Bretton Woods exchange rate system. More important for the purposes of this chapter, the postwar liberal trading order also proved increasingly difficult to maintain in the face of large-scale and often volatile international capital movements.

This was clearly demonstrated after 1982, when enormous flows of capital into the United States pushed up the value of the dollar, leading to a decrease in American competitiveness and to demands within the United States for protectionist trade policies. As Keynes had put it in earlier years, capital movements were forcing "painful" and "violent" adjustments in trading patterns that in turn were "strangling" open trade rather than "facilitating" it.[36] By the late 1980s, many were asking, as had Keynes and White, "whether free trade is antithetical to capital liberalization."[37] One Bank of England official noted that "We have freed the capital side of the balance-of-payments equation at the expense of doing the opposite on the current account of goods and services."[38] The experience of the 1980s also led many to emphasize that capital controls had facilitated rapid trade growth in the early postwar period. As one financial journalist put it, "the [postwar] 'golden era' of trade expansion was

36. For references to quotes, see notes 39 and 40 in Chapter 2.
37. Quote from Richard Levich (1988:218).
38. Quoted in Hamilton 1986:237. See also Gilpin 1987:367, Hamada and Patrick 1988:130, McMahon 1985:180, Wojnilower 1986, and Tobin in Patrick and Tachi 1986:121.

possible only because the regime governing capital flows was so il-liberal."[39]

The movement toward an open, liberal financial order in an era of considerable trade protectionism thus cannot be explained solely by differences between finance and trade. Also important is the consideration that the elements of a liberal international economic order may not necessarily be compatible. As Albert Bressand points out, free market principles in different sectors of the international economy "are assumed to be mutually coherent. But they are not. The various 'invisible hands' now at work in the world economy can often be seen to be working against each other."[40]

That the globalization of finance could take place in an era of considerable trade protectionism is *not* evidence that the process is somehow beyond the control of the states. Rather, it could occur because of differing state behavior with regard to trade and finance, for which five explanations have been given. First, the mobility and fungibility of money ensured that the collective action problems associated with the creation and maintenance of an open, liberal trade order were less relevant to the financial sector. Second, cooperation between states in finance was facilitated because central bankers have much in common with transnational epistemic communities. Third, the power and interests of three key states—the United States, Britain, and Japan—in finance and in trade differed. Fourth, the issue of financial liberalization had a lower domestic political visibility among politicians and the general public than did that of trade liberalization. Fifth, developments in the financial and trade sectors are directly related; states have found it difficult simultaneously to maintain both a liberal financial order and a liberal trading order.

These five explanations are useful to an understanding of states' different behavior in the trade and financial sectors in recent years. They also help to illuminate three broad theoretical issues concerning the ability of states to create and maintain open, liberal international economic orders. First, three of the explanations suggest that IPE scholars should become more aware of the importance of sector-specific features in analyzing the ease with which states can create and maintain such orders. Studies of trade relations have per-

39. *Financial Times*, October 25, 1987, quoted in Bienefeld 1989:36.
40. Bressand 1983:761. See Winham 1988:660 for a similar point.

suaded many scholars that their creation and maintenance will be hampered by collective action problems. The unique mobility and fungibility of money, however, ensured that collective action problems were in fact reversed in finance: an open financial order was created as a result of unilateral action and competitive pressures, whereas attempts to create and maintain a closed order encountered collective action problems. In the one area where cooperation was essential for openness—the prevention of major financial crises— cooperation was relatively successful in part because of the characteristics of the key actors concerned, central bankers. The low domestic political visibility of the issue of financial liberalization also ensured that liberalization would prove easier in this sector than in trade because those favoring liberalization had relative autonomy to pursue their goals. In sum, sector-specific considerations, such as the nature of the commodity, the characteristics of the key actors, and the political visibility of the issue concerned, strongly influence the likelihood that states will successfully create and maintain an open liberal order in different sectors of the international economy. Although such considerations work against the creation and maintenance of such an order in trade, they make its realization relatively easy in finance.

Second, the special support provided by the United States, Britain, and, more recently, Japan for the globalization process lends considerable strength to the view that hegemonic states are important for the creation and maintenance of open international economic orders. The financial case also makes clear, however, that the theory of hegemonic stability needs to be modified in several ways. The enduring power of the United States in finance into the 1980s, in contrast to its declining power in trade, highlights the importance of rejecting versions of the theory that do not break down the concept of hegemony by sector.[41] The desire of the United States to foster the globalization process also reflected a less benevolent motive—the preservation of policy autonomy—than that described in some variants of the theory.[42] In addition, to understand the special willingness of Japan and Britain to promote an open, liberal international financial order, allowance must be made for leads and lags in state behavior.

Third, the difficulties associated with reconciling policies of free trade and free finance suggest that IPE scholars must be very cau-

---

41. See also, Keohane 1980.
42. Krasner (1976) is an important exception.

tious in using the term "liberal international economic order" to describe the structure of the entire international economy at any given moment. The creation of a more liberal international trading order in the early postwar years was likely facilitated by the existence of the restrictive Bretton Woods financial order. Similarly, trade protectionism in the 1970s and 1980s may have been encouraged by the emergence of a more liberal international financial order. These incompatibilities between different elements of a liberal international economic order suggest that the term is best used only to describe a pattern of economic relations in a single sector of the international economy rather than a pattern of economic relations in the international economy as a whole.

Works Cited

Official Sources

Arthur Burns Papers, Ford Presidential Library, Ann Arbor, Michigan, Boxes 33, 34, 55, 65, 74.

Bank for International Settlements. 1984. *Fifty-Fourth Annual Report.* Basel: BIS.

European Commission. 1990. "One Market, One Money." *European Economy*, no. 44, special issue (October).

International Monetary Fund. 1972. *Summary and Proceedings*, Annual Meeting. Washington, D.C.: IMF.

———. 1974. *International Monetary Reform: Documents of the Committee of Twenty.* Washington, D.C.: IMF.

International Organization of Securities Commissions. 1989. *Capital Adequacy for Securities Firms.* United Kingdom: Royle City.

League of Nations. Economic, Financial, and Transit Department. 1944. *International Currency Experience: Lessons of the Interwar Period.* Princeton, N.J.: Princeton University Press.

Organization for Economic Cooperation and Development. 1966. Working Party Three. *Balance of Payments Adjustment Process.* Paris: OECD.

———. 1971. "OECD's Code for Liberalisation of Capital Movements." *OECD Observer* 55: 38–43.

———. 1978. *Regulations Affecting International Banking Operations*, Part 1. Paris: OECD.

———. 1981a. *Controls on International Capital Movements: Experience with Controls on International Portfolio Operations in Shares and Bonds.* Paris: OECD.

——. 1981b. *Regulations Affecting International Banking Operations*, Part 2. Paris: OECD.

——. 1982. *Controls on International Capital Movements: The Experience with Controls on International Financial Credits, Loans, and Deposits.* Paris: OECD.

——. 1984. *International Trade in Services: Banking.* Paris: OECD.

——. 1987a. *International Trade in Services: Securities.* Paris: OECD.

——. 1987b. *Introduction to the OECD Codes of Liberalization.* Paris: OECD.

——. 1987c. *Structural Adjustment and Economic Performance: A Synthesis Report.* Paris: OECD.

——. 1991. "Liberalization of Capital Markets and Financial Services in the OECD Area." *Financial Market Trends* (June).

Organization for European Economic Cooperation. 1954. *Fourth Annual Report of the Managing Board.* Paris: OEEC.

——. 1957. *Seventh Annual Report of the Managing Board.* Paris: OEEC.

——. 1961. *Liberalisation of Current Invisibles and Capital Movements.* Paris: OEEC.

United Nations Conference on Trade and Development. 1990. *Trade and Development Report, 1990.* New York: United Nations.

U.S. Congress. House. 1947. Committee on Foreign Affairs. *Emergency Foreign Aid. Hearings.* 80th Cong., 1st sess.

U.S. Congress. Senate. 1948a. Committee on Foreign Relations. *European Recovery Program. Hearings.* 80th Cong., 2nd sess.

U.S. Congress. House. 1948b. Committee on Foreign Affairs. *United States Foreign Policy for a Postwar Recovery Program. Hearings.* 80th Cong., 2nd sess.

U.S. Congress. 1963a. Joint Economic Committee. *Hearings.* 88th Cong., 1st sess.

U.S. Congress. 1963b. Joint Economic Committee. *Hearings, Part 2.* 88th Cong., 1st sess.

U.S. Congress. 1963c. Joint Economic Committee. *Hearings, Part 3.* 88th Cong., 1st sess.

U.S. Department of State. 1948. *Proceedings and Documents of the UN Monetary and Financial Conference.* Washington, D.C.: Government Printing Office.

U.S. Government. 1954a. *Majority Report, Commission on Foreign Economic Policy: Report to the President and the Congress.* Washington, D.C.: Government Printing Office.

U.S. Government. 1954b. *Minority Report, Commission on Foreign Economic Policy.* Washington, D.C.: Government Printing Office.

U.S. Government. 1973. *Economic Report of the President Transmitted to Congress, January 1973.* Washington, D.C.: Government Printing Office.

U.S. National Archives. General Records of the Department of Treasury. Record Group 56: Bretton Woods, Atlantic City Conference; Records of the National Advisory Council on International Monetary and Financial Problems; Records of the Assistant Secretary (H. D. White).

Books and Articles

Adams, Thomas, and Iwoa Hoshii. 1972. *A Financial History of the New Japan.* Tokyo: Kodansha International.

Aldrich, Winthrop. 1943. *The Problems of Postwar Monetary Stabilization.* Address to the American Section of the International Chamber of Commerce (April). Pamphlet.

——. 1944. *Some Aspects of American Foreign Economic Policy* (September). Pamphlet.

Alerassool, Mavash. 1989. "United States Freezing of Iranian Assets, 1979–87." Ph.D. diss., London School of Economics.

Allen, Chris. 1989. "The Underdevelopment of Keynesianism in the Federal Republic of Germany." In *The Political Power of Economic Ideas: Keynesianism across Nations,* edited by Peter Hall. Princeton, N.J.: Princeton University Press.

Al-Muhanna, Ibrahim. 1988. "The World System in Transition: Technology and Transnational Banking." Ph.D. diss., American University.

Altman, Oscar. 1969. "Eurodollars." In *Readings in the Eurodollar,* edited by Eric Chalmers. London: Griffith and Sons.

American Bankers Association. 1943. *The Place of the United States in the Postwar Economy.* New York: ABA.

——. 1945. *Practical International Financial Organization.* New York: ABA.

——. 1968. *The Costs of World Leadership: An Analysis of the U.S. Balance of Payments Problem.* New York: ABA.

Anderson, Benjamin. 1943. *Postwar Stabilization of Foreign Exchange: The Keynes-Morgenthau Plan Condemned.* New York: Economists' National Committee on Monetary Policy.

Aronson, Jonathan. 1977. *Money and Power: Banks and the World Monetary System.* London: Sage.

Baltensperger, Ernst, and Jean Dermine. 1987. "The Role of Public Policy in Ensuring Financial Stability: A Cross-Country Comparative Perspective." In *Threats to International Financial Stability,* edited by Alexander Swodoba and Richard Portes. Cambridge: Cambridge University Press.

Banuri, Tariq, and Juliet Schor, eds. 1992. *Financial Openness and National Autonomy.* Oxford: Clarendon Press.

Bark, Dennis, and David Cress. 1989. *A History of West Germany.* Vol. 1, *From Shadow to Substance, 1945–63.* Oxford: Basil Blackwell.

Barry, Norman. 1989. "The Political and Economic Thought of German Neo-Liberals." In *German Neo-Liberals and the Social Market Economy,* edited by Alan Peacock and Hans Willgerodt. London: Macmillan.

Bauchard, Pierre. 1986. *La Guerre des deux roses: Du Rêve à la réalité, 1981–1985.* Paris: Grasset.

Benn, Tony. 1989. *Against the Tide: Diaries, 1973–1976.* London: Hutchison.

Bernholtz, Peter. 1989. "Ordo-Liberals and the Control of the Money Supply." In *German Neo-Liberals and the Social Market Economy,* edited by Alan Peacock and Hans Willgerodt. London: Macmillan.

Bernstein, Edward. 1984. "Reflections on Bretton Woods." In *The International Monetary System; Forty Years after Bretton Woods*. Conference Series no. 28. Boston: Federal Reserve Bank of Boston.

Bertrand, Raymond. 1981. "The Liberalization of Capital Movements: An Insight." *Three Banks Review* 132: 3–22.

Beyen, Johan. 1951. *Money in a Maelstrom*. London: Macmillan.

Bienefeld, Manfred. 1989. "The Lessons of History and the Developing World." *Monthly Review* (July/August): 9–41.

Biersteker, Thomas. 1992. "The 'Triumph' of Neoclassical Economics in the Developing World: Policy Convergence and Bases of Governance in the International Economic Order." In *Governance without Government: Order and Change in World Politics*, edited by James Rosenau and Ernst-Otto Czempiel. Cambridge: Cambridge University Press.

Block, Fred. 1977. *The Origins of International Economic Disorder*. Berkeley: University of California Press.

Bloomfield, Arthur. 1946. "The Postwar Control of International Capital Movements." *American Economic Review* 36: 687–709.

——. 1950. *Capital Imports and the American Balance of Payments, 1934–39: A Study in Abnormal Capital Transfers*. Chicago: University of Chicago Press.

——. 1954. *Speculative and Flight Movements of Capital in Postwar International Finance*. Princeton, N.J.: Princeton University Press.

——. 1959. *Monetary Policy Under the International Gold Standard, 1880–1914*. New York: Federal Reserve Bank of New York.

——. 1968. "Rules of the Game of International Adjustment?" In *Essays in Money and Banking in Honour of R. S. Sayers*, edited by Charles Whittlesey and John Wilson. Oxford: Clarendon Press.

Borden, William. 1984. *The Pacific Alliance: United States Foreign Economic Policy and Japanese Trade Recovery, 1947–55*. Madison: University of Wisconsin Press.

Boston, Jonathan. 1989. "The Treasury and the Organization of Economic Advice." In *The Making of Rogernomics*, edited by Brian Easton. Auckland: Auckland University Press.

Brenner, Michael. 1976. *The Politics of International Monetary Reform: The Exchange Crisis*. Cambridge, Mass.: Ballinger.

Bressand, Albert. 1983. "Mastering the 'Worldeconomy.'" *Foreign Affairs* 61: 745–72.

Brown, Brendan. 1987. *The Flight of International Capital: A Contemporary History*. London: Croom Helm.

Brown, Edward. 1944. "The IMF: A Consideration of Certain Objections." *Journal of Business of the University of Chicago* 17: 199–208.

Bryant, Ralph. 1987. *International Financial Intermediation*. Washington: Brookings Institution.

Burke, Kathleen, and Alec Cairncross. 1992. *"Goodbye, Great Britain": The 1976 IMF Crisis*. New Haven, Conn.: Yale University Press.

Burnham, Peter. 1990. *The Political Economy of Postwar Reconstruction*. London: Macmillan.

Calder, Kent. 1988. "Japanese Foreign Economic Policy Formation: Explaining the Reactive State." *World Politics* 40: 517–41.

Callaghan, James. 1987. *Time and Change*. London: Collins.

Calleo, David. 1982. *The Imperious Economy*. Cambridge, Mass: Harvard University Press.

——. 1987. *Beyond American Hegemony*. New York: Basic Books.

Carli, Guido. 1972. "Improving the International Adjustment Process: Some Prospects." *Convertibility, Multilateralism, and Freedom: World Economic Policy in the Seventies*, edited by Wolfgang Schmitz. New York: Springer-Verlag.

Cerny, Phil. 1989. "The Little Big Bang in Paris: Financial Market Deregulation in a Dirigiste System." *European Journal of Political Research* 17: 169–92.

Chalmers, Eric. 1972. *The International Interest Rate War*. London: Macmillan.

Child, Frank. 1954. "German Exchange Control, 1931–1938: A Study in Exploitation." Ph.D. diss., Stanford University.

Clarke, Stephen. 1967. *Central Bank Cooperation, 1924–31*. New York: Federal Reserve Bank of New York.

Coakley, Jerry, and Laurence Harris. 1992. "Financial Globalisation and Deregulation." In *The Economic Legacy 1979–1992*, edited by Jonathan Michie. London: Academic Press.

Cohen, Benjamin. 1963. "The Eurodollar, the Common Market, and Currency Unification." *Journal of Finance* 18: 605–21.

——. 1981. *Banks and the Balance of Payments*. Totowa, N.J.: Allanheld, Osmum.

——. 1983. "An Explosion in the Kitchen? Economic Relations with Other Advanced Industrial States." In *Eagle Defiant: United States Foreign Policy in the 1980s*, edited by Kenneth Oye, Robert Lieber, and Donald Rothchild. Boston: Little, Brown.

——. 1986. *In Whose Interest? International Banking and American Foreign Policy*. New Haven, Conn.: Yale University Press.

Cohen, Theodore. 1987. *Remaking Japan: The American Occupation as New Deal*. New York: Free Press.

Collins, Robert. 1978. "Positive Business Response to the New Deal: The Roots of the Committee for Economic Development, 1933–42." *Business History Review* 52: 369–91.

Committee for Economic Development. 1945. *International Trade, Foreign Investment, and Domestic Employment*. New York: CED.

——. 1961. *International Position of the Dollar*. New York: CED.

——. 1966. *The Dollar and the World Monetary System*. New York: CED.

——. 1973. *The World Monetary System*. New York: CED.

Conolly, Frederick. 1936. "Memorandum on the International Short-term Indebtedness." In *The Improvement of Commercial Relations between Nations:*

The Problems of Monetary Stabilization. Paris: International Chamber of Commerce.

Conybeare, John. 1988. *U.S. Foreign Economic Policy and the International Capital Markets: The Case of Capital Export Controls, 1963–74*. New York: Garland.

Coombs, Charles. 1976. *The Arena of International Finance*. New York: John Wiley and Sons.

Cooper, Richard. 1971. "Towards an International Capital Market." In *North American and West European Economic Policies*, edited by Charles Kindleberger and Andrew Schonfield. London: Macmillan.

Costigliola, Frank. 1972. "The Other Side of Isolationism: The Establishment of the First World Bank, 1929–30." *Journal of American History* 59: 602–20.

———. 1984. *Awkward Dominion: American Political, Economic, and Cultural Relations with Europe, 1919–33*. Ithaca, N.Y.: Cornell University Press.

Cox, Robert. 1987. *Power, Production, and World Order: Social Forces in the Making of History*. New York: Columbia University Press.

Crosland, Susan. 1982. *Tony Crosland*. London: Jonathan Cape.

Crotty, James. 1983. "On Keynes and Capital Flight." *Journal of Economic Literature* 21: 59–65.

Crum, M. Colyer, and David Meerschwam. 1986. "From Relationship to Price Banking: The Loss of Regulatory Control." In *America vs. Japan*, edited by Thomas McCraw. Boston: Harvard Business School Press.

Cumby, Robert, and Richard Levich. 1987. "Definitions and Magnitudes." In *Capital Flight and Third World Debt*, edited by John Williamson and Donald Lessard. Washington, D.C.: Institute for International Economics.

Dale, Richard. 1984. *The Regulation of International Banking*. Cambridge: Woodhead-Faulkner.

———. 1992. "Finanzplatz Deutschland." *Financial Regulation Report*, Financial Times Business Information Service (February 18).

Dam, Kenneth. 1982. *The Rules of the Game*. Chicago: University of Chicago Press.

Dam, Kenneth, and George Shultz. 1977. *Economic Policy behind the Headlines*. New York: W. W. Norton.

Davis, E. P. 1989. *Instability in the Euromarkets and the Economic Theory of Financial Crisis*. Bank of England Discussion Paper no. 43.

De Cecco, Marcello. 1972. "Economic Policy in the Reconstruction Period, 1945–51." In *The Rebirth of Italy, 1943–50*, edited by Stuart Woolf. London: Longman.

———. 1976. "International Financial Markets and U.S. Domestic Policy since 1945." *International Affairs* 52: 381–99.

———. 1979. "Origins of the Postwar Payments System." *Cambridge Journal of Economics* 3: 49–61.

———. 1987a. "Financial Innovation and Monetary Theory." In *Changing Money: Financial Innovation in Developed Countries*, edited by Marcello De Cecco. Oxford: Basil Blackwell.

——. 1987b. "Inflation and the Structural Change in the Eurodollar Market." In *Monetary Theory and Economic Institutions*, edited by Marcello De Cecco and Jean-Paul Fitoussi. London: Macmillan.

——. 1989. "Keynes and Italian Economics." In *The Political Power of Economic Ideas: Keynesianism across Nations*, edited by Peter Hall. Princeton, N.J.: Princeton University Press.

Dell, Edmund. 1991. *A Hard Pounding: Politics and Economic Crisis, 1974–1976*. Oxford: Oxford University Press.

Destler, I. M., and C. Randall Henning. 1989. *Dollar Politics: Exchange Rate Policymaking in the United States*. Washington, D.C.: Institute for International Economics.

De Vegh, Imre. 1943. "International Clearing Union." *American Economic Review* 33: 534–56.

De Vries, Margaret. 1985a, b, c. *The International Monetary Fund, 1972–1978*: Vols. 1, 2, 3. Washington, D.C.: IMF.

De Vries, Rimmer. 1990. "Adam Smith: Managing the Global Capital of Nations." *World Financial Markets* (July 23).

Diaz-Alejandro, Carlos. 1984. "Latin American Debt: I Don't Think We Are in Kansas Anymore." *Brookings Papers on Economic Activity* 2: 335–403.

Diebold, William. 1952. *Trade and Payments in Western Europe: A Study in Economic Cooperation, 1947–51*. New York: Harper & Brothers.

Dobson, Alan. 1988. *The Politics of the Anglo-American Economic Special Relationship, 1940–87*. New York: St. Martin's Press.

Douglas, Roger. 1987. *Towards Prosperity*. Auckland: Bateman.

Dowd, Lawrence. 1953. "Japanese Foreign Exchange Policy, 1930–40." Ph.D. diss., University of Michigan, Ann Arbor.

Duser, J. Thorsten. 1990. *International Strategies of Japanese Banks: The European Perspective*. London: Macmillan.

Duvall, Raymond, and Alexander Wendt. 1987. "The International Capital Regime: A Cooperation Non-Problem?" Paper presented at annual meeting of the International Studies Association, Washington, D.C. (April).

Easton, Brian. 1989. "From Run to Float: The Making of the Rogernomics Exchange Rate Policy." In *The Making of Rogernomics*, edited by Brian Easton. Auckland: Auckland University Press.

Eckes, Alfred. 1975. *A Search for Solvency: Bretton Woods and the International Monetary System, 1941–71*. Austin: University of Texas Press.

Edsall, Thomas. 1984. *The New Politics of Inequality*. New York: W. W. Norton.

——. 1989. "The Changing Shape of Power." In *The Rise and Fall of the New Deal Order, 1930–80*, edited by Steven Fraser and Gary Gerstle. Princeton, N.J.: Princeton University Press.

Edwards, Richard. 1985. *International Monetary Collaboration*. New York: Transnational.

Eichengreen, Barry. 1991. "Historical Research on International Lending and Debt." *Journal of Economic Perspectives* 5: 149–69.

——. 1992. *Golden Fetters: The Gold Standard and the Great Depression, 1919–39.* Oxford: Oxford University Press.

Eichengreen, Barry, and Alec Cairncross. 1983. *Sterling in Decline: The Devaluations of 1931, 1947, 1967.* Oxford: Basil Blackwell.

——, and Richard Portes. 1987. "The Anatomy of Financial Crises." In *Threats to International Financial Stability*, edited by Richard Portes and Alexander Swodoba. Cambridge: Cambridge University Press.

Einzig, Paul. 1970. *The History of Foreign Exchange.* 2d ed. London: Macmillan.

Ellis, Howard. 1950. *The Economics of Freedom: The Progress and Future of Aid to Europe.* New York: Harper & Brothers.

Enkyo, Yoichi. 1989. "Financial Innovation and International Safeguards: Causes and Consequences of 'Structural Innovation' in the U.S. and Global Financial System: 1973–86." Ph.D. diss., London School of Economics.

Epstein, Gerald, and Juliet Schor. 1992. "Structural Determinants and Economic Effects of Capital Controls in OECD Countries." In *Financial Openness and National Autonomy*, edited by Tariq Banuri and Juliet Schor. Oxford: Clarendon Press.

Fanno, Marco. 1939. *Normal and Abnormal International Capital Transfers.* Minneapolis: University of Minnesota Press.

Fay, Stephen, and Hugo Young. 1978. *The Day the Pound Nearly Died. Sunday Times.* (London).

Feis, Herbert. 1964 (1930). *Europe, The World's Banker, 1870–1914.* New York: Augustus Kelley.

Feldman, Robert. 1986. *Japanese Financial Markets: Deficits, Dilemmas, and Deregulation.* Cambridge, Mass.: MIT Press.

Felix, David. 1985. "How to Resolve Latin America's Debt Crisis." *Challenge* (November/December): 44–51.

——. 1990. "Latin America's Debt Crisis." *World Policy Journal* 7: 733–71.

Ferguson, Thomas. 1984. "From Normalcy to New Deal: Industrial Structure, Party Competition, and American Public Policy in the Great Depression." *International Organization* 38: 41–94.

Ferguson, Thomas, and Joel Rogers. 1986. *Right Turn: The Decline of the Democrats and the Future of American Politics.* New York: Hill and Wang.

Fforde, John 1992. *The Bank of England and Public Policy, 1941–58.* Cambridge: Cambridge University Press.

Fishlow, Albert. 1986. "Lessons from the Past." In *Politics of International Debt*, edited by Miles Kahler. Ithaca, N.Y.: Cornell University Press.

Flanders, M. June. 1989. *International Monetary Economics, 1870–1960.* Cambridge: Cambridge University Press.

Frankel, Jeffrey. 1984. *The Yen-Dollar Agreement: Liberalizing Japanese Capital Markets.* Washington, D.C.: Institute for International Economics.

Fraser, Leon. 1943. "Reconstructing the World's Money." *New York Herald Tribune* (November 21), sec. 7, p. 12.

Frieden, Jeffry. 1987. *Banking on the World: The Politics of American International Finance.* New York: Harper & Row.

——. 1988. "Capital Politics: Creditors and the International Political Economy." *Journal of Public Policy* 8: 265–86.

——. 1991. "Invested Interests: The Politics of National Economic Policies in a World of Global Finance." *International Organization* 45: 425–52.

Friedman, Milton. 1953. "The Case for Flexible Exchange Rates." In *Essays in Positive Economics*, by Milton Friedman. Chicago: University of Chicago Press.

Friedrich, Carl. 1955. "The Political Thought of Neoliberalism." *American Political Science Review* 49: 509–25.

Frydl, Edward. 1982. "The Eurodollar Conundrum." *Federal Reserve Bank of New York. Quarterly Review* (Spring): 11–19.

Fujioka, M. Y. 1979. *Japan's International Finance: Today and Tomorrow.* Tokyo: Japan Times.

Funabashi, Yoichi. 1988. *Managing the Dollar: From the Plaza to the Louvre.* Washington, D.C.: Institute for International Economics.

Gardner, Richard. 1980. *Sterling-Dollar Diplomacy in Current Perspective: The Origins and the Prospects of Our International Economic Order.* New York: Columbia University Press.

Genillard, R. 1970. "The Eurobond Market." In *The Eurodollar*, edited by Herbert Prochnow. London: Rand McNally.

Giesbert, Franz-Oliver. 1990. *Le Président.* Paris: Editions de Seuil.

Gilbert, Milton. 1963. "Reconciliation of Domestic and International Objectives of Financial Policy: European Countries." *Journal of Finance* 8: 174–86.

Gill, Stephen. 1990. *American Hegemony and the Trilateral Commission.* Cambridge: Cambridge University Press.

Gilpin, Robert. 1987. *The Political Economy of International Relations.* Princeton, N.J.: Princeton University Press.

Glyn, Andrew. 1986. "Capital Flight and Exchange Controls." *New Left Review* 155: 37–49.

——. 1992. "Exchange Controls and Policy Autonomy: The Case of Australia, 1983–88." In *Financial Openness and National Autonomy*, edited by Tariq Banuri and Juliet Schor. Oxford: Clarendon Press.

Gold, Joseph. 1950. "The Fund Agreement in the Courts." *IMF Staff Papers* 1: 315–33.

——. 1971. *The Fund's Concept of Convertibility.* Pamphlet Series no. 14. Washington, D.C.: IMF.

——. 1977. *International Capital Movements under the Law of the IMF.* Pamphlet Series no. 21. Washington, D.C.: IMF.

——. 1982. *The Fund Agreement in the Courts.* Vol. 2. Washington, D.C.: IMF.

——. 1986. *The Fund Agreement in the Courts.* Vol. 3. Washington, D.C.: IMF.

Goldstein, Morris, David Folkerts-Landau, Peter Garber, Liliana Rojas-Suarez, and Michael Spencer. 1993. *International Capital Markets; Part 1: Exchange Rate Management and International Capital Flows.* Washington, D.C. IMF.

Goodhart, Charles. 1985. *The Evolution of Central Banks*. London: London School of Economics.

Goodman, John. 1992. *Monetary Sovereignty: The Politics of Central Banking in Western Europe*. Ithaca, N.Y.: Cornell University Press.

Goodman, John, and Louis Pauly. 1990. "The New Politics of International Capital Mobility." Working Paper, International Business and Trade Law Program, University of Toronto Faculty of Law.

Gowa, Joanne. 1983. *Closing the Gold Window: Domestic Politics and the End of Bretton Woods*. Ithaca, N.Y.: Cornell University Press.

Grahl, John, and Paul Teague. 1989. "The Cost of Neo-Liberal Europe." *New Left Review* 174: 33–50.

Greider, William. 1987. *Secrets of the Temple*. New York: Simon & Schuster.

Griffith-Jones, Stephany. 1988. "Debt Crisis Management: An Analytical Framework." In *Managing World Debt*, edited by Stephany Griffith-Jones. London: Harvester Wheatsheaf.

Guttentag, Jack, and Richard Herring. 1983. *The Lender-of-Last-Resort Function in an International Context*. Essays in International Finance no. 151. Princeton, N.J.: Department of Economics, Princeton University.

——. 1985. "Funding Risk in the International Interbank Market." In *International Financial Markets and Capital Movements; A Symposium in Honor of Arthur Bloomfield*. Essays in International Finance no. 157. Princeton, N.J.: Department of Economics, Princeton University.

——. 1986. *Disaster Myopia in International Lending*. Essays in International Finance no. 164. Princeton, N.J.: Department of Economics, Princeton University.

Guy, Paul. 1992. "Regulatory Harmonization to Achieve Effective International Competition." In *Regulating International Financial Markets: Issues and Policies*, edited by Franklin Edwards and Hugh Patrick. Norwell, Mass.: Kluwer Academic Publishers.

Haas, Peter. 1992. "Introduction: Epistemic Communities and International Policy Coordination." *International Organization* 46: 1–35.

Haberler, Gottfried. 1945. "The Choice of Exchange Rates after the War." *American Economic Review* 35: 308–18.

——. 1954. *Currency Convertibility*. Washington, D.C.: American Enterprise Institute.

——. 1976a. "The Case against Capital Controls for Balance of Payments Reasons." In *Capital Movements and Their Control*, edited by Alexander Swodoba. Geneva: Sijdhoff-Leiden.

——. 1976b. *The World Economy, Money, and the Great Depression*. Washington, D.C.: American Enterprise Institute.

Haggard, Stephen, and Beth Simmons. 1987. "Theories of International Regimes." *International Organization* 40: 491–517.

Hall, Peter. 1986. *Governing the Economy. The Politics of State Intervention in Britain and France*. Cambridge: Polity Press.

——. 1987. "The Evolution of Economic Policy under Mitterrand." In *The Mitterrand Experiment: Continuity and Change in Modern France*, edited by

George Ross, Stanley Hoffmann, and Sylvia Malzacher. Cambridge: Polity Press.

——. 1989. "Conclusion: The Politics of Keynesian Ideas." In *The Political Power of Economic Ideas: Keynesianism across Nations,* edited by Peter Hall. Princeton, N.J.: Princeton University Press.

Ham, Adrian 1981. *Treasury Rules: Recurrent Themes in British Economic Policy.* London: Quartet Books.

Hamada, Koichi, and Hugh Patrick. 1988. "Japan and the International Monetary Regime." In *The Political Economy of Japan.* Vol. 2, *The Changing International Context,* edited by Takashi Inoguchi and Daniel Okimoto. Stanford, Calif.: Stanford University Press.

Hamilton, Adrian. 1986. *The Financial Revolution.* New York: Free Press.

Hardach, Karl. 1976. *The Political Economy of Germany in the Twentieth Century.* Berkeley: University of California Press.

Harper, David, and Girol Karacaoglu. 1987. "Financial Policy Reform in New Zealand." In *Economic Liberalisation in New Zealand,* edited by Alan Bollard and Robert Buckle. Wellington: Allen Unwin.

Harper, John. 1986. *America and the Reconstruction of Italy, 1945–1948.* Cambridge: Cambridge University Press.

Harrod, Roy. 1969. *The Life of John Maynard Keynes.* New York: Augustus Kelley.

——. 1972. "Problems Perceived in the International Financial System." In *Bretton Woods Revisited,* edited by Archibald Acheson, John Chant, and Martin Prachowny. Toronto: University of Toronto Press.

Hart, Susan. 1989. "National Policy and the Revolution in International Banking: The British Response, 1977–86." Ph.D. diss., London School of Economics.

Hathaway, Robert. 1984. "Economic Diplomacy in a Time of Crisis, 1933–45." In *Economics and World Power: An Assessment of American Diplomacy since 1789,* edited by William Becker and Samuel Wells. New York: Columbia University Press.

Hawley, James. 1984. "Protecting Capital from Itself: U.S. Attempts to Regulate the Eurocurrency System." *International Organization* 38: 131–65.

——. 1987. *Dollars and Borders: U.S. Government Attempts to Restrict Capital Flows, 1960–1980.* Armonk, N.Y.: M. E. Sharpe.

Hayek, Friedrich. 1937. *Monetary Nationalism and International Stability.* London: Longmans, Green.

——. 1944. *The Road to Serfdom.* Chicago: University of Chicago Press.

——. 1967. *Studies in Philosophy, Politics, and Economics.* London: Routledge & Kegan Paul.

——. 1990. *Denationalisation of Money—The Argument Refined.* London: Institute of Economic Affairs.

Healey, Denis. 1989. *The Time of My Life.* London: Michael Joseph.

Heilperin, Michael. 1968. *Aspects of the Pathology of Money.* London: Michael Joseph.

Helleiner, Eric. 1989. "Money and Influence: Japanese Power in the International Monetary and Financial System." *Millennium: Journal of International Studies* 18: 343–58.

———. 1992a. "Capital Flight and the Receiving Country: Contrasting U.S. Policy in the Marshall Plan and the 1980s Debt Crisis." Paper presented at the Annual Meeting of the Canadian Political Science Association, Charlottetown, Prince Edward Island (June).

———. 1992b. "Japan and the Changing Global Financial Order." *International Journal* 47: 420–44.

———. 1992c. "States and the Future of Global Finance." *Review of International Studies* 18: 31–49.

Henderson, Hubert. 1936. "Memorandum on New Technical Arrangements for Postponing Stabilization." In *The Improvement of Commercial Relations between Nations: The Problems of Monetary Stabilization*. Paris: International Chamber of Commerce.

Henning, C. Randall. 1987. *Macroeconomic Diplomacy in the 1980s*. London: Croom Helm.

Henry, James. 1986. "Where the Money Went." *The New Republic* (April 14): 20–23.

Hewson, John, and Eisuke Sakakibara. 1975. *The Eurocurrency Markets and Their Implications*. Lexington, Ky.: Lexington Books.

Himmelstein, Jerome. 1990. *To the Right: The Transformation of American Conservatism*. Berkeley: University of California Press.

Hinshaw, Randall. 1958. *Toward European Convertibility*. Essays in International Finance no. 31. Princeton, N.J.: Princeton University.

Hirsch, Fred, 1967. *Money International*. London: Penguin.

———. 1978. "The Ideological Underlay of Inflation." In *The Political Economy of Inflation*, edited by Fred Hirsch and John Goldthorpe. Cambridge, Mass.: Harvard University Press.

Hirsch, Fred, and Michael Doyle. 1977. "Politicization in the World Economy: Necessary Conditions for an International Economic Order." In *Alternatives to Monetary Disorder*, by Fred Hirsch, Michael Doyle, and Edward Morse. New York: McGraw-Hill.

Hirsch, Fred, and Peter Oppenheimer. 1976. "The Trial of Managed Money: Currency, Credit, and Prices, 1920–70." In *Fontana Economic History of Europe: The Twentieth Century*, Part 2, edited by Carlo Cipolla. London: Fontana.

Hoffmeyer, Erik. 1986. "Danish Policy on International Capital Movements." In *The Policy of Liberalization in International Monetary and Financial Relations*, edited by Ennio Mizzau. Milan: Edizioni Giuridico Scientifiche.

Hogan, Michael. 1977. *Informal Entente: The Private Structure of Cooperation in Anglo-American Economic Diplomacy, 1918–1928*. Columbia: University of Missouri Press.

———. 1987. *The Marshall Plan: America, Britain, and the Reconstruction of Western Europe, 1947–52*. Cambridge: Cambridge University Press.

Hollerman, Leon. 1967. *Japan's Dependence on the World Economy: The Ap-*

proach toward Economic Liberalization. Princeton, N.J.: Princeton University Press.

——. 1979. "International Economic Controls in Occupied Japan." *Journal of Asian Studies* 38: 707–19.

——. 1988. *Japan, Disincorporated: The Economic Liberalization Process.* Stanford, Calif.: Hoover Institution Press.

Hoover, Calvin. 1945. *International Trade and Domestic Employment.* New York: McGraw-Hill.

Horne, James. 1985. *Japan's Financial Markets: Conflict and Consensus in Policymaking.* London: Allen & Unwin.

——. 1988. "Politics and the Japanese Financial System." In *Dynamic and Immobilist Politics in Japan*, edited by James Stockwin, Alan Rix, Aurelia George, James Horne, Daiichi Ito, and Martin Collick. London: Macmillan.

Horsefield, John. 1969a, b, c. *The International Monetary Fund, 1945–1965*, Vols. 1, 2, 3. Washington, D.C.: IMF.

Howson, Susan, and Donald Moggridge. 1990. *The Wartime Diaries of Lionel Robbins and James Meade, 1943–45.* London: Macmillan.

Hudson, Michael. 1977. *Global Fracture: The New International Economic Order.* New York: Harper & Row.

Hutton, Graham. 1981. "Why Did It Happen . . . Just Then?" In *The Emerging Consensus . . . ?*, edited by Arthur Seldon. London: Institute of Economic Affairs.

Hyman, Sidney. 1976. *Marriner S. Eccles.* Stanford, Calif.: Stanford University Graduate School of Business.

Ikenberry, John. 1989. "Rethinking the Origins of American Hegemony." *Political Science Quarterly* 104: 375–400.

——. 1992. "A World Economy Restored: Expert Consensus and the Anglo-American Postwar Settlement." *International Organization* 46: 289–321.

Ikle, Max. 1972. "The Eurocurrency Market in the Monetary Crisis." In *Convertibility, Multilateralism, and Freedom: World Economic Policy in the Seventies*, edited by Wolfgang Schmitz. New York: Springer-Verlag.

Ilgen, T. L. 1985. *Autonomy and Interdependence: U.S.-Western European Monetary and Trade Relations, 1958–1984.* Totowa, N.J.: Rowman and Allanheld.

Ingham, Geoffrey. 1984. *Capitalism Divided: The City and Industry in British Social Development.* London: Macmillan.

Iriye, Akira. 1977. "Continuities in U.S.-Japanese Relations, 1941–49." In *The Origins of the Cold War in Asia*, edited by Akira Iriye and Yonosuke Nagai. New York: Columbia University Press.

Iwasa, Yoshizane. 1970. "The Eurodollar Market: A View from Japan." In *The Eurodollar*, edited by H. V. Prochnow. London: Rand McNally.

Jacobsson, Erin. 1979. *A Life for Sound Money: Per Jacobsson.* Oxford: Clarendon Press.

Jesson, Bruce. 1987. *Behind the Mirror Glass: The Growth of Wealth and Power in New Zealand.* Auckland: Allen & Unwin.

Johnson, Arthur. 1968. *Winthrop W. Aldrich: Lawyer, Banker, Diplomat.* Boston: Harvard University Graduate School of Business Administration.

Johnson, Daniel. 1989. "Exiles and Half-Exiles: Wilhelm Ropke, Alexander Rustow, and Water Eucken." In *German Neo-Liberals and the Social Market Economy*, edited by Alan Peacock and Hans Willgerodt. London: Macmillan.

Kahler, Miles. 1990. "Orthodoxy and Its Alternatives: Explaining Approaches to Stabilization and Adjustment." In *Economic Crisis and Policy Choice: The Politics of Adjustment in the Third World*, edited by Joan Nelson. Princeton, N.J.: Princeton University Press.

Kahn, Richard. 1976. "Historical Origins of the International Monetary Fund." In *Keynes and International Monetary Relations*, edited by A. P. Thirlwall. London: Macmillan.

Kaletsky, Anatole. 1985. *The Costs of Default.* New York: Twentieth Century Fund.

Kaplan, Jacob, and Gunther Schleiminger. 1989. *The European Payments Union: Financial Diplomacy in the 1950s.* Oxford: Clarendon Press.

Kapstein, Ethan. 1989. "Resolving the Regulator's Dilemma: International Co-ordination of Banking Regulations." *International Organization* 43: 323–47.

———. 1992. "Between Power and Purpose: Central Bankers and the Politics of Regulatory Convergence." *International Organization* 46: 265–87.

Katz, Samuel. 1961. *Sterling Speculation and European Convertibility, 1955–58.* Essays in International Finance no. 37. Princeton, N.J.: Princeton University.

———. 1969. *External Surpluses, Capital Flows, and Credit Policy in the EEC 1958–67.* Princeton Studies in International Finance no. 22. Princeton, N.J.: Department of Economics, Princeton University.

Katz, Samuel, ed. 1979. *U.S.-European Monetary Relations.* Washington, D.C.: American Enterprise Institute.

Kaufman, Robert. 1990. "Stabilization and Adjustment in Argentina, Brazil, and Mexico." In *Economic Crisis and Policy Choice: The Politics of Adjustment in the Third World*, edited by Joan Nelson. Princeton, N.J.: Princeton University Press.

Kaufmann, Hugo. 1985. *Germany's International Monetary Policy and the European Monetary System.* New York: Brooklyn College Press.

Kaushik, S. K., ed. 1987. *International Banking and World Economic Growth: The Outlook for the late 1980s.* New York: Praeger.

Kawasaki, Tsuyoshi. 1993. *In the Defence of Economic Sovereignty: The Japanese Ministry of Finance in Macroeconomic Diplomacy, 1985–1987.* Toronto: Joint Centre for Asia-Pacific Studies.

Kazuhide, Uejkusa. 1991. "The Making and Breaking of a Bubble Economy." *Japan Echo* 18: 23–27.

Keegan, William. 1984. *Mrs. Thatcher's Economic Experiment.* New York: Penguin.

Keegan, William, and Rupert Pennant-Rea. 1979. *Who Runs the Economy? Control and Influence in British Economic Policy.* London: Maurice Temple Smith.

Kelly, Janet. 1976. *Bankers and Borders: The Case of American Banks in Britain*. Cambridge, Mass.: Ballinger.

Kennedy, Ellen. 1991. *The Bundesbank: Germany's Central Bank in the International Monetary System*. London: Pinter.

Keohane, Robert. 1979. "U.S. Foreign Economic Policy towards Other Advanced Capitalist States: The Struggle to Make Others Adjust." In *Eagle Entangled: U.S. Foreign Policy in a Complex World*, edited by Kenneth Oye, Robert Lieber, and Donald Rothchild. London: Longman.

——. 1980. "The Theory of Hegemonic Stability and Changes in International Economic Regimes." In *Change in the International System*, edited by Ole Holsti, Randolph Silverson, and Alexander George. Boulder, Colo.: Westview Press.

——. 1984. *After Hegemony: Cooperation and Discord in the World Political Economy*. Princeton, N.J.: Princeton University Press.

Keynes, John Maynard. 1930. *A Treatise on Money*. Vol. 2, *The Applied Theory of Money*. London: Macmillan.

——. 1933. "National Self-Sufficience." *Yale Review* 22: 755–69.

——. 1980a. *The Collected Writings of J. M. Keynes*. Vol. 25, *Activities, 1940–1944: Shaping the Post-war World, the Clearing Union*, edited by Donald Moggridge. Cambridge: Cambridge University Press.

——. 1980b. *The Collected Writings of J. M. Keynes*. Vol. 26, *Activities 1941–1946: Shaping the Post-war World, Bretton Woods and Reparations*, edited by Donald Moggridge. Cambridge: Cambridge University Press.

Kindleberger, Charles. 1943. "Planning for Foreign Investment." *American Economic Review* 33: 347–54.

——. 1973. *The World in Depression, 1929–39*. Berkeley: University of California Press.

——. 1978. *Manias, Panics, and Crashes: A History of Financial Crises*. New York: Basic Books.

——. 1985. "The Functioning of Financial Centers: Britain in the Nineteenth Century, the United States since 1945." In *International Financial Markets and Capital Movements: A Symposium in Honor of Arthur Bloomfield*. Essays in International Finance no. 157. Princeton, N.J.: Department of Economics, Princeton University.

——. 1986. "International Public Goods without International Government." *American Economic Review* 76: 1–11.

——. 1987a. "A Historical Perspective." In *Capital Flight and Third World Debt*, edited by Donald Lessard and John Williamson. Washington, D.C.: Institute for International Economics.

——. 1987b. *International Capital Movements*. Cambridge: Cambridge University Press.

——. 1988. "Reflections on Current Changes in National and International Capital Markets." In *The International Economic Order*, by Charles Kindleberger. Cambridge, Mass.: MIT Press.

——. 1989. *Manias, Panics, and Crashes: A History of Financial Crises*. 2d ed. London: Macmillan.

Kissinger, Henry. 1979. *White House Years.* Boston: Little, Brown.

Klopstock, Fred. 1949. "Monetary Reform in Western Germany." *Journal of Political Economy* 59: 277–92.

Kloss, Hans. 1972. "Monetary Policy and Liberalization of Capital Markets." In *Convertibility, Multilateralism, and Freedom: World Economic Policy in the Seventies*, edited by Wolfgang Schmitz. New York: Springer-Verlag.

Kraft, Joseph. 1984. *The Mexican Rescue.* New York: Group of Thirty.

Krasner, Stephen. 1976. "State Power and the Structure of International Trade." *World Politics* 28: 317–47.

——. 1978. "U.S. Commercial and Monetary Policy: Unraveling the Paradox of External Strength and Internal Weakness." In *Between Power and Plenty: Foreign Economic Policies of Advanced Industrial States*, edited by Peter Katzenstein. Madison: University of Wisconsin Press.

Krasner, Stephen, ed. 1983. *International Regimes.* Ithaca, N.Y.: Cornell University Press.

Krasner, Stephen, and Janice Thomson. 1989. "Global Transactions and the Consolidation of Sovereignty." In *Global Changes and Theoretical Challenges*, edited by James Rosenau and Ernst-Otto Czempiel. Lexington, Ky.: Lexington Books.

Krause, Lawrence. 1971. "Private International Finance." *International Organization* 25: 523–40.

Krieger, Joel. 1986. *Reagan, Thatcher, and the Politics of Decline.* Cambridge: Polity Press.

Kuisel, Roland. 1981. *Capitalism and the State in Modern France.* Cambridge: Cambridge University Press.

Kunz, Diane. 1987. *The Battle for Britain's Gold Standard in 1931.* London: Croom Helm.

Labour Party. 1976. "Report of the Seventy-fifth Annual Conference of the Labour Party." Blackpool.

Lebegue, Daniel. 1985. "Modernizing the French Capital Market." *The Banker* 135 (December): 23–29.

Leffler, Melvyn. 1979. *The Elusive Quest: America's Pursuit of European Stability and French Security, 1919–33.* Chapel Hill: University of North Carolina Press.

Lenel, Hans Otto. 1989. "Evolution of the Social Market Economy." In *German Neo-Liberals and the Social Market Economy*, edited by Alan Peacock and Hans Willgerodt. London: Macmillan.

Lepetit, Jean-Pierre. 1982. "Comment." In *Financial Crises: Theory, History, and Policy*, edited by Charles Kindleberger and Jean-Pierre Laffargue. Cambridge: Cambridge University Press.

Levich, Richard. 1988. "Financial Innovations in International Financial Markets." In *The United States in the World Economy*, edited by Martin Feldstein. Chicago: University of Chicago Press.

Ley, Robert. 1989. "Liberating Capital Movements: A New OECD Commitment." *OECD Observer* 159: 22–26.

Lincoln, Eric. 1986. "Infrastructural Deficiencies, Budget Policy, and Capital

Flows." In *Japan's Response to Crisis and Change in the World Economy*, edited by Michele Schmiegelow. Armonk, N.Y.: M. E. Sharpe.

——. 1988. *Japan: Facing Economic Maturity*. Washington, D.C.: Brookings Institution.

Lipson, Charles. 1986. "International Debt and International Institutions." In *The Politics of International Debt*, edited by Miles Kahler. Ithaca, N.Y.: Cornell University Press.

Lissakers, Karin. 1991. *Banks, Borrowers, and the Establishment: A Revisionist Account of the International Debt Crisis*. New York: Basic Books.

Loriaux, Michael. 1991. *France after Hegemony: International Change and Financial Reform*. Ithaca, N.Y.: Cornell University Press.

Ludlow, Peter. 1982. *The Making of the European Monetary System*. London: Butterworth Scientific.

Lundstrom, Hans. 1961. *Capital Movements and Economic Integration*. The Netherlands: A. W. Sythoff-Leyden.

Lutz, Friedrich. 1943. *The Keynes and White Proposals.* Princeton, N.J.: Princeton University Press.

Machlup, Fritz. 1968. *Remaking the International Monetary System: The Rio Agreement and Beyond*. Baltimore: Johns Hopkins University Press.

Machlup, Fritz, ed. 1976. *Essays on Hayek*. New York: New York University Press.

McKenzie, Richard, and Dwight Lee. 1991. *Quicksilver Capital: How the Rapid Movement of Wealth Has Changed the World*. New York: Free Press.

McMahon, Chris. 1985. "The Global Financial Structure in Transition: Consequences for International Finance and Trade." In *Global Financial Structure in Transition*, edited by Joel McClellan. Lexington, Ky.: Lexington Books.

McNeil, William. 1986. *American Money and the Weimar Republic*. New York: Columbia University Press.

McQuaid, Kim. 1976. "The Business Advisory Council of the Department of Commerce, 1933–61: A Study of Corporate/Government Relations." In *Research in Economic History*. Vol. 1, edited by Paul Uselding. Greenwich, Conn.: JAI Press

——. 1982. *Big Business and Presidential Power: From Roosevelt to Reagan*. New York: William Morrow.

Maier, Charles. 1987a. "The Politics of Productivity: Foundations of American International Economic Policy after World War Two." In *In Search of Stability: Explorations in Historical Political Economy*, by Charles Maier. Cambridge: Cambridge University Press.

——. 1987b. "The Two Postwar Eras and the Conditions for Stability in Twentieth-Century Western Europe." In *In Search of Stability: Explorations in Historical Political Economy*, by Charles Maier. Cambridge: Cambridge University Press.

Marris, Stephen. 1985. *Deficits and the Dollar*. Washington, D.C.: Institute for International Economics.

Mattione, Richard. 1985. *OPEC's Investments and the International Financial System*. Washington, D.C.: Brookings Institution.

Maxfield, Sylvia. 1990. *Governing Capital: International Finance and Mexican Politics.* Ithaca, N.Y.: Cornell University Press.

———. 1992. "The International Political Economy of Bank Nationalization: Mexico in Comparative Perspective." *Latin American Research Review* 27: 75–103.

Maxfield, Sylvia, and James Nolt. 1990. "Protectionism and the Internationalization of Capital: U.S. Sponsorship of Import Substitution Industrialization in the Philippines, Turkey, and Argentina." *International Studies Quarterly* 34: 49–82.

Mendelsohn, Michael. 1980. *Money on the Move: The Modern International Capital Market.* New York: McGraw-Hill.

Mikesell, Raymond. 1954. *Foreign Exchange in the Postwar World.* New York: Twentieth Century Fund.

Miller, Robert, and John Wood. 1979. *Exchange Control For Ever?* London: Institute of Economic Affairs.

Mills, R. 1976. "The Regulation of Short-Term Capital Movements in Major Industrial Countries." In *Capital Movements and Their Control,* edited by Alexander Swodoba. Geneva: Sijdhoff-Leiden.

Milward, Alan 1984. *The Reconstruction of Western Europe, 1945–51.* London: Methuen.

———. 1990. "Motives for Currency Convertibility: The Pound and the Deutschmark, 1950–59." In *Interactions in the World Economy,* edited by Carl-Ludwig Holtfrerich. New York: New York University Press.

Minsky, Hyman. 1982. "The Financial Instability Thesis: Capitalist Processes and the Behavior of the Economy." In *Financial Crises: Theory, History, and Policy,* edited by Charles Kindleberger and Jean-Pierre Laffargue. Cambridge: Cambridge University Press.

Mitsuru, Yamamoto. 1977. "The Cold War and U.S.-Japan Economic Cooperation." In *The Origins of the Cold War in Asia,* edited by Akira Iriye and Yonosuke Nagai. New York: Columbia University Press.

Moggridge, Donald. 1986. "Keynes and the International Monetary System, 1906–46." In *International Monetary Problems and Supply-Side Economics,* edited by Jon Cohen and Geoffrey Harcourt. London: Macmillan.

Monroe, Wilber. 1973. *Japan: Financial Markets and the World Economy.* New York: Praeger.

Moran, Michael. 1991. *The Politics of the Financial Services Revolution: The U.S.A., U.K., and Japan.* London: Macmillan.

Moravcsik, Andrew. 1991. "Negotiating the Single European Act: National Interests and Conventional Statecraft." *International Organization* 45: 19–56.

Morris, Frank. 1982. "Discussion." In *The Political Economy of Monetary Policy: National and International Aspects,* edited by Donald Hodgeman. Illinois: University of Illinois Press.

Murphy, R. Taggart. 1989. "Power without Purpose: The Crisis of Japan's Global Financial Dominance." *Harvard Business Review* (March/April): 71–83.

Nash, George 1976. *The Conservative Intellectual Movement in America since 1945*. New York: Basic Books.

Nau, Henry. 1984–85. "Where Reaganomics Works." *Foreign Policy* 57: 14–38.

——. 1985. "Or the Solution." *Foreign Policy* 59: 144–53.

——. 1990. *The Myth of America's Decline*. Oxford: Oxford University Press.

Naylor, Tom. 1987. *Hot Money and the Politics of Debt*. Toronto: McClelland & Stewart.

Neikirk, William. 1989. *Volcker: Portrait of the Money Man*. New York: Congdon & Weed.

Nelson, Joan. 1990. "Introduction." In *Economic Crisis and Policy Choice*, edited by Joan Nelson. Princeton, N.J.: Princeton University Press.

Newton, Scott, and Dilwyn Porter. 1988. *Modernization Frustrated: The Politics of Industrial Decline in Britain since 1900*. London: Unwin Hyman.

O'Brien, Richard. 1992. *Global Financial Integration: The End of Geography*. London: Pinter.

Ocampo, Jose. 1990. "New Economic Thinking in Latin America." *Journal of Latin American Studies* 22: 168–81.

Odell, John. 1982. *U.S. International Monetary Policy: Markets, Power, and Ideas as Sources of Change*. Princeton, N.J.: Princeton University Press.

Ohlin, Bertil. 1936. "International Economic Reconstruction." In *International Economic Reconstruction*. Paris: International Chamber of Commerce.

Oliver, Robert. 1971. *Early Plans for a World Bank*. Princeton Studies in International Finance no. 29. Princeton, N.J.: Department of Economics, Princeton University.

Oliver, W. Hugh. 1989. "The Labour Caucus and Economic Policy Formation, 1981–84." In *The Making of Rogernomics*, edited by Brian Easton. Auckland: Auckland University Press.

Ozaki, Robert. 1972. *The Control of Imports and Foreign Capital in Japan*. New York: Praeger.

Padoan, Pier Carlo. 1986. *The Political Economy of International Financial Instability*. London: Croom Helm.

Padoa-Schioppa, Tommasso. 1988. "Milan, Hanover, 1992." *Review of Economic Conditions in Italy* 3: 435–43.

Palma, Gabriel. 1978. "Dependency: A Formal Theory of Underdevelopment or a Methodology for the Analysis of Concrete Situations of Underdevelopment." *World Development* 6: 881–924.

Parboni, Ricardo. 1986. "The Dollar Weapon: From Nixon to Reagan." *New Left Review* 158: 5–18.

Parsons, Wayne. 1989. *The Power of the Financial Press: Journalism and Economic Opinion in Britain and America*. Aldershot: Edward Elgar.

Patrick, Hugh, and Ryuichiro Tachi, eds. 1986. *Japan and the United States Today*. New York: Columbia University Center on Japanese Economy and Business.

Pauly, Louis. 1987a. *Foreign Banks in Australia: The Politics of Deregulation*. Sydney: Australian Professional Publications.

——. 1987b. *Regulatory Politics in Japan: The Case of Foreign Banking.* Ithaca, N.Y.: Cornell University East Asia Paper no. 45.

——. 1988. *Opening Financial Markets: Banking Politics on the Pacific Rim.* Ithaca, N.Y.: Cornell University Press.

——. 1992. "The Political Foundations of Multilateral Economic Surveillance." *International Journal* 47: 293–327.

Penrose, Edith. 1953. *Economic Planning for the Peace.* Princeton, N.J.: Princeton University Press.

Peschek, Joseph. 1987. *Policy-Planning Organizations: Elite Agendas and America's Rightward Turn.* Philadelphia: Temple University Press.

Pfister, Ulrich, and Christian Suter. 1987. "International Financial Relations as Part of the World System." *International Studies Quarterly* 31: 239–72.

Plender, John. 1986–87. "London's Big Bang in International Context." *International Affairs* 63: 39–48.

Plumptre, Arthur. 1977. *Three Decades of Decision: Canada and the World Monetary System, 1944–75.* Toronto: McClelland & Stewart.

Polanyi, Karl. 1957. *The Great Transformation: The Political and Economic Origins of Our Time.* Boston: Beacon Press.

Porter, Tony. 1992a. "International Financial Collaboration under Stress: The Basel Capital Adequacy Accord." Paper presented at the Annual Meeting of the Canadian Political Science Association, Charlottetown, Prince Edward Island (June).

——. 1992b. "Regimes for Financial Firms." Paper presented at the International Studies Association Conference, Atlanta (April).

Pressnell, Leslie. 1986. *External Economic Policy since the War.* Vol. 1, *The Post-war Financial Settlement.* London: Her Majesty's Stationery Office.

Pringle, Robert. 1989. *Financial Markets and Governments.* Working Paper no. 57. Helsinki: World Institute for Development Economics Research.

Putnam, Robert. 1984. "The Western Economic Summits: A Political Interpretation." *Economic Summitry and Western Decision-Making,* edited by Cesare Merlini. Beckenham: Croom Helm.

Pyle, Kenneth. 1987. "In Pursuit of a Grand Design: Nakasone betwixt the Past and Future." *Journal of Japanese Studies* 13: 243–70.

Randall, Clarence. 1954. *A Foreign Economic Policy for the U.S.* Chicago: University of Chicago Press.

Rasminsky, Louis. 1972. "Canadian Views." In *Bretton Woods Revisited,* edited by Archibald Acheson, John Chant, and Martin Prachowny. Toronto: University of Toronto Press.

Rees, David. 1973. *Harry Dexter White: A Study in Paradox.* New York: Coward, McCann and Geoghegan.

Rees, Graham. 1963. *Britain and the Postwar European Payments System.* Cardiff: University of Wales Press.

Riddle, J. H. 1943. *British and American Plans for International Currency Stabilization.* Our Economy in War Occasional Paper no. 16. New York: National Bureau of Economic Research.

Ridgeway, George. 1959. *Merchants of Peace: The History of the International Chamber of Commerce*. Boston: Little, Brown.

Robbins, Lionel. 1937. *Economic Planning and International Order*. London: Macmillan.

———. 1971. *Autobiography of an Economist*. London: Macmillan.

Robinson, Joan. 1944. "The United States in the World Economy." *Economic Journal* 54: 430–37.

Robinson, Stuart. 1972. *Multinational Banking*. Geneva: Sijdhoff-Leiden.

Roll, Eric. 1971. *International Capital Movements: Past, Present, and Future*. Washington, D.C.: International Monetary Fund.

Ropke, Wilhelm. 1942. *International Economic Disintegration*. London: William Hodge.

———. 1950. *The Social Crisis of Our Time*. London: William Hodge.

———. 1952. *The Economics of Full Employment*. New York: American Enterprise Association.

———. 1959. *International Order and Economic Integration*. Dordrecht, the Netherlands: Reidel.

Rosanvallon, Pierre. 1989. "The Development of Keynesianism in France." In *The Political Power of Economic Ideas: Keynesianism across Nations*, edited by Peter Hall. Princeton, N.J.: Princeton University Press.

Rosenbluth, Frances M. 1989. *Financial Politics in Contemporary Japan*. Ithaca, N.Y.: Cornell University Press.

Ruggie, John. 1982. "International Regimes, Transactions, and Change: Embedded Liberalism in the Postwar Economic Order." *International Organization* 36: 379–415.

Russell, Robert. 1973. "Transgovernmental Interaction in the International Monetary System, 1960–72." *International Organization* 27: 431–64.

Sakakibara, Eisuke. 1986. "The Internationalization of Tokyo's Financial Markets." In *Pacific Growth and Financial Interdependence*, edited by Augustine Tan and Basant Kapur. London: Allen & Unwin.

Salant, Walter. 1989. "The Spread of Keynesian Doctrine and Practice in the United States." In *The Political Power of Economic Ideas: Keynesianism across Nations*, edited by Peter Hall. Princeton, N.J.: Princeton University Press.

Sandholtz, Wayne, and John Zysman. 1989. "1992: Recasting the European Bargain." *World Politics* 42: 95–128.

Schloss, Hans. 1958. *The Bank for International Settlements*. Amsterdam: North-Holland.

———. 1970. *The Bank for International Settlements*. New York: New York University Graduate School of Business Administration.

Schmidt, Helmut. 1989. *Men and Powers*. London: Jonathan Cape.

Schonberger, Howard. 1977. "The Japan Lobby in American Diplomacy, 1947–52." *Pacific Historical Review* 46: 327–60.

———. 1989. *Aftermath of War: Americans and the Remaking of Japan, 1945–52*. Kent, Ohio: Kent State University Press.

Schor, Juliet. 1992. "Introduction." In *Financial Openness and National Autonomy*, edited by Tariq Banuri and Juliet Schor. Oxford: Clarendon Press.

Schriftgiesser, Karl. 1960. *Business Comes of Age: The Story of the Committee for Economic Development and Its Impact upon the Economic Policies of the U.S. 1942–1960*. New York: Harper & Bros.

Schwartz, Herman. 1991. "Can Orthodox Stabilization and Adjustment Work? Lessons from New Zealand, 1984–90." *International Organization* 45: 221–56.

Schweitzer, Pierre-Paul. 1966. "International Aspects of the Full Employment Economy." In *Managing a Full Employment Economy*. New York: Committee for Economic Development.

Sebald, William. 1965. *With MacArthur in Japan: A Personal History of the Occupation*. New York: W. W. Norton.

Simmons, Beth. 1992. "Why Innovate? Founding the Bank for International Settlements." Paper presented at the Annual Meeting of the American Political Science Association, Chicago (September).

Singer, Daniel. 1988. *Is Socialism Doomed? The Meaning of Mitterrand*. Oxford: Oxford University Press.

Spero, Joan. 1980. *The Failure of the Franklin National Bank: Challenge to the International Banking System*. New York: Columbia University Press.

———. 1989. "Guiding Global Finance." *Foreign Policy* 73: 114–34.

———. 1990. *The Politics of International Economic Relations*. 4th ed. New York: St. Martin's Press.

Spiro, David. 1989. "Policy Coordination in the International Political Economy: The Politics of Recycling Petrodollars." Ph.D. diss., Princeton University.

Stigler, George. 1988. *Memoirs of an Unregulated Economist*. New York: Basic Books.

Story, Jonathan. 1986. "Comment 3." In *Europe, America, and the World Economy*, edited by Loukas Tsoukalis. Oxford: Basil Blackwell.

———. 1988. "The Launching of the EMS: An Analysis of Change in Foreign Economic Policy." *Political Studies* 36: 397–412.

Strange, Susan. 1971. *Sterling and British Policy*. London: Oxford University Press.

———. 1976. *International Monetary Relations*. Vol. 2 of *International Economic Relations of the Western World, 1959–71*, edited by Andrew Shonfield. Oxford: Oxford University Press.

———. 1982. "Still an Extraordinary Power: America's Role in a Global Monetary System." In *The Political Economy of International and Domestic Monetary Relations*, edited by Raymond Lombra and Willard Witte. Ames: Iowa State University Press.

———. 1986. *Casino Capitalism*. Oxford: Basil Blackwell.

———. 1988. *States and Markets: An Introduction to International Political Economy*. London: Pinter.

———. 1990. "Finance, Information, and Power." *Review of International Studies* 16: 259–74.

Strange Susan, ed. 1984. *Paths to International Political Economy*. London: Allen & Unwin.

Suzuki, Yoshio. 1987. "Financial Innovation in Japan: Its Origins, Diffusion, and Impacts." In *Changing Money*, edited by Marcello De Cecco. Oxford: Basil Blackwell.

Tavlas, George. 1991. *On the International Use of Currencies: The Case of the Deutsche Mark*. Essays in International Finance no. 181. Princeton, N.J.: Department of Economics, Princeton University.

Thurn, Max. 1972. "The Burden of the Balance of Payments." In *Convertibility, Multilateralism, and Freedom: World Economic Policy in the Seventies*. New York: Springer-Verlag.

Tobin, James. 1974. *The New Economics: One Decade Older*. Princeton, N.J.: Princeton University Press.

——. 1978. "A Proposal for International Monetary Reform." *Eastern Economic Journal* 4: 153–59.

Tooze, Roger, and Craig Murphy. 1991. "Getting Beyond the 'Common Sense' of the IPE Orthodoxy." In *The New International Political Economy*, edited by Roger Tooze and Craig Murphy. Boulder, Colo.: Lynne Reiner.

Tsoukalis, Loukas. 1977. *The Politics and Economics of European Monetary Integration*. London: Allen & Unwin.

Turner, Philip. 1991. *Capital Flows in the 1980s: A Survey of the Major Trends*. Basel: Bank for International Settlements.

Underhill, Geoffrey. 1991. "Markets beyond Politics? The State and the Internationalization of Financial Markets." *European Journal of Political Research* 19: 197–225.

Van Der Pijl, Kees. 1984. *The Making of an Atlantic Ruling Class*. London: Verso.

Van Dormael, Armand. 1978. *Bretton Woods: Birth of a Monetary System*. London: Macmillan.

Versluysen, Eugene. 1981. *The Political Economy of International Finance*. New York: St. Martin's Press.

Viner, Jacob. 1926. "International Free Trade in Capital." *Scientia* 39: 39–48.

——. 1943. "Two Plans for International Monetary Stabilization." *Yale Review* 33: 77–107.

——. 1951. "International Finance and Balance of Power Diplomacy, 1880–1914." In *International Economics*, by Jacob Viner. Glencoe, Ill.: Free Press.

——. 1958. *The Long View and the Short*. Glencoe, Ill.: Free Press.

Vipond, Peter. 1991."The Liberalisation of Capital Movements and Financial Services in the European Single Market: A Case Study in Regulation." *European Journal of Political Research* 19: 227–44.

Volcker, Paul. 1979. "The Role of Private Capital in the World Economy." In *Private Enterprise and the New Global Economic Challenge*, edited by Stephen Guisinger. Indianapolis: Bobbs-Merrill.

Volcker, Paul, and Toyoo Gyohten. 1992. *Changing Fortunes: The World's Money and the Threat to American Leadership*. New York: Times Books.

Wachtel, Howard. 1986. *The Money Mandarins: The Making of a New Supranational Economic Order*. New York: Pantheon.

Wallerstein, Immanuel. 1980. *The Modern World System 2*. New York: Academic Press.

Wallich, Henry. 1985. "U.S. Monetary Policy in an Interdependent World." In *International Financial Markets and Capital Movements; A Symposium in Honor of Arthur Bloomfield*. Essays in International Finance no. 157. Princeton, N.J.: Department of Economics, Princeton University.

Walter, Andrew. 1991. *World Power and World Money: The Role of Hegemony and International Monetary Order*. London: Harvester Wheatsheaf.

Walter, Ingo. 1989. *Secret Money*. 2d ed. London: Unwin.

Warren, Robert. 1937. "The International Movement of Capital." *Proceedings of the Academy of Political Science* 17: 357–64.

Welfield, John. 1988. *An Empire in Eclipse: Japan in the Postwar American Alliance System*. London: Athlone Press.

Wexler, Imanuel. 1983. *The Marshall Plan Revisited*. Westport, Conn.: Greenwood Press.

White, Harry Dexter. 1933. *The French International Accounts, 1880–1913*. Cambridge, Mass.: Harvard University Press.

Willett, Thomas. 1977. *Floating Exchange Rates and International Monetary Policy*. Washington, D.C.: American Enterprise Institute.

Williams, Benjamin. 1939. *Foreign Loan Policy of the United States Since 1933*. A report to the Twelfth International Studies Conference, Bergen, Norway (August 27–Sept 2).

Williams, John H. 1936. "International Monetary Organization and Policy." In *Postwar Monetary Plans, and Other Essays*, by John Williams (1947). New York: Knopf.

——. 1943. "Currency Stabilization: The Keynes and White Plans." In *Postwar Monetary Plans, and Other Essays*, by John Williams (1947). New York: Knopf.

——. 1944. "Postwar Monetary Plans." In *Postwar Monetary Plans, and Other Essays*, by John Williams (1947). New York: Knopf.

——. 1949. "International Trade with Planned Economies." In *Postwar Monetary Plans, and Other Essays*, by John Williams (1949). Oxford: Basil Blackwell.

Williamson, John. 1977. *The Failure of World Monetary Reform, 1971–74*. Sunbury-on-Thames: T. Nelson and Sons.

——. 1991. "On Liberalising the Capital Account." In *Finance and the International Economy 5*, edited by Richard O'Brien. Oxford: Oxford University Press.

Williamson, John, and Donald Lessard, eds. 1987. *Capital Flight and Third World Debt*. Washington, D.C.: Institute for International Economics.

Winham, Gilbert. 1988. "Review of Robert Gilpin's Political Economy of International Relations." *Canadian Journal of Political Science* 21: 660–61.

Wojnilower, Albert. 1986. "Japan and the United States: Some Observations on Economic Policy." In *Japan and the United States Today*, edited by Hugh

Patrick and Ryuichiro Tachi. New York: Columbia University Center on Japanese Economy and Business.

Wood, John. 1981. "How It All Began—Personal Recollections." In *The Emerging Consensus . . . ?*, edited by Arthur Seldon. London: Institute of Economic Affairs.

Woolley, John. 1984. *Monetary Politics: The Federal Reserve and the Politics of Monetary Policy*. Cambridge: Cambridge University Press.

Wriston, Walter. 1986. *Risk and Other Four-Letter Words*. New York: Harper & Row.

———. 1988. "Technology and Sovereignty." *Foreign Affairs* 67: 63–75.

Yoshitomi, Masaru. 1985. *Japan as Capital Exporter and the World Economy*. Occasional Paper no. 18. New York: Group of Thirty.

Zacchia, Carlo. 1976. "International Trade and Capital Movements, 1920–70." In *Fontana Economic History of Europe: The Twentieth Century*, Part 2, edited by Carlo Cipolla. London: Fontana.

Zweig, Konrad. 1980. *The Origins of the German Social Market Economy: The Leading Ideas and Their Intellectual Roots*. London: Adam Smith Institute.

Zysman, John. 1983. *Government, Markets, and Growth: Financial Systems and the Politics of Industrial Change*. Ithaca, N.Y.: Cornell University Press.

Index